TALK TREATY TO ME

TALK TREATY TO ME

UNDERSTANDING THE BASICS OF TREATIES AND LAND IN CANADA

CRYSTAL GAIL FRASER
AND SARA KOMARNISKY

Collins

Talk Treaty to Me

Published by Collins, an imprint of HarperCollins Publishers Ltd

FIRST EDITION

The authors wish to acknowledge the contribution of Stefanie Kennedy to the original concept for this book.

HarperCollins books may be purchased for educational, business, or sales promotional use through our Special Markets Department.

HarperCollins Publishers Ltd, Bay Adelaide Centre, East Tower,
22 Adelaide Street West, 41st Floor, Toronto, Ontario, Canada, M5H 4E3

www.harpercollins.ca

HarperCollins Publishers, Macken House, 39/40 Mayor Street Upper
Dublin 1, D01 C9W8, Ireland
www.harpercollins.com

Library and Archives Canada Cataloguing in Publication

Title: Talk treaty to me : understanding the basics of treaties and land in Canada / Crystal Gail Fraser and Sara Komarnisky.
Names: Fraser, Crystal, author | Komarnisky, Sara V., author
Description: Includes bibliographical references and index.
Identifiers: Canadiana (print) 20250318172 | Canadiana (ebook) 20250318180 | ISBN 9781443471169 (softcover) | ISBN 9781443471176 (EPUB)
Subjects: LCSH: Indigenous peoples—Legal status, laws, etc.—Canada. | LCSH: Indigenous peoples—Land tenure—Canada. | LCSH: Indigenous peoples—Canada—Government relations. | CSH: First Nations—Treaties.
Classification: LCC KIB490 .F73 2026 | LCC KF8210.P76 F73 2026 | DDC 346.7104/3208997—dc23

Printed and bound in the United States of America

25 26 27 28 29 LBC 5 4 3 2 1

For our ancestors and children and for yours, too.

To get to the future, we need a vision, then we must imagine the steps we must take to get to that vision. We cannot ignore our vision because it seems utopian, too grand, unachievable. Neither can we refuse to take the first steps because they are too small, too inconsequential. . . . We will both be part of whatever future we create, kiciwamanawak.

—Harold Johnson

CONTENTS

A NOTE TO READERS

Some readers might find it challenging to read about the topics in this book. If you are a Survivor or an intergenerational Survivor of an Indian residential school and need help, there's a free twenty-four-hour support line in Canada. Please call the Residential School Crisis Line at 1-866-925-4419.

INTRODUCTION
TALK TREATY TO ME

AH GWIĮNZII! WELCOME, IT IS GOOD TO SEE YOU. IN this book, we invite you to talk treaty with us. Maybe grab a cup of tea and sit around the kitchen table with an open mind. We'll tell you what we've learned about what treaties are, how they were made, what meaning they hold today, and how we can talk treaty together.

What is a treaty? Treaties are

- "agreements or arrangements establishing and organizing good relations or relations of friendship between sovereigns";[1]
- ways "for realizing separate jurisdictions within a shared territory [that outline] the 'rights' and 'responsibilities' of both parties in the ongoing relationship";[2]
- a "settlement or arrangement arrived at by treating or negotiation; an agreement, covenant, compact, contract";[3]
- "a contract between two or more states, relating to peace, truce, alliance, commerce, or other international relation; also, the document embodying such contract, in modern usage formally signed by plenipotentiaries appointed by the government of each state";[4] and
- active relationships that affirm "the continuity of Indigenous peoples' legal, political, economic, spiritual, and societal practices."[5]

By the end of this book, all of these definitions might ring true for you. Or one might resonate with you more than the others. You might also disagree with how the word *treaty* is defined above. There are truths held in apparent contradiction with each other, and multiple definitions are true. This is the reality of treaty making and how treaties are interpreted. In other words, it's complicated.

We think that it's essential for all Canadians to have some knowledge about treaties between the Crown and Indigenous Peoples. We also think that everyone should have enough knowledge about treaties to engage in truth and reconciliation.

In 2008, the Truth and Reconciliation Commission of Canada (TRC) set Canada on a new course. This was a national effort to address the historical and ongoing impacts of the Indian residential school system and the broader injustices faced by Indigenous Peoples because of colonialism. Reconciliation is ongoing. It focuses on restoring and building equitable and respectful relationships between Indigenous Peoples and non-Indigenous peoples. But we must not forget about truth. The pursuit of truth means a commitment to learning about and acknowledging the realities of Canada's colonial history. Although "truth and reconciliation" emerged in the context of the TRC, we continue to search for truths—about treaties included—as we strengthen our commitment to reconciliation.

This book is a part of that critical project. After all, treaties are foundational to the creation of the country, to our provinces and territories, and to our cities and towns. They are also central to our future: to live up to multiple federal commissions and the promises of past generations, we need to fully honour all treaties and enter into new ones that create and maintain good relationships between Indigenous Peoples and non-Indigenous institutions, governments, and peoples.

Unfortunately, Canada has a terrible track record of dishonouring treaties and actively works to diminish or destroy the sovereignty of Indigenous Peoples, whether First Nations, Métis, or Inuit. Treaties were often used as tools to facilitate settlement and resource extraction while undermining the rights of Indigenous Peoples to their Lands, languages, cultures, and ways of life. Time and time again, Canada did not implement the promises made in treaties and ensured that the laws that it created were always in its own favour. Canada's official policy of assimilation and genocide, enacted through the Indian Act (1876; amended many times since then and still in effect today), sought to eliminate Indigenous cultures, governance systems, and identities by imposing absolute control over nearly all aspects of daily life and enforcing harmful policies such as residential schools and legislated Land dispossession.

We started writing together over the summer of 2017, when celebrations of Canada's 150th year were in full swing. We experienced it as a time of glossy, celebratory, and uncritical Canadian nationalism. And we didn't like it. At the time, Crystal was writing a dissertation on the history of residential schooling in the Northwest Territories, and Sara was working on a project about art and craft made by Indigenous patients in tuberculosis hospitals. We were studying how Indigenous families and communities were fractured because of Canadian policies. We watched the federal government in Ottawa, and Canadians more generally, celebrate

150 years of colonialism while some Indigenous communities did not even have clean drinking water. The excessive celebrations felt inappropriate.

The TRC's foundational 94 Calls to Action, issued only two years prior to the celebrations, continued to inspire and energize us. But the 94 Calls to Action were neither swiftly nor enthusiastically taken up by governments, churches, and other organizations. As a response, we wrote "150 Acts of Reconciliation for the Last 150 Days of Canada's 150." It was a list of 150 ideas to inspire Canadians to continue to engage with truth and reconciliation in everyday and accessible ways. Our list was designed to reach Canadians at home, in the workplace, with family members and friends, and in a way that felt welcoming and educational. "150 Acts" was also about our journey, as a Gwichyà Gwich'in and a settler Canadian, as we tried to figure out our roles in truth and reconciliation and what we could do to move the process forward. This piece continues to be available online at activehistory.ca/150Acts.

As it turned out, we weren't the only ones who wanted something more from Canada. When we published "150 Acts" in August 2017, it went viral, with people posting and reposting each day. We had written one act for each day remaining in the year, something that anyone could do to work toward truth and reconciliation. People immediately began sharing how they were engaging with the acts, such as writing letters to elected leaders to request that Indigenous flags be raised in front of public buildings or reading to their children storybooks by Indigenous authors, such as Phyllis Webstad and Richard Van Camp. Educators incorporated "150 Acts" into classrooms at all levels, from elementary schools to university graduate seminars. We admired all of the ways in which Canadians took up our final act in the list, number 150: "Why stop at 150? After all, Indigenous Nations are celebrating millennia on this land. Build on this list or start and share your own."

In the following years, we gave presentations, webinars, and workshops on "150 Acts" and developed posters with Wolf Clan and Tagé Cho Hudän artist Lianne Marie Leda Charlie. By 2021, we had completed graduate studies and added more children to our respective families, and Sara had moved to Sǫǫ̀mbak'è (Yellowknife). As Eva Jewell and Ian Mosby have shown over the years, the 94 Calls to Action continue to be neglected by the federal government.[6] We continued to look for ways to advance truth and reconciliation while always sharing about "150 Acts." We considered writing a book about the acts, but, as it turned out, something else was in the works.

This book, and our perspectives on treaties, come out of our own backgrounds and experiences as a Gwichyà Gwich'in–settler writing team. Like you, we are reflections of our ancestral and contemporary worlds, and our life experiences. For most of our lives, we have lived on Lands governed by the Numbered Treaties.

Crystal (she/her) is Gwichyà Gwich'in and grew up in Inuuvik (Inuvik) and at her family's fish camp, Dachan Choo Gę̀hnjik (Tree River), both located in the Northwest Territories. Crystal also has Scottish and English ancestry. Her ancestors—on both sides—were the signatories of Treaty 11 in 1921. Her homeland is Treaty 11, sometimes also called the Gwich'in Settlement Area or Nahnkak Thak. But discussions of treaties were not centrally important in her life until she moved to Treaty 6 territory. Rather, her connection to the Land was characterized by catching and processing fish, travelling to the mountains to be with and learn from caribou, learning Dinjii Zhuh Ginjìk, and working with Elders and Knowledge Keepers. Crystal has lived on Treaty 6 and Métis Lands for more than twenty years.

Sara (she/her) is of Ukrainian, Italian, and Irish settler ancestry and grew up in Holden, Alberta, a small town about 100 kilometres east of amiskwaciwâskahikan (Edmonton) in Treaty 6 territory and within the homeland of the Métis Nation. She doesn't have any ancestors who signed Treaty 6, but certainly its signing made it possible for the new government of Canada to invite immigrants from Eastern Europe to "settle" parts of the Prairies. So, too, her Irish and Italian ancestors were able to settle in Ontario and Saskatchewan because of treaties. In rural Ukrainian and white settler society, treaties were not talked about at home or school, and neither was the process by which our families came to live on and own property. It wasn't until well into adulthood that Sara learned anything about treaties. She now lives in Treaty 8 territory, in Yellowknives Dene territory, and she often works and travels in Treaty 11 territory.

We both have academic backgrounds and PhDs (Crystal in history and Sara in anthropology), and our thinking and work have been informed by academia and the pursuit of higher education. Over the years we have been active witnesses to events and conversations related to Idle No More, the TRC, Canada 150, the tragic death of Colten Boushie, the National Inquiry into Missing and Murdered Indigenous Women and Girls, and the news of thousands of unmarked graves found at the former sites of Canada's Indian residential schools.

We are writing this book from who we are and where we're from, but we are also writing it as an invitation to newcomers to Canada, Canadians with multiple generations here already, and Indigenous Peoples of many nations who have been here since time immemorial to reflect on the importance of treaties in Canada. Through our experiences with "150 Acts" and as public scholars and educators, we realize that there is an ongoing and dire need to present truthful information in an accessible way. We think that everyone can take something from learning more about treaties, especially from Indigenous perspectives. After all, these agreements were intended to structure relationships on these Lands forever, for as long as the sun shines, the grass grows, and the river flows. These histories matter, and Indigenous Peoples come from many lines of strong, sovereign, and powerful leaders who sought to establish a foundation to live in partnership with others.

ABOUT THIS BOOK

Since time immemorial, Indigenous Peoples have had vibrant and complex relationships with each other. Sophisticated systems of Indigenous governance, laws, and politics guided policies, practices, and relationships. Indigenous Nations and communities had their own sovereign political structures and formed confederacies. Indigenous Peoples were political allies and economic, cultural, and spiritual partners, and folks blended their families by marrying into neighbouring cultures and communities. Before the arrival of settlers, Indigenous Peoples had a unique relationship with the Land, including principles for and agreements on how they harvested, traversed, and shared it. The arrival of newcomers and the imposition of settler colonialism and genocide changed and eliminated some of these practices.

In the chapters that follow, we start with Indigenous treaty making, then tell the story of treaty making between Indigenous Peoples and Britain, and then Canada, over the centuries from the 1400s to today. Canada—in all of its forms—made treaties with Indigenous Peoples, and each treaty was made under different circumstances and during different time periods. We discuss some of the confusion about how treaties were and are interpreted, according to Indigenous and settler perspectives. We also write about how treaties have been dishonoured—and continue to be dishonoured—in Canada, in many ways, from defining treaties as simple land ownership transactions, to not living up to promises, to implementing policies grounded in racism and intended to eliminate or assimilate Indigenous Peoples, to not prioritizing modern treaty making or underfunding the implementation of modern treaties. We follow Cree and Saulteaux scholar Gina Starblanket, who inspires us to use the treaty lens to better understand multiple issues and current events, and we look at mobility and gender from a treaty perspective.

Treaty histories can be hard to access, and we must remember that no singular source or perspective provides a complete picture of the past. Every treaty is unique, with complex and diverse oral histories and archival and documentary records. Here we only skim the surface of the depth of knowledge and understanding of each treaty. And, when it comes to Indigenous histories of treaties, there are several challenges that can complicate the story that we are able to tell. As one example, most written histories are from the perspective of men, more often non-Indigenous men the farther back in history you go. This is not specific to treaty histories in Canada and is true for history more generally. We draw from scholarship, oral histories, and popular works in print and online to share stories of the treaties on these Lands. We are not trying to tell a complete history of treaty making in Canada, but we are trying to share the main points of the story, get readers interested in learning more, and share suggestions for how to do that. We are not treaty experts, and you don't have to be either.

Each chapter tells its own story, of course, but there are several cross-cutting themes in this book. Language, violence, and gender are key elements of each chapter. As well, we write from (and to) northern Canada since that is where our connections and roots lie. At the same time, we take a global lens on treaty making in Canada. Yet there is so much more to learn and explore.

ON LANGUAGE

First Nations, Métis, and Inuit are extremely diverse Peoples. This diversity can be difficult to grasp because different Indigenous Peoples have not only unique cultures and histories but also points of overlap and commonality. Canada recognizes more than 630 First Nations across these diverse Lands who speak more than seventy different languages. That does not even include Métis people and Inuit! Throughout this book, we avoid homogenizing Indigenous cultures and their histories while also providing room to discuss shared experiences and world views. On the one hand, colonial authorities did not always adopt one basic policy or apply directives in the same way for all Indigenous Peoples in Canada. On the other, Indigenous Peoples in Canada share common experiences: being in relation to the Land and with each other, harvesting food from the Land, sharing experiences of colonialism and genocide, and engaging in direct relationships between their nations and the Crown. We do our best to be nation-specific, but there are times in this book when we write in general terms.

Appropriate words to refer to Indigenous Peoples (in Canada and elsewhere) have changed over time. It is always important to be aware of the ways that stereotypical or flattened language about Indigenous Peoples can function to perpetuate misrepresentations. Métis scholar Chelsea Vowel talks about this in *Indigenous Writes: A Guide to First Nations, Métis and Inuit Issues in Canada* (still a fantastic resource, by the way). A good practice is to take the time and make the effort to be as specific as possible. For instance, someone might describe a person as Indigenous or First Nation, Métis, or Inuit. But historically they might have been called something else. For instance, Crystal is Dinjii Zhuh, but she also calls herself Gwichyà Gwich'in. Her ancestors were also sometimes called Indian, Kutchin, Loucheux, Quarreller, or Dindji; some of these terms are derogatory and insulting. To complicate matters, people continue to use a wide variety of terms to describe themselves in different contexts. We acknowledge that terminology can be confusing. Knowing which words to use often means developing relationships with Indigenous

Peoples and territories, knowing their histories, and having someone knowledgeable to ask.

We seek to be nation-specific with naming and do our best to use the names that people themselves have adopted. We use additional Indigenous words from languages that we have relationships with or as used by the people whose writing and ideas we cite. Some of these words might be unfamiliar to you at first, but remain committed and try to become familiar with them. Try to pronounce them and feel the shape of another language on your tongue. We also use the general terms "First Nations," "Métis," and "Inuit" while acknowledging that many sub-communities comprise those groups.

In Canada, Section 35 of the Constitution defines First Nations, Métis, and Inuit as "Aboriginal." However, we use the umbrella term "Indigenous" instead. This is the preferred term today and links to global Indigenous movements. You will notice at times that we use the outdated term "Indian," but we do so only when sharing a direct quotation from a historical person or when referring to named legislation, such as the Indian Act. We use the term "settler" to refer to members of the white Euro-descendant population that make up the Canadian majority and mainstream; "settler" was the term, in fact, that non-Indigenous newcomers used to refer to themselves and their intention to stay on these Lands. We also use "settler" to describe the cultures and institutions of this group that are dominant or mainstream in Canada. We acknowledge that "settler" can be problematic or have different meanings in other socio-political contexts; our use of the term here is specific to the Canadian context.

We should mention some specifics about treaties and

treaty making. As you will read, Indigenous Peoples made treaties among themselves well before the arrival of newcomers. Treaties were then made between Indigenous Peoples and the Crown before 1923. When we refer to the Crown, we mean the British Crown: that is, the Dominion of Canada was created via the British North America (BNA) Act of 1867. After the Second World War, the term "dominion" fell out of favour, and nowadays we refer to the government of Canada or the federal government. In 1982, Canada patriated its Constitution from the authority of the British Parliament. Canada continues to be a constitutional monarchy where the reigning king or queen of England is Canada's head of state. Treaties made beginning in 1975 are referred to as modern treaties. These are treaties made with Canada, not Great Britain.

You will also note that we alternate between the pronouns *we/us* and *they/them* when writing about Indigenous Peoples. We have done so intentionally. Indigenous Peoples are so often othered with "them" in written works. We might wonder whether a book was written for us at all. We write from both settler and Gwichyà Gwich'in perspectives since one of us is Indigenous and the other is not.

In general, we do our best to be attentive to and respectful of language using Gregory Younging's *Elements of Indigenous Style: A Guide for Writing by and about Indigenous Peoples* as our main guide and encourage others to do so as well.

ON COLONIALISM, GENOCIDE, AND STATE VIOLENCE

Political theorists note that nation-states have a monopoly on the use of violence. This is true in Canada as well. It's why police and law enforcement agents carry guns: the rule of law is enforced through violence and even death. You will notice that police actions appear in nearly every chapter of this book. The police were part of treaty making on the Prairies, and they removed (and continue to remove) Land defenders from their Lands. It is important to note that Indigenous Peoples have a complicated relationship with the Royal Canadian Mounted Police (RCMP) and other policing bodies. Contemporary interactions with police officers, especially aggressive or violent ones, trigger memories of forced child apprehension, residential schools, the pass system, the so-called Oka Crisis, and other events.

Colonialism and genocide are running themes throughout every chapter. In fact, they are essential to the story that this book tells. We don't use the word *genocide* rhetorically here either. Raphaël Lemkin, a Polish Jewish jurist, fled Poland after the German and Soviet invasions of 1939. While in the United States, he coined the word "genocide" in 1943, later publishing it in his 1944 book *Axis Rule in Occupied Europe.* He defined genocide as "a coordinated plan of different actions aiming at the destruction of essential foundations of the life of national groups, with the aim of annihilating the groups themselves." This annihilation can take place through mass killings or destruction of the "national pattern" or way of life of the oppressed group and its replacement by the "national pattern of the oppressor."[7]

In Canada, the TRC asserted that what happened to Indigenous children at residential schools was cultural genocide. The National Inquiry into Missing and Murdered Indigenous Women and Girls concluded that violence against Indigenous women and girls amounts to genocide.

Unfortunately, the creation of Canada has been violent and damaging to Indigenous Peoples, even as settler society has gained great benefits. We have written this book with a great deal of care for the reader, but we do not sugar-coat these disturbing histories. To advance a shared understanding of treaties, we need to understand the truth of our shared history.

WRITING FROM AND FOR THE NORTH

We are all always in relationship with the Land. As authors, we are both connected to the North in different ways, and this relationship figures prominently in this book. Additionally, the North is regularly overlooked in important conversations about Indigenous Peoples and Canada. Often conditions in northern Canada have been very different from those in southern Canada. As you will see, northern Canada has been important for conversations about treaties and Indigenous rights, and it is where many modern treaty agreements are located. There is also a tendency among researchers and academics to focus solely on First Nations' histories. There are several reasons for this, but the point here is that we cannot talk about the history of Canada and the Land without including northern Indigenous Peoples, among them First Nations, Métis, and Inuit communities.

We wrote this book on Treaty 6 Lands, near the North Saskatchewan River, and on Treaty 8 and Treaty 11 Lands, in the boreal forest and the Arctic. We wrote it in the summertime, when the wild roses are blooming and the aspen leaves rustle in the wind, and we wrote it through the long, dark wintertime, when snow blankets the Land and the call of the raven breaks through the frozen air. We wrote through break-up and freeze-up, from the first leaves of spring to the last ones of fall. These Lands and the relationships that they hold have guided our writing and given us purpose and strength. We write this book in the spirit of truth and reconciliation. We write it in awe and recognition of all those who fight and have fought in defence of Indigenous Lands, for Indigenous rights, and toward cultural resurgence. And we write it with hope for the future.

1.

TREATY MAKING SINCE TIME IMMEMORIAL

> We come from the land, our language comes from the land, our visions come from the land, everything we are comes from the land. The land is alive and that's why we are alive, because of its magic.[1]
>
> —Elizabeth Yakeleya (née Blondin) and Joe Blondin, Dene

Indigenous Peoples have made treaties since time immemorial. Time immemorial harks back to the earliest days of the Land. On other occasions, time immemorial can signify the period before the arrival of colonizers and before these Lands were called the Americas. Other Indigenous Peoples refer to time immemorial to signify their connections with Lands that can go back a few centuries. This concept can shift and be used differently according to the story being shared, the storyteller, the social setting, the audience, and the story's lesson. It does not follow European conventions of time and should be understood in a non-linear way.

Regardless of how one defines time immemorial, we know that Indigenous Peoples have used the concept of a treaty for a very, very long time. It is important to start here, at the beginning, because these concepts are foundational when we seek to understand more about the agreements on Lands now called Canada. Indigenous Peoples were making treaties with each other and the natural world way back in the distant past. Here we share examples from the North, including ideas from Inuvialuit, Dinjii Zhuh, Sahtú, Tłı̨chǫ, and Yellowknives Dene cultures. We also incorporate teachings about early treaties from Nêhiyawak (Cree), Dene, Haudenosaunee, and Anishinaabeg.

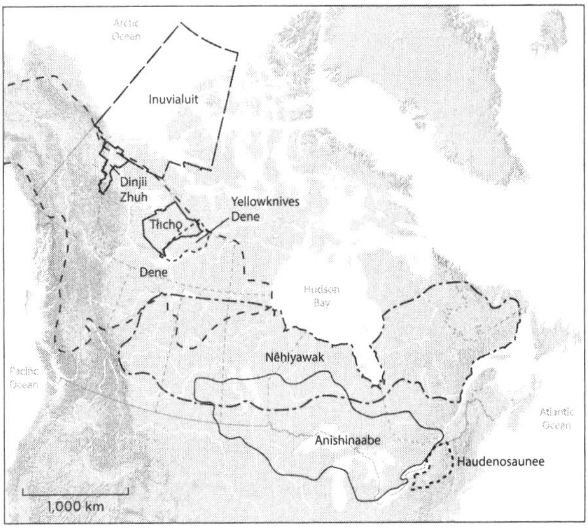

Map locating Inuvialuit, Dinjii Zhuh, Tłı̨chǫ, Yellowknives Dene, Nêhiyawak, Dene, Haudenosaunee, and Anishinaabeg Peoples. Map by Eric Leinberger.

TIME IMMEMORIAL, INGILRAANI, AND TS'II DĘĮĮ

Some Indigenous Peoples describe time immemorial as a creation period and tell origin stories about it. They might include sacred knowledge or accounts about how the Earth was created or what early human life looked like. Included in some of these stories are accounts about agreements, relationships, or treaties made with animals, plants, and the Land. One example is the well-known story of Turtle Island. In some Anishinaabe tellings, it begins in a time when the Earth was flooded by the Creator. Nanabush asked the animals to swim deep into the water to collect soil with which to recreate the world. One by one the animals tried but failed. The last animal was the muskrat, and it was underwater for a long time. When the muskrat finally resurfaced, it had a bit of wet soil in its paws. Nanabush took the soil and put it on a willing turtle's back. This became Turtle Island, the centre of creation, and what is now called North America.

Another example comes from Inuvialuit culture in the Arctic and takes place during Ingilraani (time immemorial), when a man, his wife, and their son, along with an orphaned girl, overcome a devastating flood. The son is sometimes spoken of as having the spirit of a raven. In the story, the son spears the top of a pingo in the rising water, which causes the water to recede and renew the Land.[2]

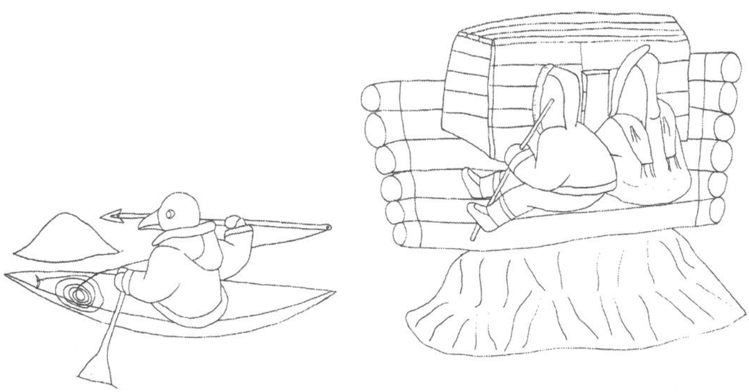

Illustration of the flood story by Mona Ohoveluk. Image from Herbert T. Schwarz's *Elik, and Other Stories of the MacKenzie Eskimos* (McClelland and Stewart, 1970).

These stories also sometimes recount how animals were prominent and influential. For Gwichyà Gwich'in, the concept of ts'ii dęįį (time immemorial) is so old that its exact meaning in English cannot be fully translated. Tsiigehtshik Elder and former Chief Hyacinthe Andre described it as the earliest days of the Land, when humans and animals were equals and could change forms. Many Gwichyà Gwich'in stories and historical accounts that originate in ts'ii dęįį capture the relationship between animals and humans, when they could communicate with each other, use powerful forces such as medicine power, and shapeshift. Shapeshifting, for them, was when humans transformed into animals and animals into humans. Animal-human relationships, including the trials and tribulations within those relationships, are documented in many stories about the tricky raven, destructive wolverine, and sympathetic loon.

During ts'ii dęįį, animals such as the beaver, fish, or wolverine were sometimes giant and could live a long time. They also left strange marks on the Land and were responsible for unique and memorable Land formations. The large creatures or spirit animals, which disturbed and imprinted themselves onto Land formations, were called chijuudiee. They were not humans who shapeshifted into animals but something else entirely. Giant animals might still be present today.

Chii Akàn, or Rock-Its Beaver Lodge, was the home of giant beavers. Teetł'it Gwich'in Elder Robert Alexie Sr. said that, before the construction of the Dempster Highway, there used to be many boulders and sticks at Chii Akàn, just like a giant beaver lodge.[3]

Chii Akàn, also known as Beaverhouse Mountain or Churchward Hill in the Gwich'in Nation. Ingrid Kritsch, Department of Culture and Heritage, Gwich'in Tribal Council.

In many northern Indigenous cultures, there are stories about a powerful warrior and traveller. For Gwichyà Gwich'in, his name is Atachuukąįį. Elder Gabe Andre tells the story about Atachuukąįį and a giant named Chii Choo who travelled the Land. English was Elder Andre's second language, and the story below is told in his original wording:

> Atachuukaii did not kill him, he starved him to death. Every time he killed good things to eat, he cooked them real good, but then he wanted to go and have a good wash before he was going to eat the food. Well, every time that happened, Atachuukaii sent a whole lot of animals there to clean up what Chii choo was going to eat, so, nothing more to eat.
>
> The giant cut a piece of his own backside off, and made pemmican from it. He should have eaten it right there! But instead he said, "I wonder who can freeze

> it for me?" And Atachuukaii was sitting nearby, could hear this. Now he saw a rat swimming by, and he said to that rat, "Why don't you go over there and freeze that grease?" (That's what they called it, grease.) He could have eaten it like that, I wonder why he wanted to freeze it? The rat went over to Chii choo and said, "There's a creek over here with cold water. I'll freeze it for you." So he gave it to that rat, and the rat swam over close to where Atachuukaii was sitting. He took a little rock, threw it at the rat and hit him in the mouth.
>
> The rat let go of the fat, and it all floated away. So Atachuukaii went down to where the fat was floating. He took the water with that fat like that [gesture of hands scooping up water], and he drank it. And since that time people drink water in that way.
>
> Then he went back to Chii choo, and he told him, "I lost that meat, it all fell in the water."
>
> That's when Chii choo started crying—talking about sunrise and sunset, saying that he'd never see it again. That's the song he sang, but I don't know how it goes. Then at last he starved to death. That's how Atachuukaii was able to beat Chii choo. That's what was told to me by the old people.[4]

Atachuukąįį travelled the landscape and overcame adversity, finding a way to outsmart the man-eating giant. Atachuukąįį also separated people from animals, establishing relationships based on mutual respect and understanding. He made things safe for the people again through agreements. In other words, Atachuukąįį might have been responsible for the first treaties among Gwichyà Gwich'in.

Atachuukąįį created Chuu Niint'aii K'it, or The Ramparts, when he left his canoe as he chased Chii Choo. A large rock that looks like an overturned canoe can still be seen there. ©NWT Archives/GNWT Dept. of Public Works and Services, G-1995-001: 0373.

Atachuukąįį also gave the people laws to enable them to live together in harmony. There are other northern stories about figures similar to Atachuukąįį, such as a leader named Yamǫ́rıa by Sahtú Dene and known as Yamǫǫ̀zha among Tłı̨chǫ. Today Yamǫ́rıa's laws are known as Dene Laws. They include

- share what you have;
- help each other;
- love each other as much as possible;
- be respectful of Elders and everything around you;
- sleep at night and work during the day;
- be polite and don't argue with anyone;
- young girls and boys should behave respectfully;
- pass on the teachings; and
- be happy at all times.

These laws, found in the oldest stories, appear in the everyday practices of Dene today. Other laws also include how to live respectfully with animals. Teetł'it Gwich'in Elder Sharon Snowshoe recounts a story called "The Boy in the Moon," shared by Johnny Semple, to explain how Dinjii Zhuh have a special relationship with caribou and thus call themselves "caribou people." The story teaches readers and listeners how to respect caribou. As she tells it, when humans and animals were separated and could no longer communicate or change places, their close relationship persisted.

Elder Snowshoe shares that "every caribou has a bit of human heart in them, and every human has a bit of caribou heart. It is because of this that we have partial knowledge of what the other is thinking and feeling. This makes it critical that we always show respect to the caribou."[5] Showing respect is demonstrated by best practices for engaging with caribou, including never trivializing or disrespecting them, never wasting the meat, and sharing the meat after the hunt. Caribou continue to be central to Dinjii Zhuh understandings of life. This is Dinjii Zhuh law, governance, and culture.

Ts'ii dęįį lasted until non-Indigenous newcomers arrived in the North. But not all ts'ii dęįį stories have come to an end, and that means we still have ts'ii dęįį knowledge. Simply put, the relationships among our ancestors, animals, and the natural world are ongoing. We are active players in this story, and we can determine how the story ends.

These creation or origin stories continue to be shared among generations of Indigenous Peoples. They are also being taught in school classrooms, on social media, in museums and books, and by cultural organizations.

TREATIES AMONG INDIGENOUS PEOPLES

Indigenous Peoples traded, travelled, and gathered across territories and long distances. We know this through storytelling, relationships, intimate unions, treaties, economic development, and how the Land has been used and shared. Distant nations travelled to gather, engage in ceremonies, and share news. Nations traded wild rice and corn, shells, pigments, minerals and metals, fish and furs, ceremonies, clothing, and horses. In other words, there was an extensive network of inter-Indigenous trade and diplomacy before the arrival of Europeans.[6] There is no doubt that formal alliances were made between nations to facilitate these continental networks.

Moreover, treaties were made and remade between Indigenous Peoples on how to use Lands and territories, share resources, and maintain peace. Nahkawininiwak (Saulteaux) Elder Danny Musqua, of the Keeseekoose First Nation, said that "all of the agreements they have had between one another as peoples and as nations were always based on [land] use—on how they were going to use that land. And . . . when I say . . . the use of that land, we had agreements between one another, hunting territories that we shared, trapping lands that we shared, gathering lands that we shared, medicinal lands that we shared [sacred lands], . . . lands that we designated for the shelter and safety of all people."[7]

There is a notable example from around current-day Sǫǫ̀mbak'è. Sometime during the 1800s, Tłı̨chǫ leader Edzo and Yellowknives Dene leader Akaitcho created a peace treaty, which ended years of hostility and warfare. Tłı̨chǫ lived between Tinde'e (Great Slave Lake) and Sahtú (Great Bear Lake), and Yellowknives Dene inhabited the forest and tundra north and east of Tinde'e.[8] They sealed the agreement at Gots'ǫkàtì (Mesa Lake) with a huge celebration at which they danced for two days. People danced for so long that they wore a circular imprint into the earth with their feet, which can still be seen today. Akaitcho and Edzo also asked their people to marry each other so that the treaty would live on in perpetuity. In a paper written for the Dene Nation and the Royal Commission on Aboriginal Peoples (RCAP), Rene Lamothe shared that it takes about five days to tell the full history of this treaty-making process between Edzo and Akaitcho.[9]

Nêhiyawak and Dene also made peace with each other through a treaty. This was during a time of illness marked by epidemics resulting from pathogens that newcomers brought. Nêhiyawak pushed Dene northward, sparking a war between the two Peoples. Nêhiyawak and Dene leaders met in what is now northwest Alberta after three battles with each other. At this meeting, Nêhiyawak explained to Dene what was happening in the South. Nêhiyawak further explained that they needed Land away from the newcomers and their diseases. Although they won the war, Dene agreed to give Nêhiyawak all the Lands south and east of the Peace River. The river became the new boundary between the two territories.[10] That is why, today, it is called Peace River.

Nêhiyawak and Niitsitapi (Blackfoot) also made a treaty together in the Prairies. They entered into a treaty titled Wîtaskêwin. This is a word from nêhiyawêwin (the Cree language), meaning "to live together on the Land." Many people also translate it as "peace hills," and indeed the treaty was made in the hills near the present-day town of Wetaskiwin, Alberta. Following local protocols, the treaty would have been marked by a pipe ceremony, at which leaders would have shared the pipe and sealed the agreement, ensuring that it "would be blessed by the Great Spirit and bound on earth and in the spiritual realm."[11] Nêhiyawak and Niitsitapi also secured peace through kinship relationships, such as adoption. After his only son was killed in battle, Siksika Chief Isapo-muxika (Crowfoot) adopted Nêhiyaw Chief Pitikwahanapiwiyin (Poundmaker). Pitikwahanapiwiyin stayed with his adopted father at Blackfoot Crossing and eventually returned to his people. This adoption created a bond and lasting peace between these enemy nations.

Based on oral histories of his people, Little Pine First Nation journalist Doug Cuthand describes the last treaty between Nêhiyawak and Niitsitapi at the Bear Hills in 1871. Rather than continuing to make war, diplomats from both sides met, exchanged tobacco, and requested a peace meeting. As Cuthand writes, "the chiefs sealed the deal with a pipe ceremony pledging their word to the treaty. Next, the warriors of both nations mounted their horses and formed two long lines across the prairie about a kilometre apart. Someone gave the war whoop and the two groups galloped toward each other. When they met, they dismounted and shook hands. In that manner they pledged to end the war and not fight again." There were adoptions too. Families met and shared their children with each other to dissuade future attacks on both sides and to nurture long-lasting relationships. According to Cuthand, this treaty "has never been breached and is still in effect. The treaty brought peace to the plains, and we were able to move on to the uncertain future."[12]

Further east, the Great Law of Peace brought together the Haudenosaunee Confederacy. Incorrectly called the Iroquois Confederacy by the French, and the League of Five Nations by the English, the Haudenosaunee Confederacy means "People of the Long House." Following a period of intense warfare sometime between 1000 and 1450 CE, a confederacy of five nations—Cayuga, Kanien'keha:ka, Oneida, Onondaga, and Seneca—was founded by the prophet known as the Peacemaker with the help of Aionwatha (Hiawatha) during time immemorial, making it "one of the first and longest lasting participatory democracies in the world."[13]

The imagery used is of nations sitting together under a tree of peace: "I Dekanwidah, and the Union Lords now uproot the tallest pine tree and into the cavity thereby made we cast all weapons of war. . . . We bury them from sight and we plant again the tree. Thus shall the Great Peace be established and hostilities shall no longer be known between the Five Nations but peace of the United People."[14] The confederacy is structured and bound by the Great Law of Peace, the constitution for the confederacy, with policies, procedures, philosophy, and mechanisms of amendment. The confederacy later worked toward diplomacy and peace negotiations with European newcomers as member nations hoped to secure Lands and the benefits of trade.[15] The Haudenosaunee Confederacy is still strong and sovereign today.

Treaty making among these Indigenous Peoples included otgó'ä (wampum). Otgó'ä beads were white and purple, made from rounded, sanded, and drilled North Atlantic mollusc shells. The beads were woven together into belts that marked agreements among peoples across Haudenosaunee,

Mi'kmaq, Anishinaabeg, and Wendat territories. According to the Onondaga Nation, "the shell is thought of as a living record of the Haudenosaunee. The speaker puts the words of the agreement into the wampum as the strings or belts are woven together. Each speaker thereafter uses the wampum to remember the initial agreement and the history that has happened to date. To us, the belts are our living history." Wampum was used as a sacred ceremonial marker to invite other nations to council meetings, to symbolize titles within the Haudenosaunee Confederacy, and to signify the importance or the authority of the message being delivered.

Again, according to the Onondaga Nation, "when a string of wampum . . . is held in a person's hand, they are said to be speaking truthfully. During ceremonies, the wampum strings are used to convey that the speaker's words are true. People listening to a speaker holding the wampum also know this and are very attentive [to] and respectful of the speaker's message."[16]

One such treaty made with wampum was the Dish with One Spoon. The rights and responsibilities within the Dish with One Spoon date back at least 900 years, way before European treaty making on these Lands.[17] Haudenosaunee artist and educator Lorrie Gallant explains that the Dish with One Spoon "uses purple and white beads that represent friendship and peace. The purple 'dish' represents the continent (Turtle Island) and all the different Nations. The white centre represents the tail of a beaver, or the resources of this part of Turtle Island. Nations are only to eat from the dish with one spoon, meaning that resources should be shared, each territory should be respected, and nations will not war with each other for the domination of the resources."[18] In this sense, the concept is about respect for the people and animals on the Lands on which we live.

Leanne Betasamosake Simpson has written about the foundation of Anishinaabeg treaty making with the natural world, which she calls a "set of ethics, values, and practices known as Bimaadiziwin or 'living the good life.'" Bimaadiziwin ensures that humans live in balance with the natural world, from the individual to the broader nation, and centres the Seven Grandfather teachings: humility, bravery, honesty, wisdom, truth, respect, and love. Because of Bimaadiziwin, leaders considered how their decisions could affect not only animals and plants, relationships both within and outside the nation, but also the next seven generations of Anishinaabeg.

Simpson says that Anishinaabeg call the Dish with One Spoon treaty with Haudenosaunee Gdoo-naaganinaa, or Our Dish. Both nations hold rights and responsibilities in this treaty, including shared responsibility for hunting territories and ecological connections. She says that the treaty "did not involve interfering with one another's sovereignty as nations. It represented harmony and interconnection, as

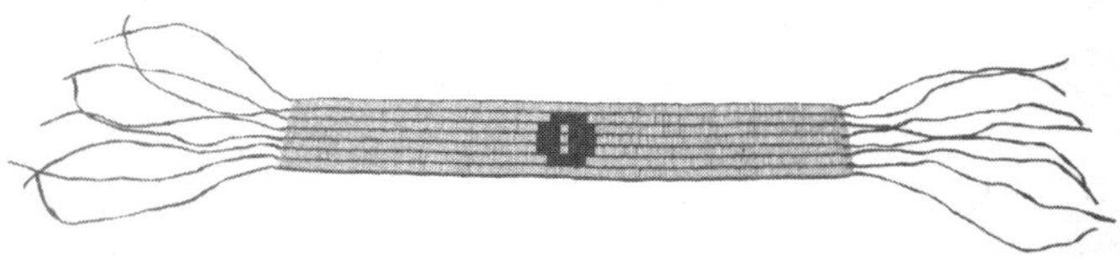

Dish with One Spoon wampum. Replica made out of resin beads and animal sinew by Yvonne Thomas, knowledge keeper and co-founder of the Jake Thomas Learning Centre, for Toronto Metropolitan University Libraries, 2020. Photo courtesy of Toronto Metropolitan University Libraries.

both parties were to be responsible for taking care of the dish."[19] This is vastly different from how Canada acts as a treaty partner today.

Other confederacies or alliances existed as well. The Nêhiyaw-Pwât (sometimes called the Iron Confederacy) was a political system of multicultural bands in the Prairies linked through shared understandings and practices of kinship. Through the mid-1800s, the Nêhiyaw-Pwât, as a regional collective, maintained an alliance of dozens of local bands of Nêhiyawak, Métis, Nahkawininiwak, and Nakota (Assiniboine). Nations were independent but interconnected through kin relationships. The alliance dominated what is now western Canada and controlled access to European trade goods, becoming wealthy and powerful in the fur trade era. Oceti Sakowin (Seven Council Fires or the Great Sioux Nation) was also a confederacy of nations that speak dialects of the same language: Dakota, Nakota, and Lakota. They share a common culture, kinship, traditions, and history as autonomous social groups living within original Oceti Sakowin territory, which extended across a vast region, including what are now four Canadian provinces and multiple US-American states. They gathered annually to reaffirm their connection and perform the Sundance ceremony. In recent years, the Oceti Sakowin powerfully resisted the Dakota Access Pipeline and environmental injustice on their Lands.

So treaty making clearly has been a long-standing practice for Indigenous Peoples. There are examples of treaty making among Indigenous Peoples across the continent that predate any treaties with colonizing nations or do not involve those nations. However, when we search online or in libraries for Indigenous treaties, the available resources are overwhelmingly about treaties between Indigenous Peoples and colonizing settler nations. Yet Indigenous treaty making reflects thousands of years of making and maintaining relationships with Lands, plants and animals, and other nations on this continent. The goal was to overcome conflict and live with each other in peace and balance. These practices shaped and continue to shape new relationships on these Lands.

THE BROADENING OF POLITICAL HORIZONS

The possibilities of treaty making inherently lead to a broadening of horizons, especially during times of contact and change. Gina Starblanket analyzes treaties in terms of relationships or how treaty-making practices reflect diplomatic practices that Indigenous Peoples have followed with other living beings, and with each other, since time immemorial. Indeed, Indigenous traditions in treaty making mediated relationships among individuals, collectives, and Lands and waters within shared territories. We are dependent on one another and the environments that surround us. This relationality is evident in the kinship terms and metaphors used in treaties between Indigenous Peoples as well as those with European countries that symbolize notions of sharing, care, and nurturance.

Relationality is an essential practice within many Indigenous cultures. Often it is used to speak to how we are connected to each other and answers certain questions: Who are you? Where do you come from? Who claims you? Where do you belong? In this context, relationality foregrounds the relationships inherent to a world view that sees connections among humans, animals, plants, and Lands as essential not only to survival but also to living well. The agreements that structure these relationships, the original treaties of these Lands, continue today. And getting back to treaty relationality can support living better together today. As Elizabeth Yakeleya and Joe Blondin told us, "the land is alive and that's why we are alive, because of its magic."[20] We have all felt that magic, regardless of whether we are Indigenous to the Lands on which we live or not. With the majesty of the Land comes relationships and the need to tend to and nurture them. Before the arrival of newcomers, Indigenous Peoples practised ways to accomplish that.

Treaties were not only a European or Canadian invention. These long-standing forms of governance positioned Indigenous communities to be experienced and knowledgeable in treaty making when the first explorers, missionaries, fur traders, and settlers arrived and when the first settler nation-state governments were established. Ancient ancestral knowledge combined with contemporary Indigenous political and ceremonial practices shaped the process of and participation in treaty making between nations and the Crown or Canada.

2.

WHEN THINGS BEGAN TO CHANGE

> There were lots of people. They had everything, but he never mentioned what they ate. Well, he said they had everything, that's all that Daįį dhakhaįį needed to say. They gave him some things, too, to take home—a plate, I think, a plate, and a pot. But it was a plate made from steel. That's why it's funny.[1]
>
> —Gabe Andre, Gwichyà Gwich'in Elder

Gwichyà Gwich'in told stories that predicted cultural change before European newcomers arrived on their Lands. Gabe Andre tells a story about a man named Daįį dhakhaįį. He visited a place called Daįį dhakhaįį chì' (Bluefly Killer's Hill) because he had dreamt about it. He found a door at the side of the cliff and went in. He found a buffalo tied up and saw many people who had everything. Those people gave him some things, such as a plate and a pot made from steel. When Daįį dhakhaįį was ready to leave, the people pointed out a second door. They said that, if he left through the second door, "your country is going to be like it is now, forever. But if you go back the same way, some day this country will change."[2] Daįį dhakhaįį was worried, though, that if he went through the new door he wouldn't find his partner again. He also didn't want to change anything. Fearful of losing his partner, Daįį dhakhaįį left the way that he had come, thus initiating a time of great change and new relationships for Gwichyà Gwich'in.

This can be read as a story about newcomers to Dinjii Zhuh Lands and the North, with trade goods like metal axes, pots, and other items representing the massive changes to come. We will never know if the course of history would have changed had Daįį dhakhaįį chosen the other door. But we do know that there is no way that he—or his relatives—could have predicted which changes were to come.

As you've already read, Indigenous Peoples in North America had treaties with each other and the natural world. They had rich and vibrant cultures and societies, but history books have not focused on them. Instead, it is more common to learn about European history, such as the Hundred Years' War (1337–1453), the (in)famous trial of Joan of Arc (1431), the invention of the printing press (1440–50s), the fall of the Byzantine Empire (1453), the Scientific Revolution (1543–1687), and the Enlightenment (1685–1815). A part of the story of treaty making between Indigenous Peoples and newcomers, though, begins around the time of the voyages of Christopher Columbus (1492–1504), which marked a new period when Europeans began exploring and conquering Lands.

COLONIAL BEGINNINGS

During the fifteenth century, European sovereigns—kings and queens—were subject only to the Christian God, and they were understood as God's representatives on Earth via the Catholic Church. Much changed in the following century with the Reformation and the rise of Protestantism, but that's a story for a different book. Suffice it to say that, at the time, the pope (the head of the Catholic Church and the Vatican's head of state) had immense power, influencing kings and queens and setting out directives in the name of Christianity through papal bulls. A papal bull is a public decree or charter—or an official public statement—made by the pope. When colonizing nations first began to claim territories, it was the pope who decided which European nations would be granted the rights to those territories.

An international law of colonization called the Doctrine of Discovery was first initiated through a series of papal bulls in the late 1400s. In 1436, Pope Eugenius IV issued a papal bull confirming Portuguese rights of conquest and trade in parts of West Africa. Later papal bulls extended these rights, including *Romanus Pontifex* (1455), which gave Portugal authority along the African coast. In 1493, three papal bulls granted the Lands discovered by Columbus to Spain as well as any Lands that it would discover in the future (if not already in the possession of any Christian king). The pope drew a line through the Atlantic Ocean, allowing Spain the first opportunity to conquer Lands "discovered and to be discovered" west of that line.

Portugal was entitled to the same rights east of that line. Spain and Portugal later amended these papal bulls in the Treaty of Tordesillas (1494) when they moved the line farther west, thereby allowing Portugal to claim the eastern coast of Brazil. This gave the Spanish and Portuguese Empires the authorization to continue exploring, discovering,

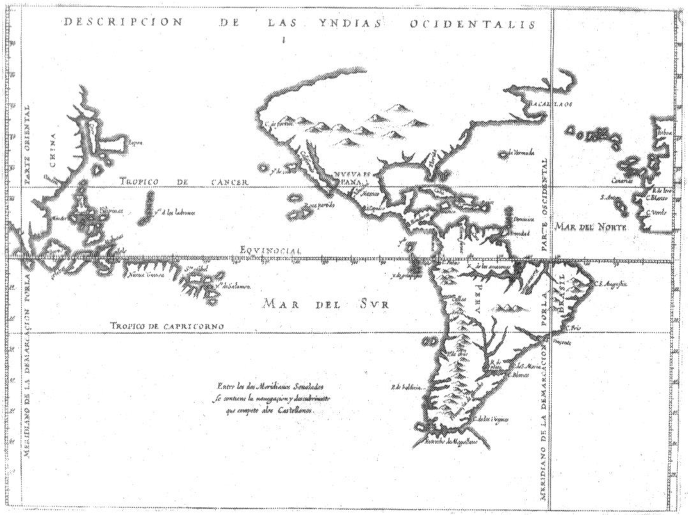

In 1494, the Treaty of Tordesillas drew a boundary through the "New World," granting Spain and Portugal control over Lands, resources, and Indigenous Peoples. The line cutting through eastern Brazil marks this division. This map is from *Novus orbis, sive, Descriptio Indiae Occidentalis* by Antonio de Herrera y Tordesillas, published in 1622. Library of Congress, 09014008.

and conquering territories. At the time, these Lands were home to over 50 million Indigenous Peoples living in well-established societies across the Americas. Spain and Portugal applied their claims using the Doctrine of Discovery across the South Pacific, Africa, Asia, and the Americas. These claims were dependent not on dealing with people living in those territories but on mutual recognition between European authorities. The Spanish initially claimed territorial rights in what is now Newfoundland and Labrador based on the Treaty of Tordesillas, even as the British explorer John Cabot was navigating those coasts and the Portuguese were establishing fishing outposts on the east coast of modern-day Canada.

Scholars point out that the Doctrine of Discovery not only was used to justify conquest and colonization but also remains an applicable principle today, one that continues to limit the rights of Indigenous Peoples and their governments. As international law, the Doctrine of Discovery had elements reflected today in the laws, treaties, court cases, policies, and histories of almost all European settler societies. These elements include:

- Europeans had a right and a duty to convert non-Christians and to civilize Indigenous Peoples.
- European cultures and civilizations were superior to Indigenous cultures and civilizations.
- The first European country that discovered Lands claimed rights over those Lands and the Indigenous Peoples who inhabited them.
- A claim of discovery meant that an Indigenous Nation's rights to Land, sovereignty, self-determination, and human rights were dependent on negotiating with the discovering authority for recognition of those rights, otherwise known as pre-emption.
- Pre-emption meant that the Euro-American country that first discovered new Lands had an exclusive right to buy the Lands of Indigenous Peoples if it chose to do so. Pre-emption greatly limited the negotiating position of Indigenous Peoples.
- Upon discovery, Indigenous Nations lost aspects of their sovereignty and their rights to engage in international trade and treaty making. Colonial governments treated Indigenous Peoples as domestic concerns instead of allowing them to be part of an international order. This is called

domestication, and, once domesticated, Indigenous Nations could interact politically only with the government of the country that discovered them.

- A claim of discovery also meant that Euro-American countries could claim Lands contiguous to and surrounding actual discoveries and settlements (as when an entire watershed is claimed by discovering the mouth of a river).[3]

Of course, we know that these Lands were not "new" or "empty" and that newcomers did not "discover" them. Indigenous Peoples have lived on and cared for these Lands since time immemorial.

Nevertheless, England, Holland, and France later used this international law to claim rights in North America and elsewhere. These nations didn't have papal bulls to legitimize their claims, but it didn't really matter because by the sixteenth century the Doctrine of Discovery was beginning to be applied as secular and international law. After the sixteenth century, French, English, Dutch, Danish, Flemish, German, Italian, Swedish, and Russian states all claimed territories around the world and established themselves as colonial powers.

European countries spent centuries exercising sovereignty, claiming Lands that were not theirs, enslaving, conquering, colonizing, and "civilizing" Indigenous Peoples, and developing further legal techniques and institutions to do so.

Interestingly, the Doctrine of Discovery and associated concepts that today ground international laws regarding sovereignty, nationhood, trade, rights, and so on weren't developed all at once and then exported to different colonial contexts around the world. The doctrine was created *because* of the encounter between Europeans and Indigenous Peoples in the era of discovery and colonization.

In other words, international law in the age of exploration posited a set of universal rules and rights that applied to all humans: Europeans, Indigenous Peoples, everyone. But Europeans understood Indigenous Peoples as too culturally different: they didn't follow these (European-developed) universal norms, they lived in a state of nature instead of civilization, and as a result they were defined (by Europeans) as inherently unable to be sovereign. Indigenous Peoples were thus excluded by European thinkers of the day from possessing the characteristic and unique powers of the sovereign: the power to wage war and acquire title to territories and authority over alien peoples. Europeans could wage a just war against Indigenous Peoples if they did not allow Europeans to trade and spread Christianity.

A perfect example of the ritual of discovery exists within the founding narrative of what would become Canada when French Breton explorer Jacques Cartier sailed with his crew into the Gulf of St. Lawrence in 1534 and erected a giant cross in the earth with the words *Long Live the King of France*, claiming possession of the territory in the name of King Francis I.

As mentioned, the Land that Cartier planted his cross on was not empty or unoccupied—quite the opposite actually! And he would have known this. Indeed, part of the story of the planting of the cross is that Chief Donnacona of the St. Lawrence Haudenosaunee protested the raising of the cross. European newcomers quickly realized that Indigenous communities were vibrant and powerful, accustomed

An artist's representation of the scene in which Cartier erects the cross and claims the Land for his king. We imagine it to have been much less glorious in real life. Charles William Jefferys. Library and Archives Canada, Acc. No. 1996-282-1.

to diplomacy with other nations and able to wage war when necessary. But Cartier's king, as a European sovereign, had the right to sovereignty and could acquire territory and claim authority over the people living there. Indigenous Peoples could not.

However, if European countries had the right to sovereignty, then why make treaties with Indigenous Peoples at all? The doctrine provided a framework for European entities to claim Lands and for their claims to be recognized by other European authorities. The Doctrine of Discovery did recognize Aboriginal title, but it was only the right to use and occupy Lands until that title was extinguished by a discovering authority. From a European perspective, it was through treaties that Aboriginal title could be extinguished.

This is very different from the perspective of Indigenous Peoples, who saw treaties as sacred agreements in which peoples committed to sharing the Lands.

In North America, Holland, France, and Great Britain all made treaties with First Nations. The tentacles of the British and French Empires and the Dutch West India Company extended around the globe, and they devoted significant resources to establishing and expanding settlement and trade in North America. Throughout the 1600s and 1700s, Britain, France, and Holland made alliances with Indigenous Peoples to facilitate trade, settlement, and war (or peace) with each other. The Europeans were vying for Lands and resources and formalizing allies in the so-called New World to establish commercial rights and settlements in what is now eastern Canada and the United States (today's Nova Scotia, New Brunswick, Quebec, Massachusetts, and New Hampshire).

We find it unlikely that Indigenous Peoples bought in to the hierarchical international law developed by colonizing nations. Indeed, First Nations would have understood themselves as entities on par with European nations with developed practices and protocols for treaties and agreements with each other and all creation. Political theorist Carole Pateman writes that, by the early eighteenth century, the British Crown had already acknowledged the sovereignty of Indigenous Peoples. First Nations at the time insisted on treaties and agreements emphasizing peace and friendship to limit settlement, formalize alliances, and ensure that their ways of life on their Lands were protected.

The concepts underlying the Doctrine of Discovery were taken forward into these treaties, thus justifying the conquering of Lands already inhabited by rich Indigenous civilizations. The losses have been immeasurable and devastating, and we continue to feel their effects. In April 2023, resulting from the TRC's 94 Calls to Action (specifically Call to Action 45) and conversations about the unmarked graves of Indigenous children at the sites of former Indian residential schools in Canada, the Vatican repudiated the Doctrine of Discovery.

What does that mean? Although the Catholic Church received accolades for making this announcement, neither the Vatican nor Pope Francis had legal authority or decision-making power in Canada. But the Catholic Church failed to acknowledge that the Doctrine of Discovery was really one example of a broader world view of conquering Lands, accumulating wealth, and gaining converts. That ideology and those practices persist.

Mi'kmaw lawyer and activist Pam Palmater is hopeful that this will produce systemic changes but points out that the repudiation of the Doctrine of Discovery has not resulted in any meaningful change in Canada to date. The doctrine is part of the creation of Canada in all kinds of ways and continues to be part of how Canada functions today: structuring how Land and property rights are regulated, grounding the existence of Canadian sovereignty, shaping how our courts function, and more.

PEACE AND FRIENDSHIP WITH NEWCOMERS

The earliest treaties between Europeans and First Nations were grounded in long-standing governance practices of Indigenous Peoples in eastern North America. These practices were focused on diplomacy and concepts of peace, friendship, and noninterference. As in treaties made before the arrival of colonizing nations, First Nations sought to continue to exist as autonomous groups within relationships of peace and friendship with newcomers. For example, the Haudenosaunee Confederacy carried out more than 400 negotiations between 1613 and 1842 with Dutch, French, English, and American entities. Gaswéñdah, or the Two Row Wampum Treaty, is the agreement made in 1613 between the Haudenosaunee and representatives of the Dutch government in what is now upstate New York. According to Kanien'keha:ka historian Ray Fadden, the Dutch initially proposed a paternalistic relationship: the Dutch as fathers and the Haudenosaunee as children. The Haudenosaunee rejected this notion:

> We will not be like Father and Son, but like Brothers. [Our treaties] symbolize two paths or two vessels, travelling down the same river together. One, a birchbark canoe, will be for the Indian People, their laws, their customs, and their ways. The other, a ship, will be for the white people and their laws, their customs, and their ways. We shall each travel the river together, side by side, but in our own boat. Neither of us will make compulsory laws nor interfere in the internal affairs of the other. Neither of us will try to steer the other's vessel.[4]

For the Haudenosaunee, this treaty is the basis of all subsequent treaties. It is still valid today and guides how different peoples can live together on these Lands. Fully implementing Gaswéñdah means supporting the rights of

Indigenous Peoples to maintain themselves on their own Lands, according to their own systems of governance, organization, and economics, but alongside settler systems. These are two parallel paths, side by side, and do not converge, and one does not dominate or oppress the other. This treaty has been broken many times by programs of assimilation in both Canada and the United States.

The Haudenosaunee also made treaties with the Dutch and then the British colonies through the Covenant Chain alliances in the seventeenth and eighteenth centuries. This agreement is sometimes called the Silver Covenant Chain. According to the Onondaga Nation, the term "chain" is an English translation of words that mean "arms linked together" or "they have joined hands/arms." It also says that, "even when the term 'chain' does not appear in the records, it is implied, at least from the Haudenosaunee point of view, in the English term 'treaty.'"[5] This reflects the Haudenosaunee principle of balance.

The term "silver" in the phrase signifies the increasing strength of friendship bonds. In its entirety, the Silver Covenant Chain represents two linked entities in a cooperative and mutually beneficial pact. This needs to be maintained continually; for example, a silver chain needs to be polished regularly, or it will tarnish. The Covenant Chain's key metaphors are thus about the links between peoples and the ongoing maintenance needed for an effective treaty alliance. The chain of friendship between settlers and Indigenous Peoples needed to be actively cared for and not neglected. Indigenous Peoples said as much about all treaties in general: maintenance needs to be ongoing on both sides. These agreements are about relationships and relationality.

There are also peace and friendship treaties written on parchment or paper from this era. One of them is the Treaty of Mascarene, or Mascarene's Treaty, ratified by the Wabanaki Nations of Mi'kmaq, Wolastoqiyik (Maliseet), Peskotomuhkati (Passamaquoddy), and Penawahpskek (Penobscot) and the Nova Scotia government in 1725. Maliseet scholar Andrea Bear Nicholas encourages its use in Nova Scotia and New Brunswick today, even though both provinces have either ignored or totally rejected it as a legitimate treaty.[6] Over the years, Wolastoqiyik had been consistently charged and found guilty of violating provincial fish and game rules because the justice system said that no treaty gave them rights to fish and hunt on their own Lands.

Bear Nicholas, quoting the treaty itself, showed otherwise, demonstrating that the agreement made in Mascarene's Treaty promised that the people of the Wabanaki Nations "shall not be molested in their persons, Hunting, Fishing, and Planting grounds nor in any other [of] their Lawfull Occasions by His Majestys Subjects or their Dependants nor in the exercise of their religion provided the missionaries residing amongst them have leave from the Governour or Commander in Chief of His Majesty's said province of Nova Scotia or Acadie for so doing."[7] The agreement and documents that make up Mascarene's Treaty also show a separate but mutually respectful relationship between very different nations that would coexist on the same Lands.

MAKING A ROYAL PROCLAMATION

The balance of power in Europe and North America changed over time. In particular, and as with the Doctrine of Discovery, European nations continued to take actions and apply their laws in ways that had lasting consequences for Indigenous Lands in North America.

In 1674, the Dutch relinquished New Netherland (later called the British colony of New York and then the independent state of New York) to the British following Anglo-Dutch wars in the Treaty of Westminster. In 1713, France ceded the mainland of the Maritimes to Great Britain with the signing of the Treaty of Utrecht. Following the Seven Years' War and as part of the terms of the Treaty of Paris in 1763, France renounced its claims to territory in mainland North America to Great Britain.

Indigenous Peoples were excluded from these processes even though they had made alliances with the French and Dutch. Some were suspicious of the British. Anishinaabe leader Minavavana issued a warning to a group of English traders: "Englishman, although you have conquered the French, you have not yet conquered us. We are not your slaves. These lakes, these woods and mountains, were left to us by our ancestors. They are our inheritance; and we will part with them to none."[8] Other Indigenous Nations echoed these sentiments and were deeply dissatisfied with evolving conditions.

Obwandiyag (Pontiac), an Ottawa war Chief at the time, led a coalition of Indigenous Nations—including the Ottawa, Huron, and Potawatomi Nations—in calling for the total annihilation of the English. At a Grand Council in May 1763, he said that

> it is important for us, my brothers, that we exterminate from our lands this nation which seeks only to destroy

> us. You see as well as I that we can no longer supply our needs, as we have done, from our brothers, the French. The English sell us goods twice as dear as the French do. . . . When I go to the English commander and . . . ask anything for our sick, he refuses with the reply that he has no use for us. . . . [Y]ou can well see that they are seeking our ruin. Therefore, my brothers, we must all swear their destruction and wait no longer. Nothing prevents us; they are few in numbers, and we can accomplish it. All the nations who are our brothers attack them. . . . [W]hy should we not attack? Are we not men like them?[9]

Obwandiyag's coalition forced the British to reconsider their approach. King George III issued the Royal Proclamation in October 1763 to organize and consolidate Great Britain's new North American empire. The Royal Proclamation set out British settlement terms in Indigenous territories in North America. To do so, the document first clarified that King George III had "ownership" of North America. According to Anishinaabe legal scholar John Borrows, it also clearly stated that all Lands are Indigenous Lands until ceded by treaties. Colonial governments were not allowed to survey or grant any unceded Lands, settlers could not claim Lands unless they had been bought by the Crown, and only the Crown could buy Lands from Indigenous Peoples. Finally, the proclamation created an official system of public purchases developed to extinguish "Indian title" to Lands.

Great Britain and Indigenous Nations also made treaties alongside the Royal Proclamation. In fact, Borrows

A Covenant Chain Wampum belt was presented at the Treaty of Niagara in 1764. This is a replica made out of resin beads and animal sinew by Yvonne Thomas, knowledge keeper and co-founder of the Jake Thomas Learning Centre, for Toronto Metropolitan University Libraries, 2020. Photo courtesy of Toronto Metropolitan University Libraries.

argues that the Royal Proclamation and the Treaty of Niagara should be understood together, not separately, for a comprehensive understanding of these agreements. The Royal Proclamation includes only the Crown's interpretation, whereas the Treaty of Niagara was negotiated between the Crown and First Nations who participated. During the summer of 1764, approximately 2,000 people gathered at Niagara. There were representatives of twenty-four Indigenous Nations from "as far east as Nova Scotia, as far west as Mississippi, and as far north as Hudson's Bay" who travelled long distances to meet with the British. They met to renew and extend a nation-to-nation relationship between settlers and Indigenous Peoples and to reaffirm the Covenant Chain.

Borrows argues that the Royal Proclamation, written unilaterally by Great Britain, became a treaty at Niagara.[10] It became a treaty since representatives of Great Britain and Indigenous Peoples united and made an agreement. Oral statements were made, and exchanges of gifts, medals, and wampum bound participants to their promises. Moreover, the agreement made at Niagara and the words of the Royal Proclamation were expressed with wampum belts. Borrows says that the Two Row Wampum Belt reflects the principles of mutual noninterference grounded in peace, friendship, and respect also agreed to in the Treaty of Niagara. The Royal Proclamation and the Treaty of Niagara, taken together, once again affirmed that Indigenous Peoples were (and are!) sovereign and self-determining.

The Royal Proclamation marked a shift in relations between Indigenous Nations and the British Crown in terms of treaty making. It set out protocols and processes for making treaties and clarified that agreements had to be made with Indigenous Nations before settlement. British treaty making after the Royal Proclamation was led by the "Indian Department," created to oversee relations between the British Empire and Indigenous Peoples in North America.

HISTORICAL TREATIES

Following the Royal Proclamation and the Treaty of Niagara, treaties were made in what is now Ontario. They were called the Upper Canada Land Surrenders or Upper Canada Treaties.

One of the first was when the Onöndowa'ga (Seneca), a member of the Haudenosaunee Confederacy, were compelled to surrender Land to allow the British unimpeded access to two miles on either side of the Niagara River. This happened shortly after the Royal Proclamation in 1764. Other Upper Canada Treaties contained wording about Land surrenders to facilitate settlement, especially for Loyalists coming to Canada after the American Revolution and the War of 1812. Indigenous signatories to these treaties might have received cash payments (one-time or annual), reserves, or other goods in return for the surrender of their Lands to the Crown. There were many treaties signed in

Upper Canada, somewhere between thirty and forty agreements between 1764 and the 1860s. Some of these treaty Lands are now located in the United States since the border at the forty-ninth parallel was in flux during this time. From a British perspective, Upper Canada Treaties were about securing access to territories for travel or settlement. We discuss these details later but note here that, when terms such as "cede" or "surrender" are used, it is unlikely that Indigenous Peoples intended to permanently give away their Lands. It's much more likely that sharing was at the core of these agreements, just as in the Covenant Chain, Gaswéñdah, and Mascarene's Treaty.

The Robinson Treaties consisted of two treaties (the Robinson-Huron Treaty and the Robinson-Superior Treaty) signed in the 1850s for settlers to access resources along the northern shores of Lake Huron and Lake Superior. In the 1840s, Upper and Lower Canada (now called Ontario and Quebec) were combined into the Province of Canada. It had its own government but remained a colony of Great Britain. At this time, and without a treaty, the Province of Canada claimed authority over the north shores of both lakes, provided funds to the Geological Survey of Canada to map potential resources, and began issuing mining leases and allowing surveyors into the territory.

Anishinaabeg in the area were unimpressed. They wanted a treaty and to benefit from mining, alongside the settlers, on their Lands. Anishinaabeg leaders Nebenaigoching and Shingwaukonse first attempted to peacefully engage with the government to secure rights to their Lands and resources and determine who could access and profit

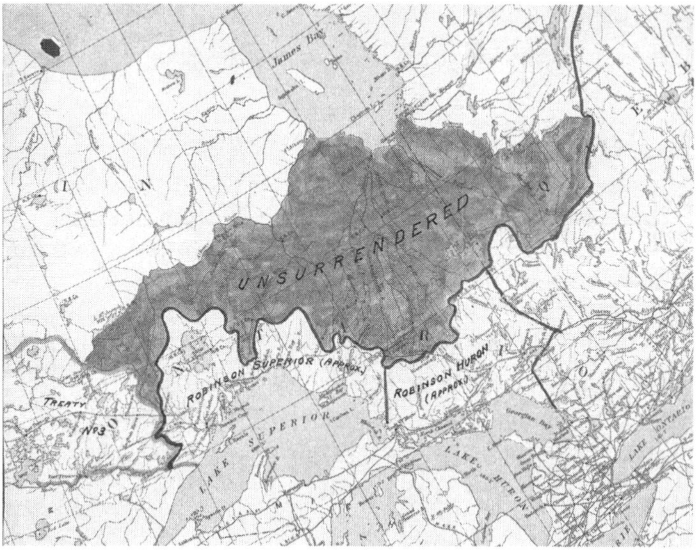

This map of Ontario and Quebec shows the Robinson Treaties, Treaty 3, and a large swath of unsurrendered territories to the north. One could argue (and we do) that none of it was ever surrendered. Library and Archives Canada, RG10M 78903/78, Box number: 2000002024, File number: 235225-1.

from them. Shingwaukonse understood the principles of the Covenant Chain and that wampum belts represented treaties in which the British had recognized Anishinaabeg as allies, acknowledged that Anishinaabeg owned the Land, and promised that the British would offer protection against unscrupulous traders and businessmen. According to Anishinaabe historian Alan Ojiig Corbiere, "Chief Shingwaukonse saw the great wampum belts, heard the speeches recited, committed them to memory, and knew the channels that he was to follow if he had a grievance." So the Anishinaabeg stopped surveyors, petitioned the government, and sought an audience with settler government leaders to plead their case. As printed in the Montreal *Gazette* in 1848, Shingwaukonse said to the lieutenant-governor that

> Three years have passed since your white children, the miners, first came among us, and occupied our lands; they told us that we should be paid for them, but they wished to find their value. With this reply, at the time we were satisfied; but our lands being still occupied and claimed by them we became uneasy, and sent some of our Chiefs to see you in Montreal. You promised that justice should be done us, a year passed, and there is no appearance of a treaty; again we sent, again the same reply, and again last Autumn we sent and still there is no appearance of a treaty.[11]

Anishinaabeg also leased various islands and Lands to Allan Macdonell, a mineral speculator, lawyer, and staunch supporter of Indigenous rights and Land claims who saw Anishinaabeg claims and aspirations as integral to the success of the colonial state. He represented the Anishinaabeg in dealings with the federal government, and Nebenaigoching, Shingwaukonse, and Macdonell together argued convincingly that the Anishinaabeg had rights to their Land with mineral rights as a path to growth and prosperity for peoples along the Great Lakes.

Although action was promised, nothing happened. Meanwhile, mining activities in the region continued. Shingwaukonse, Nebenaigoching, a group of Anishinaabeg, people of mixed settler-Anishinaabeg heritage, and two settler supporters (including Macdonell) compelled the miners to withdraw from the Mica Bay mine site on the shores of

Shingwaukonse, his son Menissinowinnini, and Nebenaigoching are depicted during the trip to Montreal for the *Illustrated London News* in 1849. They appear to be wearing medals or coins with Queen Victoria's profile on them. *The Illustrated London News*, September 15, 1849.

Lake Superior. This was an illegal mine since the Land had not been surrendered or leased by the Anishinaabeg to the Crown, as required by the Royal Proclamation. Afterward, the group surrendered themselves to authorities but were released when it was determined that the arrests were illegal. This "Mica Bay Incident" finally forced real action and the creation of a treaty commission in 1850.

Fur trader and politician William Benjamin Robinson was to negotiate the treaty, and he was given instructions on the parameters of the terms that he could offer on behalf of the Crown. Throughout the negotiations, Nebenaigoching consistently demanded security of Lands, access to resources, and inclusion of mixed-ancestry residents in the treaty. Shingwaukonse knew that his band had rights to their Land and everything on and in it, including timber, hay, fish, animals, and minerals. He wanted a monetary share from anything removed from his territory.

Robinson travelled to Sault Ste. Marie in September 1850 and had the two treaties—the Robinson-Huron Treaty and the Robinson-Superior Treaty—signed. The commissioners, with practice in the art of "divide and conquer," apparently split the Chiefs' opinions to force those resisting to sign. Shingwaukonse signed the treaty, but he did so grudgingly since he did not get the terms that he had wanted. Nebenaigoching's efforts failed to see mixed-ancestry people included in the treaty or a higher annuity or guaranteed protection of mineral access. Nebenaigoching did manage to retain Whitefish Island as a fishing station for his people, and he was successful in the creation of a large reserve on Batchawana Bay.

There are lessons to learn from the Robinson Treaties. First, Anishinaabeg knew their rights and were familiar with the Royal Proclamation, and they demanded that treaties be made before settlers surveyed their Land. In the aftermath of Mica Bay, perhaps because of the success of the Chiefs with Allan Macdonell as their lawyer, a law was passed to restrict Indigenous Peoples from hiring lawyers. This restriction later became part of federal legislation—the Indian Act of 1876—designed to oppress and eliminate Indigenous Peoples. Second, the Robinson Treaties set many precedents for the future Numbered Treaties in terms of the texts of the treaties, the protocols offered, and the structure of negotiations. The Robinson Treaties saw

First Nations and mixed-ancestry people who sought treaties together but were met with a "divide and conquer" strategy by the settler negotiators. Third, these leaders had a vision for the future prosperity of Indigenous Peoples in that they demanded the right to benefit alongside settlers in emerging regional economies.

At the same time, treaties were being formed in the west. The first was the Selkirk Treaty, which allowed for settlement along the Red and Assiniboine Rivers. This was a way for the Hudson's Bay Company (HBC) to claim Lands. King Charles II had already granted the HBC a huge territory (Rupert's Land), and to eliminate its competitors, the HBC proposed to establish a permanent settement as well. To this end, in 1811, the company granted Lands in the Winnipeg Basin—300,000 square kilometres—to the Earl of Selkirk, Thomas Douglas. This became known as the Grant of Assiniboia or the Selkirk Grant.

Six years later, in 1817, Lord Selkirk and five Nêhiyawak and Nahkawininiwak Chiefs signed the Selkirk Treaty to allow newcomers to settle along the rivers in exchange for 100 pounds of tobacco per year. This treaty ensured the establishment of the Red River Colony, which became a major metropole in the region and the centre of the Métis Nation.

Farther west, on what is now called Vancouver Island, fourteen Douglas Treaties were negotiated and made between 1850 and 1854 with Teechamitsa, Kosampson, Whyomilth, Swengwhung, Chilcowitch, Che-ko-nein, Ka-ky-aakan, Chewhaytsum, T'Sou-ke, Saanich, Saalequun, Queackar, and Quakiolth Peoples. These treaties were named after James Douglas, both the HBC Chief Factor at Fort Victoria and

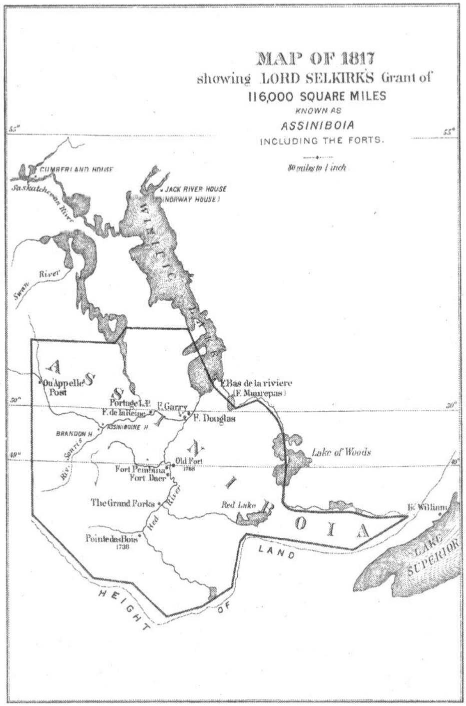

This map shows the area of the Selkirk Grant. It was drawn in 1881 by George Bryce. Located at the confluence of the Red and Assiniboine Rivers, this area was called Assiniboine or Red River. It is the ancestral home of the Red River Métis. Today the US-Canada border cuts across the map at the forty-ninth parallel, and the city of Winnipeg is located where the historic Fort Garry appears on the map. George Bryce, Five Forts of Winnipeg (Royal Society of Canada, 1885), plate III.

the governor of the colony. Talk about a conflict of interest: Douglas was in charge of both a multinational corporation and the local government at the same time. Administrators in the British Colonial Office were anxious about increasing numbers of American citizens in the Pacific Northwest and possible threats to its claims there. They promised the HBC exclusive trading rights for the next ten years if they could colonize the region with settlers.

Douglas intended to accomplish this by securing Lands for settlement through treaties. Negotiations were conducted orally and only later written down in English. Some accounts allege that signatures or marks were made on largely blank forms that were afterward filled in with the treaty text—a point that remains contested. Surviving records suggest that First Nations understood the treaties as agreements to share parts of their territories to allow settlement. Colonial officials, however, framed them as permanent surrenders of land in exchange for material goods such as cash, clothing, and blankets, along with promises that First Nations could continue to use their village sites and fields, and to hunt, fish, and harvest from the sea.

By 1867, missionaries, surveyors, newcomers, and corporate interests were already present in territories across western and northern Canada. In 1870, the Dominion of Canada purchased Rupert's Land (discussed in Chapter 4) from the

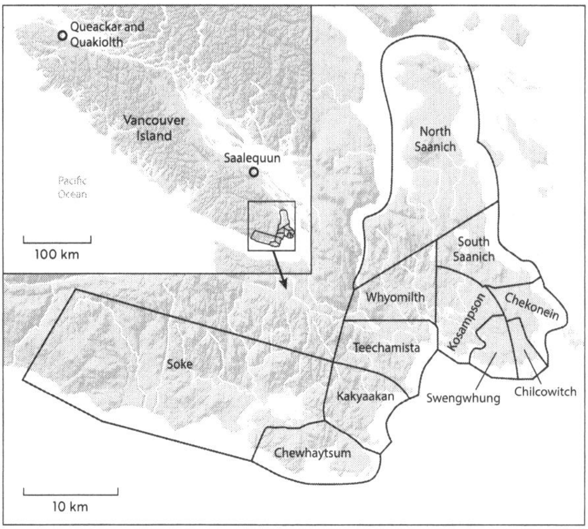

The Douglas Treaties were land purchases made by James Douglas with First Nations on southern Vancouver Island. Because the terms of the treaty were written in after signing, it is unlikely the Chiefs who signed them were fully informed about what they were agreeing to. Map by Eric Leinberger.

HBC, effectively extending its domain over Indigenous Peoples living in that area but without any treaties. Within this context, the new dominion government began planning a federal police force to bring settler law and order to the new Lands. This force began as the North West Mounted Police (NWMP, 1873) and became the RCMP (1920). Throughout the late 1800s, the NWMP established posts and played a role in all of the Numbered Treaty negotiations. They helped to prepare for treaty signings and were included in the treaty parties, along with church and dominion representatives. Church, state, and police—all powerful entities representing the settler state—played essential roles in treaty making with Indigenous Peoples.

Between 1871 and 1921, the Crown and First Nations negotiated and signed the Numbered Treaties across the Prairies and the northern boreal forest in what is now Ontario, Manitoba, Saskatchewan, Alberta, Northwest Territories, and parts of British Columbia, Yukon, and Nunavut. Unlike previous treaties, they were made after the British North America Act, or Canadian Confederation, which came into effect on July 1, 1867. At the time, the Dominion of Canada was made up of four provinces (Ontario, Quebec, Nova Scotia, and New Brunswick), and the act outlined how powers were divided among federal and provincial governments. Among other things, the BNA Act put "Indians and lands reserved for Indians" under the jurisdiction of the federal government.

After 1867, the Dominion of Canada (still under the British Crown) sought to unite west with east. This union was desired for many reasons, including to prevent American encroachment, secure Lands for settlement, profit from west-

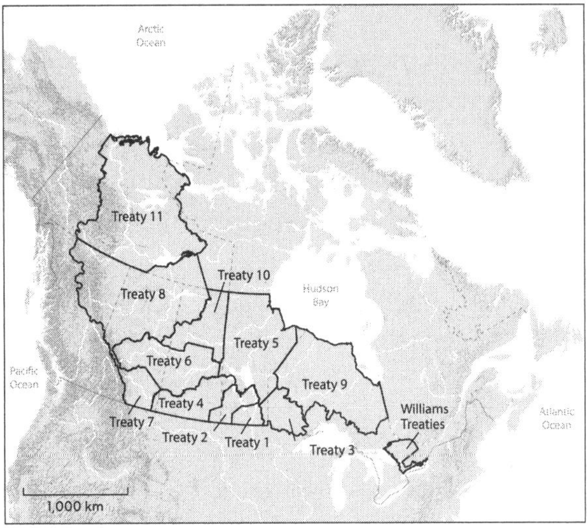

This map shows all Confederation-era treaties signed between 1871 and 1923, including Treaties 1–11 and the Williams Treaties. Map by Eric Leinberger.

ern economies, and use the Pacific Ocean shipping ports. To accomplish this goal, treaties were required. Cree lawyer Sharon Venne (masko-nôcokwêsiw manitoukan) wrote, in reference to Treaty 6, that "sharing the land through treaty-making was a known process. The treaty-making process with the British Crown and others followed the Cree laws. The only way to access the territories of the Cree, Assiniboine, Saulteau, and Dene was to enter into a treaty."[12]

Treaties 1–7 were made between 1871 and 1877 in Nêhiyawak, Nahkawininiwak, Anishinaabeg, Siksika, Piikani, Kainai, Tsuu T'ina, and Nakoda territories, and they enabled the creation of the Provinces of Ontario, Manitoba, Saskatchewan, and Alberta as we know them today. These treaties made it possible to create those provinces in line with the Royal Proclamation, which established that, before settlement and the creation of settler governments, agreements had to be made first with Indigenous Nations.

Adhesions to previously negotiated and signed treaties were also sought and made with Indigenous communities that could not attend scheduled treaty signings, were not initially included in treaty negotiations, or did not want to make treaties at the time. By signing adhesions, Indigenous Peoples entered the terms of treaties as already written.

The Numbered Treaties made before 1878 include the following:

- Treaty 1, 1871, negotiated and signed at Upper and Lower Fort Garry;
- Treaty 2, 1871, negotiated and signed at Manitoba House;
- Treaty 3, 1873, negotiated at Fort Frances in 1871 and 1872, negotiated and signed at Northwest Angle, Lake of the Woods, with adhesions in 1874 and 1875;
- Treaty 4, 1874, negotiated and signed at Fort Qu'Appelle, with adhesions in 1875, 1876, and 1877;
- Treaty 5, 1875, negotiated and signed at Norway House and Berens River, with adhesions in 1875 and 1908;
- Treaty 6, 1876, negotiated and signed at Fort Pitt and Fort Carlton, with adhesions in 1877, 1878, 1879, 1882, 1889, 1944, 1950, 1954, and 1956; and
- Treaty 7, 1877, negotiated and signed at Blackfoot Crossing, with an adhesion in 1877.

The written texts of the Numbered Treaties were based on a format established in the Robinson Treaties, with some additions depending on local negotiations. Terms agreed to in earlier treaties also set a precedent for subsequent treaties. These treaties were made between Indigenous leaders and the British Crown as the ultimate authority in Canada. To this day, some First Nations see their treaty relationships as being with the British Crown rather than the government of Canada.

There was a twenty-one-year break in treaty making from 1878 to 1899. This break represented a shift in geography and context. After 1899, Treaties 8–11 were made in northern Canada, where resource extraction, not agricultural settlement, was the focus of state expansion. Indigenous northerners were concerned about trappers, prospectors, surveyors, and other newcomers in their territories. Like the earlier Numbered Treaties, these treaties were made at multiple locations throughout the territory with subsequent adhesions. But unlike in earlier treaties no reserves were established.

Key to those signing Treaties 8 and 11 was the promise that Indigenous northerners would be free to continue their ways of life. As Oblate missionary René Fumoleau wrote, "only when the Treaty Commissioners promised them that they would be free to hunt and trap and fish for a living, and that their rights would be protected against the abuses of white hunters and trappers, did the Indians at each trading post of the Treaty 8 area consent to sign the Treaty."[13]

Numbered Treaties made in 1899 and after include the following:

- Treaty 8, negotiated and signed in 1899 at Lesser Slave Lake, Peace River Landing, Vermilion, Dunvegan, Red River Post, Peace River, Fort Chipewyan, Smith's Landing, Fond Du Lac, Fort McMurray, and Wabiscow, with an adhesion in 1900;

- Treaty 9, negotiated and signed from 1905–06 at Osnaburg, Fort Hope, Marten Falls, Fort Albany, Moose Factory, New Post, Abitibi, Matachewan, Mattagami, Flying Post, New Brunswick House, and Long Lake, with an adhesion in 1929;
- Treaty 10, negotiated and signed in 1906 at Île-à-la-Crosse and Lac du Brochet; and
- Treaty 11, negotiated and signed from 1921–22 at Fort Providence, Fort Simpson, Fort Wrigley, Fort Norman, Fort Good Hope, Arctic Red River, Fort McPherson, Fort Rae, and Fort Liard.

The Williams Treaties (1923) were the last of the historical treaties. The Ontario government had already allowed settlement in the upper Ottawa River and Muskoka regions but had failed to secure a treaty agreement with the Anishinaabeg who lived there. The Williams Treaties were designed to extinguish Indigenous title to the Lands in question, with no negotiation, no legal representation for the Indigenous signatories, and unfavourable terms compared with those in previous treaties.

Anishinaabeg scholars Jackson Pind and Jack Hoggarth have called them some of the worst treaties in Canada. But the seven First Nations that signed the Williams Treaties sought justice, which resulted in a federal investigation. It affirmed Indigenous rights to territories in central and southern Ontario, and a settlement was negotiated in 2018 between the Williams Treaties First Nations and the governments of Canada and Ontario. The First Nations received financial compensation, recognition of their harvesting rights, and additional Lands for reserves. Both governments also formally apologized.

FOR AS LONG AS THE RIVER FLOWS, THE GRASS GROWS, AND THE SUN SHINES

Many historical treaties are meaningfully celebrated across the country. At treaty anniversaries and celebrations, the Crown continues to distribute nominal annuities agreed to in treaties (where they exist), but they are also chances to revisit the agreements and to remind us of what was promised. After all, the agreements made were intended to last forever.

The 100th anniversary of Treaty 11 was celebrated across the Northwest Territories, with many communities hosting events over the summer of 2021 or 2022 (some celebrations had to be postponed because of the COVID-19 pandemic). Treaty 11 was the last of the Numbered Treaties made between First Nations and the government of Canada. One of these celebrations took place in Behchokǫ̀, Northwest Territories, where Chief Zephirin Monfwi signed Treaty 11 in 1921. On a hot and sunny summer day, Sara and her children stood at the edge of a playground looking toward a series of canvas tents set up on a grassy area nearby. Flags of the Tłı̨chǫ government and Canada flew beside the Union Jack.

This was a re-enactment of the signing of Treaty 11, with costumed actors playing a priest, an RCMP officer, and a government representative awaiting the arrival of actors playing Tłı̨chǫ leaders, soon to land nearby in a canoe. Women in old-style shawls worked nearby, and narrators recounted the scene in Tłı̨chǫ and English. A descendant of Chief Zephirin Monfwi played the role of Chief that day: he arrived by canoe with his party, and they made their way to the tents to re-enact the signing of the treaty.

Treaty 11 re-enactment in Behchokǫ̀, August 2022. This play was performed as part of the 100th anniversary celebrations of Treaty 11. Photo by Sara Komarnisky.

On this day, the narrators talked about what the treaty has meant for the Indigenous Peoples: "Despite our history and our experience with colonization, we never ceased to be self-governing, we never ceased to practice our language, culture and way of life, and we never ceased to be who we are as distinct Tłįchǫ peoples and a distinct Tłįchǫ Nation."[14] Afterward, everyone in attendance celebrated with a prayer song and a drum dance.

3.

WRITTEN TREATIES, FALSEHOODS, AND ORAL HISTORIES

They said all this beautiful stuff—why aren't they doing it? It was my first inkling of racism. The world, I was starting to see, was not perfect.[1]

—Stephen Kakfwi, Dene leader

Stephen Kakfwi was born in the bush near Rádeyîlîkóé (Fort Good Hope), Northwest Territories. When he was older, he went to residential schools in Inuuvik, Sǫǫ̀mbak'è, and Thebacha (Fort Smith). The institution at Thebacha was called Grandin College, and it was run by the Catholic Church and funded by the territorial and federal governments. Despite the oppressive intentions of the residential school system, some children were able to use what they learned at Grandin College, in part, to build careers in northern leadership. Kakfwi became an activist and later president of the Dene Nation (1983–87) and premier of the Northwest Territories (2000–03). His "success," or the "success" of any residential school Survivor, does not mean that residential schools were positive or for the benefit of the children. In his memoir, *Stoneface: A Defiant Dene*, Kakfwi outlines the cost of residential schooling and what he had to do to rebuild his life.

He also wrote about encountering the written version of Treaty 11 in the library at Grandin College, noting that it diverged from what Elders in his community had told him. They were shocked to hear the language of "cede and surrender." According to Kakfwi, Elders did not see the treaty as being about Land at all. As Kakfwi explained, "I told my grandfather about it the next summer, and I think he just about pulled me out of school when I asked him why he sold our land for five dollars a year."[2] Years later, Dene Elders and the Council of Young Canadians gathered oral histories of Treaty 11 from community members who had attended the actual treaty signing. Oral histories and living memories of Treaty 11 are clear that no one had agreed to give up the Land.

How could this be? First, we know that different understandings of treaties are common. Across Canada, oral histories of treaties do not align with "official" written versions of them, especially the idea that Lands were "ceded and surrendered." To generalize, Indigenous Peoples understood these treaties to be based on peace and friendship and that they were agreements about how to live well together on these Lands. This is often referred to as the "spirit and intent" of a treaty. The written texts of these treaties say otherwise and contain clauses in which First Nations signatories "cede, release, surrender and yield up" their Lands. This language does not appear in the earlier peace and friendship treaties, but the language of "cede and surrender" is present in Upper Canada Treaties and the later Numbered Treaties.

It is not uncommon for people to interpret an agreement in different ways, especially when they come from diverse world views, practise various cultures, speak multiple languages, hold distinct loyalties, and recall unique details. But the ability to "cede and surrender" Lands is based on elements of the Doctrine of Discovery and beliefs about property ownership that originated in Europe. European colonizers have often imposed their own understandings as superior, dominant, and binding compared with those of Indigenous Peoples.

When we think about the bigger picture unfolding on these Lands, though, and the intent of British and Canadian treaties in the first place, we are reminded that they were a means to conquer, colonize, extract, and settle. Treaties involved high stakes, especially for First Nations who faced starvation or other desperate circumstances because of changing socio-economic conditions caused by colonial forces. For Canada and for settler Canadians, treaties often paved the way for benefits from resource extraction, settlement, and new profits.

OMISSIONS, COERCION, AND DECEIT

For every Treaty, there is far more to the story than the written treaty and the formal report by the treaty commissioner or whoever was the representative of the Crown or the government of Canada. In *No Surrender: The Land Remains Indigenous*, settler historian Sheldon Krasowski tells the story of the Numbered Treaties with historical sources written by people present at and witness to treaty negotiations and signings, including newspaper columns written by reporters, private diaries of treaty party members, and other eyewitness accounts.[3]

Scholars generally have neglected to include these types of sources since they are outside the official narrative. In other words, by considering new or previously unused evidence, we can understand the story in more detail and nuance.

Alarmingly, Krasowski documents many instances in which, during negotiations, Canada's treaty commissioners actively deceived Indigenous leaders by focusing only on the positive aspects of the treaties. Benefits like annuity payments, agricultural supplies, education, and other so-called provisions were highlighted to motivate First Nations to sign the treaties. Completely relinquishing all power over Lands, giving them up altogether, and what is meant by "cede and surrender" were not explicitly discussed. Krasowski writes that the failure to discuss all aspects of the written treaty "was part of a strategic plan employed by the treaty commissioners to distance the Indigenous leadership from the treaty text."[4]

There was a clear difference, then, between what was discussed verbally and what treaty commissioners recorded on the treaty documents. For the Douglas Treaties, the text about what was agreed to was written in after the documents were signed. For the Numbered Treaties and adhesions, the texts were usually prepared in advance. They were crafted in Ottawa, with blank spaces provided in which to write additional terms that might be agreed to during negotiations. Generally, though, there was little room for discussion or negotiation on new or revised terms. Nêhiyaw scholar Harold Johnson writes:

> If we go to the original paper the treaties are written on, the first thing we notice is that large parts of it were pre-written, with spaces left for the Treaty Commissioner to

> fill in. These spaces that are filled in include our names and which articles of agricultural equipment would be supplied. The important terms about the relationship with our Mother the Earth were pre-written. Can you, Kiciwamanawak, in good conscience, insist upon these terms that were likely not mentioned and, even if they were, not likely understood, and were definitely not negotiated?[5]

Indeed, by the time many treaties were signed, Canada operated on the premise, rooted in the Doctrine of Discovery and formalized in the Royal Proclamation, that title could be extinguished only by treaty. It had already decided that its government was the lawful "owner" of these Lands and had developed legal mechanisms to recognize that. Other colonial entities had already established themselves in these territories: fur-trading corporations such as the HBC, various for-profit entrepreneurs, and Christian churches and missionaries. In some areas, settler laws were imposed before treaties were signed, and this was the situation in northern Canada, where federal game laws were imposed *before* Treaties 8 and 11 were signed. By Canada's own laws, Aboriginal title to Lands had to be extinguished before Canada could claim them, as spelled out in the Royal Proclamation. Yet was Canada actually open to negotiating anything?

The answer is sometimes it was. In Treaty 6, for example, First Nations were successful in negotiating the addition of a clause stipulating that a "medicine chest" would be kept for the benefit of each band. Treaty 6 also guaranteed that, if First Nations were overtaken by any pestilence or famine, then relief would be provided. Finally, Treaty 6 contained the promise of increased agricultural assistance in the form of animals and supplies compared with any other treaty before or since.

In general, though, there wasn't much added to the written treaties. In later years, there wasn't even much discussion or negotiation. This is particularly obvious in the later Numbered Treaties. According to Treaty 8 Commissioner David Laird, "we met the Indians [*sic*] on the 20th, and on the 21st the treaty was signed." How could they have had in-depth conversations, supported by informed interpreters, and followed proper protocols and ceremonies in such a short time? The answer is that the terms of the treaty were largely preset. Although the wishes or will of the Indigenous Peoples did inform the negotiations, they were not central to Canada's proposed treaty terms. Treaty commissioners' primary task was "to secure the relinquishment of the Indian title at as small a cost as possible."[6]

Moreover, treaties were sometimes negotiated and signed under dire and desperate circumstances. In *Clearing the Plains: Disease, Politics of Starvation, and the Loss of Aboriginal Life*, settler historian James Daschuk explains that First Nations in the Prairies had already endured significant economic and social changes by the first half of the eighteenth century. Daschuk writes about the widespread presence of European traders in the 1770s, which created competition, conflict, and violence between fur trade enterprises and trappers.

Increased hunting and trapping during the fur trade resulted in game depletion, changed regional economic conditions, and led to famine for many, including Nêhiyawak, Siksikaitsitapi, Nahkawininiwak, Nakota Sioux, and Métis. Increased numbers of newcomers combined with desperate conditions for First Nations led to outbreaks of contagious diseases—including tuberculosis—among Indigenous communities. In fact, Daschuk argues, tuberculosis crises in the Prairies could have been mitigated had Canada acted in good faith toward its treaty partners. Daschuk also points out how famine in Indigenous communities was used as a political tool at treaty negotiations and later.[7] Food was deliberately withheld from Indigenous Peoples, making them more vulnerable to diseases. These acts were designed to coerce Indigenous Peoples into entering into treaties with the Crown. In other words, the Canadian government used starvation and disease as tactics to come to "agreements" on Lands.

Another part of this already complicated story is the fact that Indigenous Peoples sometimes did not actually "sign" treaties. Instead, they sometimes engaged in a practice called "touching the pen" as a sign of consent. Touching the pen was used consistently in the Numbered Treaties. The practice originated with Treaty 1 when the Chiefs, rather than making their own marks, seals, or signatures on the text of the treaty, shook hands with the commissioner and then touched the pen. The clerk then made an *X* on the document.

Some leaders, though, refused to touch the pen. For example, during Treaty 7 negotiations in 1877, after much hesitation and contemplation, Siksika leader Isapo-Muxika accepted the treaty for the Niitsitapi Nations. When the Niitsitapi Chiefs agreed to this treaty, Isapo-Muxika shook hands with the treaty commissioners; David Laird, the lieutenant-governor of the Northwest Territories; and Colonel James Macleod, the NWMP commissioner. Isapo-Muxika was willing to trust that they would keep their promises, but he refused to touch the pen. Why? For him

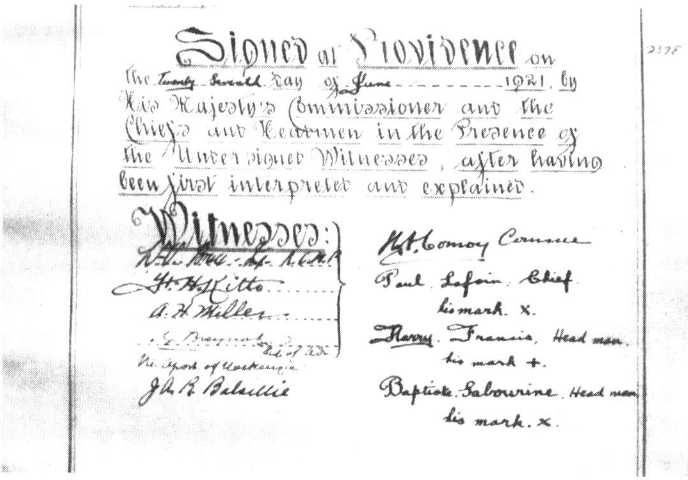
Signed at Providence on the Twenty Seventh Day of June 1921, by His Majesty's Commissioner and the Chiefs and Headmen in the Presence of the Undersigned Witnesses, after having been first interpreted and explained.

Witnesses:

A. H. Miller

J. R. Balsillie

H. A. Conroy Commissioner

Paul Lefoin Chief his mark x.

Harry Francis, Head man. his mark +.

Baptiste Sabourine, Head man his mark x.

The signature page of Treaty 11 signed at Zhati Kų́ę́ (Fort Providence). Note the *X* beside each name, intended to suffice as a signature. ©NWT Archives/René Fumoleau, N-1995–002: 9686.

and other signatories to Treaty 7, the conversations, promises, and exchanges made the treaty, not the signatures.

When we talk about a treaty, we sometimes talk about it being signed: who signed it, what the signatures reflect, and so on. Conversations about "touching the pen" or refusing to do so suggest that people had different understandings of consent and agreement. Krasowski asserts that this was another deliberate strategy used by the Canadian treaty parties to distance Indigenous signatories from the texts. Replacing signatures with handshakes created that distance and was part of a strategic attempt to mislead Indigenous Peoples about the contents of the treaty documents. Many Chiefs could not read or write at the time, and Krasowski says that they had intense mistrust of the written documents.[8] Instead, a handshake became symbolic of the trusting relationship made through a treaty and is depicted on treaty medals distributed at treaty signings.

All treaties have oral histories passed down through generations from those who signed them to make up part of living memory today. For example, in Tulít'a, Chief Albert Wright and Saul Blondin signed the treaty on behalf of Dene from the area. Afterward, the Chief sent men along the Keele River to put up signposts to notify the Shúhtaot'ınę of the treaty signing. Northern authors Paul Andrew and Patrick Scott note that these signposts are unique in Canada. They emphasize that Chief Wright understood the importance of informing the people about the signed treaty. Everyone needed to know about it. The signposts remain, as do the oral histories of Treaty 11.[9]

Oral histories also raise questions about treaty documents. The signature of Chief Julian Yendo of Pehdzeh Ki (Wrigley) is depicted as syllabics on the treaty document. Yendo himself called this signature into question and suggested fraud: "I do not remember having signed anything. Someone might have

Medals were distributed to those who signed the Numbered Treaties. This one is from Treaty 1, signed in 1871 at Lower Fort Garry, near present-day Winnipeg. Although Treaty 1 was signed in 1871, the chiefs were not happy with the initial medals. This version was designed and presented to them in 1873. The same imagery was used for medals presented to chiefs who signed the subsequent Numbered Treaties. Manitoba Museum, HBC 57-53.

signed my name. A white man, or the Bishop might have done it."[10] His peers supported his assertion, adding that Yendo was never able to read or write syllabics. Another person disagreed and said that he had previously corresponded with Yendo in syllabics. Adding to the confusion, there are contradictory memories of that day. Other testimonies further complicate the story: one person said that no one was seen physically signing the treaty, but the same person later reported having seen Yendo sign it. What we do know is that, on January 4, 1941, Yendo resigned as Chief and used an *X* in place of his signature. This supports the theory that he did not know syllabics and possibly did not sign Treaty 11 in that way.

During the Numbered Treaty negotiations, we know that different treaty parties were unlikely to understand other parties' languages fully. Representatives of the Crown generally spoke English, and the treaty text was printed in English. Given the time period, most Indigenous Peoples were unlikely to be fluent in English. The expertise of interpreters was required. At the time, few individuals could interpret English or French into an Indigenous language.

There are more than seventy Indigenous languages spoken in what is now Canada, and there might have been even more in the past since some have gone extinct because of colonialism. Those individuals (whether Indigenous or not) who spoke multiple languages would have grown up in a multilingual and multicultural environment, married into a family and community that spoke a different language, lived near other language communities, had diplomatic or other responsibilities that required communicating with newcomers, and/or were engaged in work that required them to learn new languages and develop these skills.

Christian churches and fur-trading companies needed people who spoke local languages and could navigate local cultures and economies. Additionally, Indigenous language speakers could have been forced to learn English or French as children when they were institutionalized at an Indian residential school or a hospital. These individuals sometimes worked as interpreters and, in theory, could have understood and interpreted English or French at treaty negotiations. For each treaty, it's important to ask and critically investigate who were the interpreters, who selected them, and were they able to interpret fully and without bias?

Krasowski writes about the interpreters and their interpretations of the treaties. He argues that treaty commissioners selected interpreters in favour of the treaties. Often the people selected were allies who would benefit from the Dominion of Canada in its pursuit of gaining control over the Lands. Often people selected were affiliated with the church or fur trade. And they did not work in the best interests of Indigenous communities.

Serving as an interpreter at treaty negotiations was no doubt challenging, especially given the language of the treaty texts and the fact that European legal terms do not translate well into some Indigenous languages. It's also unlikely that interpreters had sufficient time to prepare for their task. They were caught in a fraught "in-between" position, with the responsibility of working across different languages and cultures, within changing colonial power dynamics, and possibly in limited time frames.

During Treaty 4 negotiations in the 1870s, Charles Pratt served as an interpreter. He was fluent in Nêhiyawêwin, Nahkawiwin, and English and was trusted by Nêhiyawak and

Nahkawininiwak leaders. Pratt was related to Nêhiyawak and Nakoda through marriage and descent and was well respected for his oratory skills and teachings. Interestingly, he was also a lay teacher for the Anglican Church. He had been teaching elements of Euro-Canadian world views to Nêhiyawak and Nakoda for many years. One of his duties was to interpret Anglican sermons for visiting ministers. Apparently, some priests complained because Pratt did not interpret verbatim; they said that he "changed elements of the Christian teachings to soften their Eurocentric edges and avoid critiques of Indigenous traditions."[11]

Krasowski suggests that Pratt did in fact soften the translation, noting how a treaty was important in contexts in which the bison were disappearing and people were facing hardships. Pratt also likely faced challenges with the task. *The Manitoban* newspaper journalist F.L. Hunt was at the treaty signing and described the "look of dismay and consternation" on Pratt's face when Pratt was asked to translate the full text of the treaty.[12] We can imagine the many difficulties: the length of the document, the lack of time to prepare before the treaty negotiations, the legal language used, and his primary experience within Nêhiyawak and Nakoda oral cultures.

Peter Erasmus was the interpreter for Treaty 6 at Fort Carlton, by invitation of Chiefs Mistawasis and Ahtahkakoop. Erasmus was Métis and fluent in English, several nêhiyawêwin dialects, as well as Anishinaabe, Nakoda, and Niitsitapi languages. Although the Chiefs had in Erasmus probably the best translator available, it is doubtful that they were fully aware that the treaty contained wording to "cede, release, surrender and yield up . . . all rights, titles and privileges" to their Lands. In the record of the treaty negotiations that Lieutenant-Governor Alexander Morris submitted to Ottawa, there was no indication that land rights surrender was ever discussed or explained. It is documented that Erasmus read the written treaty aloud, including the legally worded surrender clause, to the assembled First Nations. But the semantic differences between the languages and cultures might well have been too vast for Erasmus to bridge. It also appears likely that a key part of the surrender clause, defining the limits of the territory actually surrendered, was absent from the written document when Erasmus read it and the Chiefs signed it.[13]

About fifty years later, in 1921, Treaty 11 interpretations were under way in the Northwest Territories and Yukon. René Fumoleau noted that, even if Treaty Commissioner Henry A. Conroy explained the treaty (which is uncertain), the concepts were rooted in a colonial legal tradition unfamiliar to Indigenous northerners, making it unlikely that a shared understanding was reached. Fumoleau shared as one example that the terms for "treaty" in Dënesųłinë́, Tłı̨chǫ, and other dialects literally translated as "money is distributed."[14] Indeed, money was distributed at treaty time and then every year after that. But the main agreements in the written text of the treaty do not seem to have been translated or explained fully to these First Nations signatories.

Oblate Bishop Gabriel Breynat accompanied the treaty parties for both Treaty 8 and Treaty 11. There are different accounts of how Indigenous communities perceived Breynat. For some, he was a trusted individual and assured Dene leaders that Canada would honour their treaty promises. A Dene man named William Squirrel, at the signing of Treaty 11 in Zhati Kų́ę́ (Fort Providence), said that "there was also a Bishop,

Peter Erasmus, a father, farmer, teacher, missionary assistant, hunter, guide, trader, chronicler, and interpreter. He was born at Red River and lived his life in the Prairies. His book *Buffalo Days and Nights* is a first-hand account of life in western Canada in the nineteenth century. Photo courtesy of Glenbow Library and Archives Collection, Libraries and Cultural Resources Digital Collections, University of Calgary.

witness to the treaty. He was good in Slavey language and translating to the Indians, he said that the government was offering good care to the Indians in return for the treaty and that the white man and the Indians were to live side by side on the land till the end of the world, and that from hereafter things would be good for the Indians."[15]

Some Elders claim that Breynat lied to Indigenous communities. Rene Lamothe asserts that "Bishop Breynat knew that the Treaty was a land deal as far as the Crown was concerned even though, according to Dene testimony, he would not admit that to the Dene during negotiations."[16] There are other examples. Pierre Mercredi, the interpreter for Treaty 8, talked about how the people were misled:

> I interpreted the words of Queen Victoria to Alexandre Laviolette, Chief of the Chipewyans and his band. . . . I know, because I read the treaty to them, that there was no clause in it which said they might have to obey regulations about hunting. They left us no copy of the treaty we signed, saying that they would have it printed and send a copy to us. When the copy came back, that second clause (that they shall promise to obey whatever hunting regulations the Dominion Government shall set) was in it. It was not in there before.[17]

TO SHARE THE LAND

All of this calls into question the validity of the written treaties.

In the oral histories of treaties that we have encountered, Indigenous Knowledge Keepers and Elders have stated that the written texts of the treaties do not align with their understandings of Land and stewardship. For example, according to Sharon Venne, in Nêhiyawak culture, Land cannot be sold for exclusive use because it cannot be separated from the people who live on it. Moreover, Venne describes how women own the Land because of their spiritual connection with the Creator and Mother Earth. "The Chiefs who entered into treaty only had the authority to share the lands, never to sell or surrender it."[18]

As well, Treaty 4 in the southern Prairies was signed in Nêhiyawak and Nahkawininiwak territories in 1874. Treaty 4 oral histories maintain that the people did not surrender any Land rights but agreed to share the Land with settlers "to the depth of a plow." Treaty 4 Elder Gordon Oakes, of the Nekaneet First Nation, in what is now southern Saskatchewan, said that "this country belongs to the Indian people; the Creator gave us this country. Then the treaties were taking place, that's what they gave up, a tip of the plough, so the people that came from elsewhere, different countries, they can farm, ranch, all that. We never gave up anything more than that."[19] There are oral histories, such as this one, from all treaty areas affirming that Indigenous Peoples did not give up their Lands. Rather, they intended to share them with newcomers. Krasowski repeatedly demonstrates that the surrender of Lands was never discussed during negotiations for Treaties 1 through 7.

Dene Elder John Blondin provides an example from the signing of Treaty 11: "When I read Treaty 11 I said to myself, how come we never talked about giving our land away when Mr. Conroy said in front of witnesses, 'It is not for your land.'"[20] Dene in the North "maintain very clearly that [a] Treaty was made, that it is a Treaty of Peace and Friendship and that there are rights and obligations on the part of both the Dene and the non-Dene."[21] Indigenous northerners did not agree to cede and surrender their Lands in Treaty 11.

In fact, there is a Dene version of Treaty 11 written by the Dene Nation in the 1970s. It is a peace treaty that honours the oral histories and provides a much different account compared with Canada's written version:

> The Dene leadership, through negotiations and discussion with their people, and with the interest and concern to provide their people with a more secure future, have been

satisfied by the repeated statements of Commissioner Conroy and Bishop Breynat that this treaty:

A. has nothing to do with The Land
B. would not give Canada [the] right to interfere in the internal affairs of the Dene; and therefore
C. has no bearing on Dene jurisdiction and governance over their territories
D. Is a symbol of a nation to nation relationship between the Dene and the Crown.

This Peace Treaty therefore provides as follows:
The Dene Agree:

1. to allow the subjects of King George to move peacefully on Dene lands to seek minerals providing their work does not interfere with the Dene
2. to meet with a delegation of the King each year to renew this treaty.

The Crown Agrees:

1. to protect the Dene against the invasion of White people on their hunting and fishing territories
2. to take care of the education of children
3. that medical services would be assured according to their needs
4. to come to the assistance of widows, orphans, and elders
5. that the Dene would not be molested in this kind of life with the geographic and climatic conditions imposed on them
6. that the Dene would continue to assure their life and that of their families by hunting and fishing

7. to supply the Dene with hunting and trapping supplies, including fishnets, bullets, food, and other basic needs to go out on the land
8. to provide the Dene with housing.

IT IS AGREED THIS TREATY WILL BE HONOURED AS LONG AS THE LAND IS HERE, AS LONG AS THE GRASS GROWS, AS LONG AS THE RIVER FLOWS, AS LONG AS THE SUN RISES IN THE EAST AND SETS IN THE WEST THIS WILL NOT CHANGE.[22]

For many Indigenous Peoples, treaties were designed to facilitate lasting peace and friendship and set guidelines for enduring relationships; they were never designed to completely give up or hand over Lands. These agreements were also meant to last forever. Nêhiyaw scholar Harold Johnson explains that agreements made between Nêhiyawak and the Crown were made in perpetuity:

> The treaties are forever. We cannot change them because the promises were made, not just between your family and mine, but between your family and mine and the Creator. There were three parties at the treaty. When my family adopted your family, we became relatives, and that cannot be undone.[23]

Dene Elder John Blondin shared an account of the signing of Treaty 11 at Tulít'a, where Albert Wright was chosen as the signing representative for his people. Wright told Treaty Commissioner Conroy that "our witnesses are Mackenzie

River, the Sun, and Bear Rock. We can't see them from inside the tent, we have to go out and look." Everybody went out of the tent. "You see these three? If anything happens to one of them, you can do what you want. But if nothing happens to them then you can change nothing."[24] We think that this speaks to how the promises made in the treaty, with witnesses from the Land, are for forever. As long as these perpetual and sacred Land features of the river, the sun, and the rock exist, the treaty stands. Treaties are about relationship, connection, and relationality, even if they were not what the treaty commissioners or governments anticipated.

Bear Rock is a sacred mountain, located just north of the community of Tulít'a. Dene oral histories recount how the great traveller and lawmaker Yamǫrıa confronted a pack of giant beavers that had been terrorizing hunters. He killed three of the beavers and draped their pelts over Bear Rock, forming three dark circles that can be seen on the mountain to this day. ©NWT Archives/Northwest Territories Department of Information, G-1979–023: 1493.

4.

REFUSAL, UNCEDED TERRITORY, MÉTIS SCRIP, AND MODERN TREATIES

they don't understand
in this place
truth is a seed
planted deep

if you want to get it
you have to dig[1]
—KATHERENA VERMETTE,
RED RIVER MÉTIS WRITER

LOOKING AT A TREATY MAP OF CANADA, ONE WILL notice quite a few blank spots where there were never historical treaties.

Indeed, exploration, missionization, and trade on these Lands did not always happen under treaties. European explorers crossed the continent, beginning from the Atlantic, Pacific, and Arctic Oceans. They traversed rivers and Lands to map and gather information. Although these explorers did not ask Indigenous Peoples if they could do so, the latter sometimes supported these activities. Indigenous Peoples shared knowledge relevant to survival and travel routes and, especially in the North, provided life-saving measures to newcomers.

Churches were also involved in the exploration, documentation, and administration of Indigenous Lands and Peoples, including bringing Christianity to fur trade outposts, educating children, providing health care, and studying the languages and cultures of Indigenous Peoples, all from a Western or European mindset. By which treaty or agreement, though, were missionaries and religious officials permitted to stay? In most cases, there was no treaty.

Colonization also came with huge financial profit and business expansion. Conquering new worlds filled the coffers of European monarchs and affiliated corporations. Items such as silver, gold, fur, and oil were (and are) very profitable. The fur trade was a major commercial enterprise in North America, and to satisfy that market, hats made of felted beaver fur were created and sold. They were highly desirable fashion statements, especially for European men. A 1670 Royal Charter by Great Britain established the Hudson's Bay Company, giving it exclusive trading rights across a vast territory. This territory was called Rupert's Land, after the first HBC governor, Prince Rupert, and it included all Lands with rivers whose waters flow into Hudson Bay. Other fur-trading outfits such as the North West Company also operated within North America, building relationships with Indigenous Peoples and claiming different areas as their exclusive interests. These companies competed for furs, relationships, and Lands. At the same time,

Christian churches expanded their influence in Indigenous territories, often working in parallel with traders and reinforcing each other's presence, though their roles were distinct: commercial versus spiritual and cultural.

Whaling was big business in the age of exploration and early colonization in North America. Whale oil and baleen were valuable commodities, and so was whalebone. Before the mainstream use of fossil fuels, lamps were lit with whale oil. Inuit have done so since time immemorial, using the qulliq, a traditional soapstone lamp in the Arctic fuelled with seal or whale oil. European and American commercial whaling ships hunted the oceans around North America, peaking in the mid-1800s. The industry ultimately greatly reduced whale populations on which coastal Indigenous Peoples had depended since time immemorial while also damaging or destroying traditional economies. Coastal Indigenous Nations, such as Inuvialuit in northern Canada, first encountered whalers and the changes that they wrought and later met representatives of the government.

EXCLUDED FROM TREATIES

Some Indigenous Peoples were excluded from treaties based on racialized understandings of them and their ways of life. Indeed, the priority for Canada was to make treaties with First Nations only. Inuit were therefore excluded from treaty negotiations. For example, when preparing for Treaty 11 in 1921, Canadian government representative Franklin H. Kitto said that, because Inuit were supposedly "a purely nonresident people, they are not in the same position as the non-treaty Indians."[2] Kitto was drawing from his own racist beliefs that Inuit were nomads, which generally meant "wanderers," with a subpar intellect and no connection to Lands or resources. We know this to be radically untrue. However, for people who did not care to learn about Indigenous societies, especially before the establishment of government-built "settlements," travelling in and harvesting from the Lands according to the seasons might have portrayed a false scenario. Even so, the proposed area for Treaty 11 excluded Inuit. Historically, they lived in the Arctic and sub-Arctic, so newcomers and their early governments did not perceive those Lands as valuable, and therefore no treaty was necessary. As Treaty Commissioner Henry A. Conroy explained, "there may be some in the barren lands who will not be included, but as these lands will not be wanted for many generations . . . it [the treaty] will give title to all the land which will be needed for probably a century."[3]

Inuvialuit were offered Treaty 11 in 1921 and refused to sign it. Inuvialuit are a group of Inuit who live in Inuvialuit Nunangat, also known as the Inuvialuit Settlement Region. Some call this the Beaufort Delta; it is where the Nagwichoonjik or Deh Cho (Mackenzie River) meets the Arctic Ocean. In 1929, Inuvialuk man Nuligak described travelling to Akłarvik (Aklavik) in the spring and, while there, meeting Oswald Finnie, then the director of the Northwest Territories and Yukon Branch of the Department of the Interior for the federal government. Finnie had accompanied Lord Julian Byng, the governor general of Canada, on a trip by paddlewheeler via river. Nuligak refused to sign Treaty 11, and he wrote about it:

> There was a meeting for the purpose of giving the Inuit money such as the Indians were receiving. The white chief asked me if I had something to say. I asked him what would be the amount we would receive for 12 months. He answered, "Five dollars." I asked the Inuit if it was worth disturbing ourselves for the amount of five dollars. They answered, "We don't want it." I said to the white chief: "We have no business to do with you. Keep your five dollars. Instead of distributing it to everyone, put that money to some purpose. Everything costs much here, and five dollars will not help us. It would be better to feed those who are in misery, the widows, the blind, the sick." Chief Finnie answered that I was right, and that the Inuit would not receive the treaty.[4]

While most First Nations in what is now British Columbia did not sign historical treaties, there are important exceptions: the fourteen Douglas Treaties on Vancouver Island and Treaty 8. The vast majority of the province, particularly in the interior and north, remains unceded. The arrival of settlers and those seeking gold in the interior of British Columbia had introduced new diseases, which nearly destroyed villages and dispossessed Indigenous Peoples of their territories. Without treaties, resources were extracted, reserves were allocated, and settler newcomers claimed the right to determine territorial boundaries. Scottish Canadian ethnographer James Teit lived and worked in what is now British Columbia's south-central interior, and he lived in close relationship with St'at'imc, Nlaka'pamux, Sylix, and Secwépemc. Writing in 1909, Teit explained that "some whites believe the Shuswap [Secwépemc] never had any permanent settlements west of the Fraser River, while others think they at one time occupied nearly all the Chilcotin country extending in a continuous line to the Bella Coola, but that they have gradually been driven out of their country." None of this was true. Instead, Teit noted the impacts of "the white man's laws, which recognized no tribal boundaries," and of mass deaths from diseases that removed Secwépemc from their Lands.[5] Teit was observant but still writing from the perspective of a white male ethnographer in the early twentieth century.

Or consider Newfoundland and Labrador. Treaties were not negotiated or signed with Mi'kmaq, Innu, Inuit, or Kablunângajuit Peoples there either. But the region became a fishing outpost for settlers, with churches and fur-trading posts operating as though they had been there since time immemorial (they had not!). When Newfoundland and Labrador entered Confederation in 1949, the terms of union between the two governments did not reference Indigenous Peoples whatsoever, and no provisions were made to safeguard Indigenous Lands or cultures. This exclusion made Mi'kmaq, Innu, Inuit, and Kablunângajuit Peoples vulnerable to outside forces, and they had little recourse or power to push back. In the 1980s, some Mi'kmaq in Newfoundland were registered under the Indian Act, and the province finalized the Labrador Inuit Land Claims Agreement with Canada and the Nunatsiavut government in 2005. Inuit of Labrador and Quebec are part of the Nunavik Inuit Land Claims Agreement, finalized in 2008. Negotiations are still under way with the Innu Nation.

After Confederation in 1867, it was uncertain how the

Métis would be included in the Dominion of Canada. Métis scholar Chris Andersen points out that Indigenous identities, and how they are defined, can be contentious. This is certainly the case for Métis. We follow the definition of the Métis National Council, which defines a Métis as "a person who self-identifies as Métis, is distinct from other Aboriginal peoples, is of historic Métis Nation Ancestry and who is accepted by the Métis Nation."[6] Indeed, being Métis is about peoplehood, culture, language, community, connection, shared history, and nationhood.

Andersen uses the term "Métis" to refer to the history, events, leaders, territories, language, and culture associated with the growth of the buffalo hunting and trading Métis of the northern Plains, in particular during the period between the beginning of the Métis buffalo brigades in the early nineteenth century and the 1885 North West Uprising."[7] Chelsea Vowel agrees and notes the vibrant and visible national culture of Métis People that can include the Michif language, Red River carts, the flag, the sash, and the jovial style of music and dance. Importantly, Vowel notes that, despite the *Daniels* decision (a 2016 Supreme Court of Canada ruling recognizing Métis and non-status Indians as "Indians" under s. 91(24) and affirming federal responsibility), Métis are not governed by the Indian Act, do not always have the right to live on reserves, and continually battle the federal government, which understands its responsibilities, under the Indian Act, to extend only to Status Indians who live on reserves.[8]

According to Andersen and Vowel, there is a persistent and incorrect idea that Métis People are just racially mixed.

In other words, there is a stereotype that, if a First Nations person and a white person have a child, then the child is Métis. If being "mixed" is all that it takes to be Métis, then all folks of mixed Indigenous ancestry would be Métis. The mixing of blood does not produce a rich and vibrant heritage and culture; in fact, this is typical of colonial blood quantum ideas that reduce and simplify Indigenous identities.

So let us return to asking how the Métis could be included in the Dominion of Canada after Confederation. The Métis Nation, centred on the Red River area and living within a wider region to engage in seasonal hunting and relationships with First Nations that encompassed the Canadian and American prairie and woodland west, had grown and coalesced into a unique social, cultural, and political force by the late eighteenth century. The Manitoba Act of 1870 moved Rupert's Land and the Northwest Territories under the power of the Dominion of Canada, and some have argued that it effectively created a Métis province. The province had protections for regional Métis, including bilingualism in institutions, Catholic schooling, and guaranteed rights to Lands. But many of Canada's promises to Métis People were unfulfilled, and Métis rights to Lands were (and are) continually undermined.

Louis Riel returned from exile in the United States in 1884 and created a coalition to fight for their rights. In March of that year, an armed force of Métis under Riel's leadership formed a provisional government, seized the parish church at Batoche, and demanded the surrender of the HBC post at Fort Carlton. Canada waged war on the Métis, engaged the military to quash the resistance, and hanged

Riel for high treason in 1885. Canada used strict administration to subjugate and oppress prairie Indigenous Peoples, and many Métis fled. Some moved farther west and north to keep their traditional lifestyles and avoid the restrictions of the government.

One way that Canada undercut Métis rights to Lands was through a process called Métis scrip. Scrip is a document that represents legal tender. It is a certificate or voucher that entitles the bearer to certain rights (in fact, gift cards are a form of scrip). Métis were usually excluded from treaty making because of racialized understandings of them and their place in colonial society. Historically, federal authorities did not deal with Métis as a separate or distinct people: to join a treaty, a Métis person had to choose between being considered white (relinquish claims and take scrip) and being considered "Indian" (join the treaty). Some Métis families were offered a treaty or scrip, but this essentially meant that they were being asked to choose how the state would recognize them. If they signed a treaty, then they were labelled "Indians." Otherwise, the "half-breeds" were eligible for scrip. Identities were more complicated than this, and families had extensive connections with each other. For example, it was not uncommon for one sibling to be included in a treaty and another in scrip.

Scrip is not cash, which can be freely spent at any establishment. In some treaties, Métis were offered either money scrip or Land scrip. Sometimes they were offered only money scrip. Scrip commissions followed the treaty commissions across the Prairies and the North and handed out scrip. The Department of the Interior issued scrip notes that looked similar to government bonds and were produced by the Canadian Bank Note Company. At first, the value of the scrip provided to the Métis was either 160 acres of Land or $160 to be used for the purchase of Land. Later the value was increased to 240 acres or $240. When the Dominion Lands Act of 1872 opened Lands in western Canada for homesteading, the federal government arbitrarily set the price of farmland at a dollar per acre. As a result, a money scrip worth $160 or $240 could be exchanged for the same number of acres. Whether for money or Land, the process to redeem scrip was convoluted and complicated, and fraudulent land speculators used malicious business tactics to purchase money or Land scrip from Métis at very low prices and then sold it to Canadian chartered banks. Andrea Sandmaier, president of the Otipemisiwak Métis government, has called it "deceit and exploitation."[9] For example, scrip commissioners left Métis with only 1 percent of Land scrip issued in northwestern Saskatchewan. The Manitoba Métis Federation estimates that up to three-quarters of those eligible for scrip ultimately lost it because of fraud,

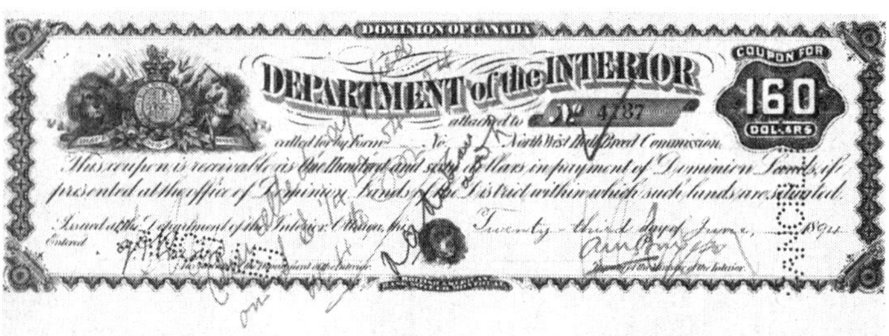

This is a cancelled Métis Land scrip for $160 dated June 23, 1894. Library and Archives Canada, RG15-D-II-8-f, Volume number: 1395, File number: 337381.

coercion by land speculators, or manipulation by government officials.

As René Fumoleau describes in his account of Treaty 11 in *As Long as This Land Shall Last*, Métis in the Northwest Territories were offered money scrip only. Treaty Commissioner Conroy argued that there was no Land valuable for agricultural settlement anyway. Those living in the "Indian mode of life" were offered a treaty, and the others were offered $240 to "[satisfy] their claims arising out of the extinguishment of Indian title." However, Métis were not paid until 1924, three years after Treaty 11 was finalized, because the Dominion Lands Act needed to be amended. Commissioner Conroy and Bishop Breynat encouraged many Métis to take the treaty. Northern Elder Adele Lafferty recalled that

> the Bishop . . . said: "Take treaty money. It will be better for you and you will benefit from it. If you do not take treaty money, you will be like the whiteman you will not get anything out of it. You will live like the wind. But if you take treaty money like the Indians, the government will help you."[10]

That is not to diminish the meaning that scrip might have had for Métis families but it is helpful to better understand Canadian systems of colonialism. The outcome was that Métis were dispossessed, repeatedly, of their Land rights. To maintain their way of life, they moved away from prairie homelands and into new areas west and north. Without access to Lands, many Métis families struggled in poverty over the years. The Supreme Court of Canada ruled in 2013 that the federal government failed to provide Métis Peoples with Lands as described in the Manitoba Act, and negotiations regarding Métis Land rights continue to this day.

Larry Chartrand, in *Métis Treaties in Canada: Past Realities and Present Promise*, argues that "the general resistance by British and Canadian authorities to accepting Métis as independent groups for the purposes of treaty is arguably one of the key injustices of the past, the present implications of which we are only now beginning to fully appreciate."[11] In fact, though, there is evidence that the government did not always exclude Métis from treaty making. Chartrand shares examples of Canada entering into treaties with self-governing Métis collectives, such as the Métis adhesion to Treaty 3 (1873), the Manitoba Act (1870), the HBC/Selkirk Treaty (1817), and the Robinson Treaties (1850s), in which those of mixed heritage were included as distinct signatories in the treaty with the Anishinaabeg. There are also examples from the Northwest Territories, where Métis are included as beneficiaries in three completed comprehensive Land claims or modern treaties: the Gwich'in Comprehensive Land Claim Agreement (1992), Sahtú Dene and Métis Comprehensive Land Claim Agreement (1993), and Tłı̨chǫ Land Claims and Self-Government Agreement (2003).

Today there is also a legislated Land base for Métis in Alberta. It began when a settlement was formed at Saint-Paul-des-Métis in 1896 after the missionary Albert Lacombe successfully petitioned the Canadian government for a Land grant for Métis to farm. Unfortunately, the colony was abandoned, and the Land was opened to homesteaders in 1909. Between approximately 1900 and 1960, many

Métis lived in poverty and hardship because of the loss of their Lands. They became known as the Road Allowance People because there was literally nowhere else to live other than the thin strips of land left between homesteads where roads or railways were to be built. In the 1930s, Métis activists pressured the Alberta government to set aside Lands for Métis. As a result, there are now eight self-governing Métis settlements across the northern and east-central parts of the province.

TOWARD MODERN TREATIES

The Manitoba Métis Federation and Canada have also signed a self-government treaty called the Red River Métis Self-Government Recognition and Implementation Treaty. This co-developed modern treaty recognizes the Manitoba Métis Federation as the government of the Red River Métis with an inherent right to self-government and law-making powers over its own citizens, elections, and other operations.

Self-government is an inherent right; however, when the Crown is willing to recognize the right to self-government, it means that an agreement has been made that recognizes the right of Indigenous Peoples to organize and govern themselves and to pass laws that apply to their citizens in a way that meets their needs, goals, and traditions. These are not Indian Act band council–type governments since they are intended to move beyond that imposed system of governance.

Starting in the 1970s, the first modern treaties were negotiated and signed. They are agreements among Indigenous Peoples, the Crown, and sometimes a province or territory.

Why the 1970s? The Indian Act, established in 1876, was created to control and oppress Indigenous Peoples. As a mechanism of assimilation and genocide, it controlled movement on and off reserve via a pass system; it criminalized cultural ceremonies and celebrations; it enfranchised First Nations persons who earned a postsecondary education or joined the military; it altered the identities of First Nations women and their children; and it imposed a system of governance for Indigenous Nations radically different from their own systems. The Indian Act, by every means, was designed to obliterate Indigenous cultures, traditions, languages, and governance.

Beginning in 1927 and until 1951, First Nations bands under the Indian Act were prohibited from raising money or using their funds to pursue a claim. This meant that people couldn't hire lawyers and could only send letters to advocate for and assert their rights. They couldn't organize politically either since there were prohibitions on the number of "Indians" allowed to gather. As Vowel explains, "Canada legislated away our ability to seek any recourse."[12] Even so, Indigenous Peoples always advocated for their rights and knew that they had never "ceded and surrendered" their Lands. By the 1960s and 1970s, the prohibitions on organizing and hiring legal representation were removed, and communities began to initiate legal action against the federal government. When it came to treaties, people knew about the agreements that their relatives and ancestors had made and that they were vastly different in terms of how the relationship with the federal government had played out. This was a time when Indigenous activism was making national headlines in the media, but historians have demonstrated that Indigenous Peoples had been protesting and working to hold the government to account for many decades already.

In 1973, led by François Paulette, a group of sixteen Dene Chiefs filed a legal caveat, noting that Treaty 8 and Treaty 11 had been differently interpreted by signatories to it, and stated a legal interest in 1 million square kilometres in the Northwest Territories. The Paulette Caveat was registered as an expression of Dene rights to "Crown Land" covered by Treaties 8 and 11 in the Northwest Territories. Preceding this, Dene, Dinjii Zhuh, Métis, and Inuvialuit in the Northwest Territories had experienced massive changes to their ways of life. The population had more than doubled from 1941 to 1971 with many white settlers and immigrants coming to the North to participate in the booming resource extraction economy. Additionally, as a result of wage labour and new economies, Indigenous northerners resided in "settlements" on a year-round basis for the first time. At the same time, medical, educational, and other government institutions expanded. Indigenous northerners were not consulted even though their Lands were being used, sold, and exploited by both the federal and the territorial governments.

The Paulette Caveat was taken to the Supreme Court of the Northwest Territories, and Justice William Morrow held hearings to understand whether the signatories of the treaties had understood what they were signing. Repeatedly, witnesses stated that they did not believe that they were extinguishing Land rights but entering into a peace treaty. In 1973, Morrow ruled in favour of the Dene and affirmed Aboriginal rights to Treaty 8 and Treaty 11 Lands.

This photo was taken during the gathering of evidence for the Paulette Caveat hearing. Shown here are James Wah-shee (*left*) of the Dene Nation; Julian Yendo (*centre*), the last surviving Treaty 11 Chief; and Justice William Morrow (*right*) in Tulít'a, July 1973. ©NWT Archives/NCS-Native Press Photo, N-2018-010-1264.

The Supreme Court of Canada overturned the caveat on a technicality: the judge ruled that the Dene and Métis had a prima facie case (meaning that their claim appeared to be valid) but that the caveat could not proceed because they did not have a written document proving legal ownership, required at the time under Canadian property law. The finding that Indigenous Peoples maintained rights to their Lands was still valid.

In other parts of Canada, there were never any treaties or agreements made between First Nations and the Crown or Canada. These Lands are called unceded territories. For example, the majority of Lands in British Columbia are not covered by treaties. White settlers arrived to claim Lands and build communities, establish a provincial government, and profit from mining, fishing, and logging. This all happened while First Nations were restricted from accessing their traditional territories, and they were moved onto reserves without a treaty or consent. But BC First Nations continually advocated for recognition of their rights and a resolution of ongoing Land issues.

For example, Nisg̱a'a have lived in the Nass River Valley, in northwestern British Columbia, since time immemorial. Upon settlement of the valley, their rights to traditional Lands were ignored. Nisg̱a'a Chiefs first took their demands for rights recognition to the BC premier in 1887 and later formed a Land committee to continue to seek a resolution. They petitioned the provincial and federal governments and the Privy Council in England. Nisg̱a'a continued to look for ways to pursue their claim, even under restrictive Indian Act amendments.

Nisg̱a'a man Frank Calder was the first Status Indian to go to the University of British Columbia and the first Indigenous person elected to the BC legislature. He dedicated his life's work to Nisg̱a'a Land rights. He asked lawyer Thomas Berger to represent his people in a court case against the provincial government to recognize that their title to Lands in and around the Nass River Valley had never been extinguished. In 1973, the *Calder* case was with the Supreme Court of Canada, and the judges ruled that Aboriginal title existed in Canadian law; in other words, there was a legal right to Lands based on use and occupation of traditional territories. The judges were split on whether or not Nisg̱a'a title had been extinguished, but in the end the Nisg̱a'a lost on a technicality: they had failed to obtain permission from the attorney general to sue the BC government.

The *Calder v. British Columbia* case (1973), the Paulette

Caveat (1973), and the (much later) *Delgamuukw v. British Columbia* case (1997) pushed the federal government to seriously reckon with the fact that Indigenous Peoples held rights to their Lands and that these rights had never been extinguished.

The 1970s were a powerful decade for Indigenous Peoples and Lands. There were visionary and influential documents written to assert Indigenous rights and share a vision for the future, such as the Red Paper (1970), *Together Today for Our Children Tomorrow* (1973), and the *Dene Declaration* (1975). The United States government signed the largest Land claims settlement of its kind and created a modern treaty in Alaska with the passing of the Alaska Native Claims Settlement Act in 1971. It was in this context that the Canadian government created a Comprehensive Land Claims policy in August 1973 and began negotiations with many Indigenous Nations. When the Quebec government sought to develop hydroelectric power in Cree and Inuit territories, and proceeded without proper consultation, the Cree and Inuit in those regions organized to voice their concerns and took legal action to force negotiations. The first modern treaty was signed in 1975: the James Bay and Northern Quebec Agreement.

TREATY MAKING TODAY

Since 1975, Canada has negotiated and signed modern treaties with Indigenous Peoples. Many outstanding claims are still in process.

Here is a list of all the modern treaties (as of the time of writing):

- James Bay and Northern Quebec Agreement (1975)
- Northeastern Quebec Agreement (1978)
- Inuvialuit Final Agreement, Northwest Territories (1984)
- shíshálh Nation Self-Government Act (1986), an Act of Parliament recognizing the shíshálh as a self-governing Nation
- Gwich'in Comprehensive Land Claim Agreement, Northwest Territories and Yukon (1992)
- Nunavut Land Claims Agreement (1993)
- Council for Yukon Indians Umbrella Final Agreement (1993)
- Sahtú Dene and Métis Comprehensive Land Claim Agreement, Northwest Territories (1993)
- Champagne and Aishihik First Nations Final Agreement, Yukon (1995)
- First Nation of Nacho Nyak Dun Final Agreement, Yukon (1995)
- Teslin Tlingit Council Final Agreement, Yukon (1995)
- Little Salmon/Carmacks First Nation Final Agreement, Yukon (1997)
- Selkirk First Nation Final Agreement, Yukon (1997)
- Tr'ondëk Hwëch'in Final Agreement, Yukon (1998)
- Nisga̱'a Final Agreement, Nass Valley, northern British Columbia (2000)
- Ta'an Kwach'an Council Final Agreement, Yukon (2002)
- Tłı̨chǫ Land Claims and Self-Government Agreement, Northwest Territories (2003)
- Kluane First Nation Final Agreement, Yukon (2004)
- Kwanlin Dun First Nation Final Agreement, Yukon (2005)
- Labrador Inuit Land Claims Agreement, Labrador (2005)
- Westbank First Nation Self-Government Agreement

(2005), which provides for self-government but is not a comprehensive claim settlement
- Carcross/Tagish First Nation Final Agreement, Yukon (2006)
- Nunavik Inuit Land Claims Agreement, northern Quebec (2008)
- Tsawwassen First Nation Final Agreement, BC Lower Mainland (2009)
- Eeyou Marine Region Land Claims Agreement, northern Quebec (2010)
- Maa-nulth First Nations Final Agreement, Vancouver Island (2011)
- Sioux Valley Dakota Nation Self-Government Agreement, Manitoba (2014)
- Tla'amin Nation Final Agreement, British Columbia (2016)
- Délı̨nę Final Self-Government Agreement, Northwest Territories (2016)
- Cree Nation Governance Agreement, northern Quebec (2018)
- A Self-Government Treaty Recognizing the Whitecap Dakota Nation/Wapaha Ska Dakota Oyate, Saskatchewan (2023)
- Red River Métis Self-Government Recognition and Implementation Treaty, Manitoba (2024)
- Chiix̱uujin/Chaaw K̲aawg̲aa (Big Tide/Low Water) Haida Title Lands Agreement (2025), recognizing Aboriginal title in Haida Gwaii

As seen in the names of these agreements, specialized terminology is used. For example, what is a "final agreement"? How is it different from a "land claim"? What is the difference between "specific claims" and "comprehensive claims"? And why do some agreements include "self-government" but others do not?

Final agreements are the outcomes of successful negotiations on a comprehensive land claim and self-government, and they describe who owns and manages the Land, how decisions are made, and how Indigenous governments will work together with other governments. These agreements take many years to negotiate, beginning with a framework agreement in which settler governments and Indigenous parties agree on issues to be discussed. Then they work toward an agreement in principle (sometimes referred to as an AIP), in which the parties try to resolve the elements of the final agreement. Land claims seek to address wrongs among Indigenous Peoples and infringements of their rights. Comprehensive claims are about Indigenous rights to Lands based on traditional use and occupancy by First Nations, Métis, and Inuit who did not sign historical treaties. Specific claims argue that the government of Canada did not fulfill its obligations under historical treaties or the Indian Act.

As discussed, Métis have also been included in some modern treaties, such as the Gwich'in Comprehensive Land Claim Agreement and the Sahtú Dene and Métis Comprehensive Land Claim Agreement. In these cases, the Métis resolved outstanding claims, including those linked to scrip, through negotiated settlements that provided recognition of treaty rights and participation as rights-bearing parties in the agreements.

The agreement that led to Nunavut entering Confederation is also a modern treaty. Indeed, it is the largest and most comprehensive Land claim agreement in North America.

Nunavut is a vast region, and the agreement covers most aspects of governance, economics, and environmental management that pertain to the Lands and waters. Moreover, Inuit leaders had co-dependent goals of both a Land claim and the implementation of a new public government. The creation of Nunavut, then, was to affirm Inuit rights to Lands, create a new legislative assembly and public government, and separate it from the remainder of the Northwest Territories.

We both have ties to modern treaty areas. Crystal is a rights holder under the Gwich'in Comprehensive Land Claim Agreement. Sara has worked on projects with the Tłı̨chǫ government, which was created after the Tłı̨chǫ Land Claims and Self-Government Agreement was signed. There are many ongoing treaty negotiations in the Northwest Territories. For example, the Akaitcho Dene First Nation is working toward an agreement in principle for Lands, resources, and self-government with the federal and territorial governments. Additionally, the North Slave Métis Alliance is seeking recognition and an eventual comprehensive agreement. We encourage you to find out which modern treaties exist or are being negotiated in different parts of the country. At their best, modern treaties provide frameworks for the management of Lands, wildlife, resources, and programs and services and ultimately a plan for how Indigenous Peoples and non-Indigenous peoples and our governments will relate to each other going forward.

5

THE ONGOING FIGHT FOR INDIGENOUS RIGHTS

Our people have never given up the right to govern themselves. Our people have never given up the right to this land.[1]

—Georges Erasmus, Dene leader

A plan to put a natural gas pipeline through the Mackenzie Valley of the Northwest Territories became a flash point for Indigenous rights in the 1970s. Canada looked to the North as Justice Thomas Berger led the Mackenzie Valley Pipeline Inquiry, established by the government of Canada, to review potential impacts of the proposed pipeline. To gauge public opinion on the project, Berger held hearings (the Berger Inquiry) in thirty-five communities along the proposed pipeline route, and in cities in southern Canada.

Conversations about the proposed pipeline occurred in the context of ongoing action for the recognition of Indigenous rights. In the Northwest Territories, the Paulette Caveat (1973) determined that Dene had rights to their Lands and the resources on them, and the Committee for Original Peoples' Entitlement (1970–84) organized to secure Inuvialuit rights. The Dene Nation (then known as the Indian Brotherhood

This is the Berger Inquiry community hearing in Tulít'a. Rod Hardy, president of local Métis, Chief Paul Andrew, interpreter Laura Yakeleya, and Robert Clement are seated at the table. The hearings were held in thirty-five communities along the proposed pipeline route, and hundreds of people spoke to the inquiry about the importance of the Land. The inquiry recommended a ten-year moratorium on constructing a pipeline to allow time to settle land claims. ©NWT Archives/NCS-Native Press Photo, N-2018–010: 02816.

of the Northwest Territories) called for a resolution of outstanding Land and governance issues with the government of Canada. Indigenous Peoples demanded recognition as having sovereignty, the right to self-determination, and the ability to make decisions over their Lands.

We know that Indigenous Peoples have inherent rights that predate colonization. These rights cannot be given up, surrendered, or extinguished. They are not created by rules or legislation but date back to time immemorial. Before colonization, Indigenous Peoples organized themselves and were sovereign, with unique economies, systems of governance, laws, and relationships with their Lands. Throughout history, Indigenous Peoples, in what is now Canada, sought agreements to live in peace and friendship with others, with the desire to maintain their own ways of life parallel to those of others.

This was carried into the Numbered Treaties. As Dene politician Georges Erasmus said, "when our ancestors entered the agreements now known as Treaties 8 and 11, it was understood that our right to be a self-determining people had been recognized. The records show that, repeatedly, throughout the [Mackenzie] valley, our leaders told the treaty commissioner that [if] signing the treaties meant that this was not our land, or we would have to follow someone else's laws, then they would never be signed."[2]

Modern treaties present an opportunity to rebuild the things that Indigenous Peoples already had and to never again be restricted from their ways of life. Indeed, speaking of the Red River Métis Self-Government Recognition and Implementation Treaty, president of the Manitoba Métis Federation David Chartrand said that "we are correcting an historic wrong done to the Red River Métis, and showing the true character of our country. Together, we are showing that Canada is a place where we can face challenges and come to terms with the mistakes of the past, and move forward in a positive way, forging a new history for future generations."[3]

Honouring the treaties, whether historical or modern, always means upholding and ensuring Indigenous rights. In some ways, this should be easy. After all, Indigenous rights are enshrined in the Royal Proclamation. Recall that, after conquering the French in the Seven Years' War (1756–63),

King George III of England made a proclamation to officially claim territories throughout North America and to establish the administrative structure for all of the newly acquired British territories. The proclamation explicitly sets out the terms by which First Nations and British would coexist in North America.

On the one hand, the Royal Proclamation was a major accomplishment for King George III in that, in one fell swoop, he claimed vast territories for Great Britain just by proclaiming it so. On the other, the Royal Proclamation also importantly affirms and enshrines the existence of Indigenous rights within British territories that would later become Canada and the United States. Specifically, it states that all Lands are Indigenous unless ceded by treaties.

The document reads that Indigenous Peoples should not be "molested or disturbed" and be able to enjoy their customary ways of life. It also states that only the Crown can enter into a treaty relationship. Settlers cannot purchase Lands directly from Indigenous Peoples. The wording is not so straightforward, though, and we invite you to read it to see for yourself. Given the legal language of the time, you will want to read it alongside the works of Indigenous legal experts, such as John Borrows, who can help with its interpretation.

When making treaties, all parties sought relationships that acknowledged their sovereignty, independence, and freedom of cultural expression. But not all parties came to treaty negotiations on an equal footing. Treaty relationships should have strengthened First Nations' rights, but historically the treaty relationships probably did more for Canada's assertion of rights.

Canada finally became fully independent from Great Britain in 1982, marked by the repatriation of the Constitution. Until then, Canada's Constitution was the British North America Act, the same legislation that had established Canada through Confederation in 1867. The passing of the Constitution Act in Canada in 1982 guaranteed, in part, the rights of Indigenous Peoples in Canada, but it did not define those rights. Specifically, Section 25 of the Canadian Charter of Rights and Freedoms ensures that any rights and freedoms guaranteed by the charter don't "abrogate or derogate" any Indigenous rights, including those recognized by the Royal Proclamation and those that exist (or will exist in the future) by way of Land claim agreements:

Section 35 of the Constitution Act states the following:

> 35. (1) The existing aboriginal and treaty rights of the aboriginal peoples of Canada are hereby recognized and affirmed.
>
> (2) In this Act, "aboriginal peoples of Canada" includes the Indian, Inuit and Métis peoples of Canada.
>
> (3) For greater certainty, in subsection (1) "treaty rights" includes rights that now exist by way of land claims agreements or may be so acquired.
>
> (4) Notwithstanding any other provision of this Act, the aboriginal and treaty rights referred to in subsection (1) are guaranteed equally to male and female persons.

Section 35 recognizes and affirms Aboriginal rights but does not create them since they are inherent and have existed since time immemorial. It also does not clarify or define those rights. Instead, it relies on previous or future agreements to define them, whether through treaties and Land claims already established or through those to be established in the future.

Despite the protection of Aboriginal rights in Section 35, Indigenous Peoples had long mistrusted the federal government and needed reassurances. In 1988, Georges Erasmus, as leader of the Assembly of First Nations (formerly the National Indian Brotherhood), called for amendments to the Constitution to explicitly recognize the right to self-government. Erasmus noted that, "because of the history of our relations with past federal and provincial governments, as well as the way we have been treated in the Canadian legal system, we have to insist, for greater certainty, on explicit recognition of our rights."[4]

Borrows agreed and similarly wrote that "inherent First Nations sovereignty must be protected further by explicitly entrenching it in the Canadian Constitution."[5] Dene lawyer Daniel T'seleie and others have further identified this framing of rights in the Constitution as unspecific to Indigenous rights and reconciliation. This lack of precision means that Canada can interpret the language however it deems suitable and can do so to serve a colonial agenda. This means that Indigenous rights in Canada are subordinate and that the Crown continues to be the ultimate sovereign authority.

In other words, Indigenous self-governments in Canada do not hold equal sovereignty compared with the nation-state of Canada. Rather, they have been "granted" the right to govern themselves in relation to matters internal to their communities as though that has not always existed. We know that it has.

INTERNATIONAL INDIGENOUS RIGHTS

> So much has changed since the United Nations General Assembly adopted the *Declaration on the Rights of Indigenous People* in 2007. And yet so much remains the same.[6]
>
> —Hayden King, Anishinaabe scholar and executive director of the Yellowhead Institute

The United Nations Declaration on the Rights of Indigenous Peoples (UNDRIP) emerged from global organizing for the recognition of Indigenous rights. The UNDRIP describes and outlines the collective and individual rights of Indigenous Peoples and identifies states and governments as responsible for protecting and upholding these rights. They include ownership rights to cultural and ceremonial expression, health, education, identity, language, employment, and intellectual and cultural property.

The declaration prohibits the infringement of these rights. The overall goal is to empower nation-states to work alongside Indigenous Peoples to tackle global issues. It is not legally binding according to international law. Rather, the United Nations describes it as a tool that will help to eliminate human rights violations against Indigenous Peoples.

The UNDRIP was inspired and led by Indigenous Peoples. Early international advocacy by Haudenosaunee Hereditary Chief Deskaheh (Levi General) in 1923 and Māori leader Tahupōtiki Wiremu Rātana in 1925, who brought treaty concerns to the League of Nations, served as important precedents and inspiration for later global organizing on Indigenous rights.

In 1982, the United Nations Economic and Social

Council formed the Working Group on Indigenous Populations. Its aim was to create a document that would help to protect the rights of Indigenous Peoples internationally. After numerous drafts of the document, the United Nations Human Rights Council adopted the draft declaration in 2006, and the United Nations General Assembly formally adopted the declaration in September 2007. In favour of the declaration were 143 countries, 4 were against it, 11 abstained from the vote, and 34 were absent. Canada was one of the countries that voted against implementing the UNDRIP.

According to investigative reporting released in 2024, documents indicate that in the early 2000s, Canada—under Jean Chrétien's Liberal government—worked with Australia to promote a 'state-friendly' alternative draft of the declaration. These accounts suggest the two governments sought to sidestep the official UN working group process, aiming to remove references to Land restitution and genocide, while adding language reinforcing state sovereignty. It's clear that both Canada and Australia were against Indigenous rights as outlined in the draft declaration.

In 2010, Stephen Harper's Conservative government endorsed the UNDRIP as an "aspirational document." In 2016, Romeo Saganash, Nêhiyaw and New Democratic Party Member of Parliament, introduced Bill C-262, An Act to Ensure that the Laws of Canada Are in Harmony with the United Nations Declaration on the Rights of Indigenous Peoples. Jim Carr, the minister of natural resources, said that the bill wasn't necessary since Canada was working on a "Canadian definition" of the UNDRIP. In late 2016, though, Minister of Indigenous and Northern Affairs Carolyn Bennett announced that Canada planned to fully implement the UNDRIP. This decision came nearly a decade after the United Nations adopted the declaration.

In December 2020, the government of Canada introduced Bill C-15, officially called the United Nations Declaration on the Rights of Indigenous Peoples Act. This bill passed and received royal assent in June 2021. At that point, the government had two years (until June 2023) to create an action plan to put the declaration into practice. In June 2023, Canada released the United Nations Declaration on the Rights of Indigenous Peoples Act Action Plan 2023–2028. The government says that this plan was developed after two years of consultations with First Nations, Inuit, and Métis from across the country.

Two objectives of the Action Plan specifically mention treaties. It notes that the "protection of Aboriginal and treaty rights—recognized and affirmed by section 35 of the Constitution Act, 1982—is an underlying principle and value of the Constitution of Canada, and Canadian courts have stated that such rights are not frozen and are capable of evolution and growth." It also states that, "whereas there is an urgent need to respect and promote the rights of Indigenous peoples affirmed in treaties, agreements and other constructive arrangements, . . . those treaties, agreements and arrangements can contribute to the implementation of the Declaration."

The declaration itself is made up of a preamble and forty-six articles. Reading the UNDRIP through the lens of treaty is enlightening, and there are several UNDRIP articles related to Indigenous Lands and sovereignty. The following articles are examples:

Article 10:

Indigenous peoples shall not be forcibly removed from their lands or territories. No relocation shall take place without the free, prior and informed consent of the indigenous peoples concerned and after agreement on just and fair compensation and, where possible, with the option of return.

Article 25:

Indigenous peoples have the right to maintain and strengthen their distinctive spiritual relationship with their traditionally owned or otherwise occupied and used lands, territories, waters and coastal seas and other resources and to uphold their responsibilities to future generations in this regard.

Article 26:

1. Indigenous peoples have the right to the lands, territories and resources which they have traditionally owned, occupied or otherwise used or acquired.
2. Indigenous peoples have the right to own, use, develop, and control the lands, territories and resources that they possess by reason of traditional ownership or other traditional occupation or use, as well as those which they have otherwise acquired.
3. States shall give legal recognition and protection to these lands, territories and resources. Such recognition shall be conducted with due respect to the customs, traditions and land tenure systems of the indigenous peoples concerned.

Article 37:

1. Indigenous peoples have the right to the recognition, observance and enforcement of treaties, agreements

and other constructive arrangements concluded with States or their successors and to have States honour and respect such treaties, agreements and other constructive arrangements.

2. Nothing in this Declaration may be interpreted as diminishing or eliminating the rights of indigenous peoples contained in treaties, agreements and other constructive arrangements.

Throughout the UNDRIP, there is reference to free, prior, and informed consent. It is derived from the right to self-determination, and it asserts that Indigenous Peoples must have control over matters affecting them and their territories. They must oversee how that control is exercised since, ideally, consent is in alignment with Indigenous laws and governance.

Implementation of the UNDRIP in Canada means revisiting and revising the foundation of Canadian institutions and thinking about how Indigenous Peoples and settler governments can relate to each other equitably and respectfully. The TRC, in its "Principles of Reconciliation," listed the UNDRIP as a "framework for reconciliation at all levels and across all sectors of Canadian society."[7]

The Assembly of First Nations has identified key areas of focus that will help to enforce the UNDRIP and protect the human rights of Indigenous Peoples in Canada. These areas include elimination of sex-based discrimination in the Indian Act; recognition of and respect for First Nations rights to travel and trade freely across the US-Canada border; rejection of the Inherent Right to Self-Government Policy, which has guided Canada's approach to self-government agreements; and oversight of Canada's Action Plan for implementation of the UNDRIP.

In a basic way, the declaration calls for the establishment of a mutually respectful treaty relationship grounded in the rights of Indigenous Peoples. Canada has not done this and continues to skirt its responsibilities as a treaty signatory.

Provinces in Canada have taken a different approach to the UNDRIP. British Columbia was the first jurisdiction to pass legislation on the declaration under the John Horgan government in 2019. However, implementation has been contested: Wet'suwet'en Land defenders, for example, argue that their human and Indigenous rights have not been fully respected under this framework. In 2023, the Northwest Territories passed legislation to implement the declaration but did so without unanimous support from territorial Indigenous governments and organizations.

The Dene Nation and some Indigenous scholars have pointed out problems with Article 46, which states (in part) that the UNDRIP does not authorize or encourage any action that would "dismember or impair, totally or in part, the territorial integrity or political unity of sovereign or independent states."[8]

According to former Dene Nation Chief Gerald Antoine, "for us, it is a big problem because it clearly places the territorial integrity, and political unity of the state, as the only consideration. And for us, you know, we're thinking, 'What about Dene territorial integrity and political unity? How come that isn't even considered? We were not engaged properly . . . and we did not give our free, prior and informed consent to that legislation." He goes on to state that, "by rejecting Canada's legislation, we're not saying we don't have rights. . . . We're rejecting Canada's presumption that it has the right to legislate our sovereign rights, and, especially, the presumption that our territory belongs to Canada."[9] Hayden King has described Article 46 as a "backdoor" of sorts through which states can choose to reject the former forty-five articles when convenient.

CONSISTENTLY INCONSISTENT

In 2019, scholar Terry Mitchell described Canada's approach to Indigenous rights as "consistently inconsistent." On the one hand, the government of Canada says that it affirms Aboriginal rights, acknowledges treaties, and promises to implement the UNDRIP. There is a strong legal framework for Aboriginal rights. On the other, Indigenous Peoples in Canada continue to experience the harms of colonization (lower educational attainment, substandard income, shorter life expectancy, and so on), and there are "significant and enduring policy failures," meaning that many historic and modern treaties and the UNDRIP have yet to be fully implemented.[10]

Negotiating and signing modern treaties are crucial, but the years that follow matter just as much. Without proper implementation, these agreements—historical or modern—cannot achieve their purpose. For treaties with Indigenous Peoples or international frameworks such as the UNDRIP, this requires engagement and commitment from all levels of government and sometimes even a society-wide shift. Why is that? Well, the scope of the UNDRIP is broad and covers almost all aspects of Indigenous lives.

One example is British Columbia's first modern treaty, the Nisg̱a'a Final Agreement (also known as the Nisg̱a'a

Treaty), signed in 1998 and in effect in 2000. The agreement includes wide-ranging provisions for fisheries management, wildlife harvesting, roads, rights of way, Lands, programs, services to citizens, environmental assessment, and more. As you can see, the treaty covers multiple aspects of daily life for both Nisg̱a'a and Canadians.

The Nisg̱a'a Treaty is an agreement between the federal government and the Nisg̱a'a Nation, but it also involves provincial jurisdictions. The federal government has tended to focus on fulfilling its specific legal obligations under the agreement, such as transfer payments, while provincial governments manage other jurisdictional aspects. This division of responsibility has sometimes led to narrow interpretations of obligations, with less attention to the broader spirit of the treaty. These are complex agreements that do not "just" affect Indigenous Peoples, but they are not necessarily treated as such. Governments treat them just like other policy-making, priority-setting, and program-management functions of the government.

Implementation of the UNDRIP is also intended to improve the human rights of Indigenous Peoples globally. Where Canadian entities operate in other countries, for example in the mining sector, where is the consideration for upholding Indigenous rights in other places? We cannot even seem to do that within our own borders.

Treaties are supposed to create relationships of mutual respect and set guidelines for coexistence. They should allow us to collectively work toward reconciliation and change existing political relationships. They can support and encourage Indigenous legal systems and governments to coexist with non-Indigenous laws and governments in Canada. This has yet to happen.

6.

THE (DIS)HONOURING OF TREATIES AND CANADIAN SETTLER COLONIALISM

I never understood how foreigners
could come and tell us where
to die and where to live.
Where to be buried and how to breed.[1]

—Tanya Tagaq, Inuk artist, singer, composer, and author

So closes one of the chapters in Tanya Tagaq's book, *Split Tooth*. Written from the perspective of an Inuk girl, the book shares the beauty and the violence of growing up in northern Canada. This is a story, in many ways, of Canada's harmful and genocidal practices within a story of broken treaties. Indeed, Canada continues to dispossess Indigenous Peoples of their Lands, languages, cultures, and ways of life. At the same time, we ask, in this context of ongoing settler colonialism, how can we honour the treaties today?

SETTLER COLONIALISM AND WHITE SUPREMACY

This drive to claim and own territories comes from the overarching structure of settler colonialism that has shaped British, and then Canadian, approaches to Lands and Indigenous Peoples. There are different kinds of colonialism. In Canada, our system is described as settler colonialism. It seeks to replace the original population of the colonized territory with a new society of settlers. This means either assimilating or eliminating Indigenous Peoples on their Lands and replacing them with new peoples, languages, cultures, and ways of life from elsewhere. Elimination is exactly what it sounds like: it means committing genocide against Indigenous Peoples through tactics such as physical violence, famine, institutionalization, forced sterilization, and neglect, all of which happened to Indigenous Peoples in Canada.

Assimilation refers to the deliberate efforts by settler governments, institutions, and society at large to absorb First Nations, Inuit, and Métis into the dominant Euro-Canadian culture. This process was premised on the notion that Indigenous societies, languages, cultural practices, and world views were inferior to or otherwise incompatible with the values of the emerging Canadian nation-state. Policies of assimilation—created by Canadians—sought to suppress Indigenous identities, traditions, and governments and to replace them with those aligned with the mainstream settler culture. Historically, and today, assimilation has been actively encouraged and sometimes accomplished through coercion.

Examples include making Indigenous cultural practices illegal while encouraging mainstream settler ones, using the legal process of enfranchisement, or removing Indigenous Peoples from their Lands or families. Often processes of elimination and assimilation occurred in tandem, as in residential schools, where many children died or disappeared because of mistreatment, neglect, and disease. Children were also forced to adopt Christianity and Euro-Canadian languages, values, and knowledge systems. Settler colonialism and genocide continue in Canada today, and some scholars and activists also identify parallels in other global contexts, such as Palestine.

When academics write or talk about "structure," they often mean a framework built over time or a system of organizational and institutional policies that guides how society operates. This is what Australian scholar of settler colonialism Patrick Wolfe meant when he described settler colonialism as a "structure not an event."[2] In Canada, settler colonialism—and the structures that have supported it—have been led by the Christian churches, European monarchies, corporations, past and present governments (municipal, provincial, territorial, and federal), institutions such as universities, and policing bodies. The enforcement of the structure can be subtle and everyday, and it is designed to operate in ways that feel normal or don't require a second thought.

At the heart of settler colonialism is state violence against the people whom it seeks to remove. In this case, it is Indigenous Peoples. Examples include the military treatment of Kanien'keha:ka activists at Oka in 1990 and the RCMP raids at Land defender camps in Wet'suwet'en territory. Military and paramilitary agencies, such as the

RCMP, are authorized to use force to uphold state laws. Even subtle forms of state violence can be deadly, which we see time and time again in the news. Brian Sinclair and Joyce Echaquan faced racism in hospitals that led to their untimely deaths. In the North, there are stories about Indigenous patients repeatedly visiting health centres and hospitals to seek care, only to be dismissed and later diagnosed with life-threatening conditions. But this happens all over Canada too.

Settler colonialism is also interwoven with white supremacy. Indeed, colonizers framed themselves as innately superior to those whom they were colonizing. Over time, white people overwhelmingly gained power and controlled material resources, and they made both conscious and unconscious decisions based on ideas related to white superiority and entitlement. In all interactions and relations, they made sure that white people were dominant. This economic, political, and cultural system that privileges whiteness is called white supremacy, and it shapes all of our lives today. Like settler colonialism, it is structural: systems and institutions in Canada uphold it. White supremacy is a part of systemic racism.

Who is a settler? We like the definition from Métis author and scholar Chelsea Vowel. For Vowel, settlers are "the non-Indigenous peoples living in Canada who form the European-descended socio-political majority."[3] Settlers can trace their roots to another country or place within living and written memory. This means that all people of European ancestry in Canada are settlers. We acknowledge that some people do not like the term "settler"; but know that it is not a pejorative term, and neither is "white settler." Rather, the term "settler" positions people in the context of our claim to Lands, resources, and domination within Canada. The term is historically accurate as well, since this is what early newcomers called themselves. Additionally, ideas about how to define the term are changing.

"Settler" is connected to structures that continually assimilate, depopulate, and attempt to remove the rights of Indigenous Peoples to their homelands. At the same time, the system allows settlers to accumulate wealth and privilege. Again there is an interaction with white supremacy so that the potential differences between settlers are set aside by whiteness. It's important to know that racism shifts over time, as does the category of whiteness. Power dynamics, however, rarely shift. Over time, whiteness is the structure that produces white privilege. Settler colonialism is the structure that privileges settlers.

For example, many of Sara's ancestors were from a region in Europe that later became Ukraine. They may not have called themselves Ukrainians, and, when they settled in Canada, they would not have been understood as white. They spoke another language, practised foreign customs, and were considered backward by government administrators of the era. But over time they started to benefit from privileges similar to those of white settlers and increasingly became a part of the dominant society.

Although Sara and her family retain cultural characteristics from past generations, they have diminished over time. Her family members do not work the Land collectively, speak Ukrainian with each other, or engage in daily Ukrainian cultural activities. Generally, they have become individualistic, English-speaking, educated professionals who have profited from access to education, land ownership, career opportunities, and social status. For now, Sara is comfortable with calling herself a white settler, which most closely reflects her own and her ancestors' relationships with the Lands and Indigenous Peoples here. She often adds "of Ukrainian heritage" because it allows her to be positioned within the prairie social-cultural landscape.

Why use the term "settler" and not another term such as "immigrant" to describe people who have come from elsewhere? Eve Tuck and K. Wayne Yang point out, in their famous essay "Decolonization Is Not a Metaphor," that immigrants assimilate into a society upon their arrival. Settlers, conversely, take over and dominate societies in which they arrive, making them their own and reflecting their own world views. Or, as Tuck and Yang put it, "immigrants are beholden to the Indigenous laws and epistemologies of the lands they migrate to. Settlers *become* the law, supplanting Indigenous laws and epistemologies" [emphasis added].[4]

That said, not every newcomer to Canada is a settler. Vowel points out that the descendants of enslaved African people cannot, and should not, be considered settlers.[5] Enslaved people did not consent to be brought here, and their presence cannot confer on their descendants acceptance into the settler-colonial system, especially since, being inherently white supremacist, settler colonialism is also anti-Black.

Métis scholar Chris Andersen notes that the term "settler" might not adequately capture relationships and relations of power and dominance. For example, in the North, there is no agricultural settlement, and those who move there from elsewhere often do so temporarily. Perhaps there is a different dynamic, and a term such as "colonizing sojourner" or "extractor" would be more appropriate to signify the taking of resources and the accumulation of profits and then moving back to southern Canada.

There are also terms for white people in Indigenous languages that can be insightful when thinking about relationships in different territories. As you learn more about treaties in your area, you might also learn some of these terms. For example, in the Tłı̨chǫ region, "mola" means a French-speaking person or a white person, and "kwet'ı̨ı̨̀" refers to white people of English-speaking descent and might have been specifically used to refer to early prospectors or geologists.[6]

In Dinjii Zhuh Ginjìk, the term for white people is "uunjit." In Inuktitut, "qallunaat" is used in the same way, although in the 2006 satirical film *Qallunaat! Why White People Are Funny* directors Mark Sandiford and Zebedee Nungak say that the term can also be defined as "participants in mainstream Euro-American culture."[7]

Concepts used to describe people and their relationships with each other change over time. Reading this might make you feel uncomfortable if you are a white settler. You might feel angry or disappointed because you did not expect this book to be about this, and that is okay. But be aware that others might consider this "settler fragility."

Robin DiAngelo coined the term "white fragility" to explain the defensive reactions that so many people have when one's racial world views, positions, or advantages are questioned or challenged.[8] There is a related kind of settler fragility, too, in which suggesting that someone is a settler, or has benefited from colonialism, triggers a deep defensive response. We admit that this work can be hard.

WHAT DOES THIS HAVE TO DO WITH TREATIES?

> The Indians and the Metis of the Northwest will be held down with a firm hand until the country is overrun, owned and operated by White settlers.[9]
>
> —John A. Macdonald, prime minister of Canada (1867–73, 1878–91)

Settler colonialism and white supremacy shaped the attitudes and actions of colonial treaty makers and, later, federal government administrators, and they grounded the decisions made by many actors to implement laws and policies harmful and even deadly to Indigenous Peoples and their cultures, languages, and ways of life. Indigenous Peoples entered into treaties in good faith, agreeing to peace and friendship with the newcomers. However, those agreements were profoundly dishonoured by settler governments.

In his important and bestselling book *21 Things You May not Know about the Indian Act*, Bob Joseph says that there was an important change between the Royal Proclamation (1763) and the British North America Act (1867; also known as the Constitution Act, which created the Dominion of Canada as a self-governing colony within the British Empire, not yet fully independent from Great Britain). The Royal Proclamation set out the terms by which Indigenous Peoples and colonizers would relate to each other and how settlement could happen. It explicitly stated that Indigenous Peoples have title to their Lands and that, for colonizers to gain title to those Lands, they first needed to extinguish Aboriginal title.

The British North America Act gave the Dominion of Canada exclusive jurisdiction over "Indians and lands reserved for Indians." It also gave the government the responsibility of negotiating treaties on behalf of the Crown. This was a clear conflict of interest: The same entity given jurisdiction over Lands was responsible for fairly negotiated treaties? And then just two years later, in 1870, Rupert's Land was transferred to the HBC without the consent of Indigenous Peoples, from the Hudson's Bay Company to Britain, and then to Canada, for $1.5 million. At no point was the consent of Indigenous Peoples sought. Canada unilaterally took control of those Lands, and Indigenous Peoples had no say in the matter.

Then in 1876 the federal government consolidated all existing legislation on Indigenous Peoples and passed the Indian Act. With it, the government set out to implement a colonizing, assimilatory, and genocidal agenda. This was not at all the relationship that Indigenous Peoples envisioned when they entered into treaties. Indigenous Peoples signed treaties in the hope of achieving a better life for future generations, with the intention not only to maintain their own languages, cultures, and ways of life but *also* to benefit from a relationship with settlers and newcomers and make use of new technologies, knowledge, and medical innovations.

That didn't happen.

"TREATY DOUBLETALK" AND THE INDIAN ACT

Cree lawyer Sharon Venne uses the concept of "treaty doubletalk" to better understand how the British Crown and Canada, on the one hand, could actively sign treaties with Indigenous Peoples and, on the other, implement oppressive and harmful policies that brought about trauma, cultural devastation, and death. These treaties were supposed to represent mutually agreed-upon terms between sovereign nations on how to live together in peace and friendship. How could these two things have happened at once?

Venne explains that the answer lies in the wording. She writes that some Indigenous Peoples "are talking about their 'treaty rights' but the Canadian Government is talking about the 'rule of law.'"[10] One might think that treaties became part of the laws of the state of Canada. Yet Canada worked to ignore the treaties and impose its own version of the law, which really was just rules and regulations. Treaties are different from rules and regulations. Indigenous Peoples made treaties with the understanding that they would continue their ways of life and assert their sovereignty.

But the Indian Act imposed rules and regulations that made that impossible. You can see this "doubletalk" clearly when you compare the agreements made in the treaties and the harmful policies of the Indian Act. Consider that, when it was passed in 1876, the Crown signed Treaty 6 the same year. It had not yet negotiated or signed Treaties 7, 8, 9, 10, and 11. That means that the Crown negotiated treaties with First Nations already governed by the Indian Act. Vine Deloria has a phrase for the fiction of treaty making in a US context: "conquest masquerading as law."[11] This, to us, describes the Crown's approach to treaty making and the legislative acts that prevented those treaties from being fully realized.

One of the most powerful tools that the Canadian government developed to acquire complete dominion over Indigenous Lands and lives was the Indian Act. There are several examples of Indian Act policies and other rules and regulations that violated the spirit and intent of treaties and caused irreparable harm to individuals, families, communities, and their languages, cultures, and ways of life.

INDIAN RESIDENTIAL SCHOOLS

The first residential schools opened in the early seventeenth century (1620, to be exact), but they were not a national project until Prime Minister John A. Macdonald's government decided to organize, fund, and support these institutions in 1880. For both the Christian churches and the government, the goal was to remove Indigenous Peoples from the Lands and to destroy their cultures, languages, systems of governance, and family connections.

The easiest way to do so was through harmful and traumatic child apprehension policies: that is, remove and institutionalize children at residential schools, sometimes thousands of kilometres away from their families and for years. Not only that, but also white settlers such as Macdonald believed Indigenous Peoples to be savage, dirty, and immoral. They needed to be radically changed if Canada was going to become a prosperous, productive, and Christian settler state.

Macdonald himself supported this agenda, writing in 1879 that, "when the school is on the reserve, the child lives with its parents, who are savages, and though he may learn to read and write, his habits and training [and] mode of thought are Indian. He is simply a savage who can read and write. It has been strongly impressed upon myself, as head of the Department, that Indian children should be withdrawn as much as possible from parental influence, and the only way to do that would be to put them in central training industrial schools where they will acquire the habits and modes of thought of white men."[12]

To achieve its goals, the Canadian government created laws and policies that encouraged what it called "assimilation." Residential schools were one part of this larger colonial agenda, and the last two institutions finally shut their doors in 1996. All Canadians should now know about the traumatic experiences that many children had at these schools and the damage done to families and communities. All Canadians should now also recognize how non-Indigenous families benefited and continue to benefit from the legacy of the residential school system.

Particularly since the national conversation on unmarked graves and the disappearance of Indigenous children at the former sites of residential schools has emerged, an explosion of resources has been published. There are landmark documents, though, such as the Truth and Reconciliation Commission's 94 Calls to Action and final report. In October 2024, the Office of the Independent Special Interlocutor for Missing Children and Unmarked Graves and Burial Sites associated with Indian residential schools released its final report, which calls on the government to take the next steps in this work of reconciliation.

BAND COUNCILS AND GOVERNANCE

Every society develops a system to govern itself, and over time there has been great diversity worldwide in governance structures. Anthropologists erroneously called this "social organization" instead of governance, but that's exactly what it is: the system of leadership and decision-making bodies within a society. Even within the borders of colonial Canada, Indigenous governance has varied widely from Haudenosaunee Longhouses to Coast Salish clan-based winter villages to extended family camps among Inuit. Indigenous Peoples have been governing themselves since time immemorial.

The Indian Act changed all of this and violated the spirit and intent of the treaties. When it was enacted in 1876, it imposed an elected Chief and band council governance structure on all First Nations regardless of their existing traditional governance structures. The Indian Act defined a "band" as "a body of Indians," and elected positions were open only to men and largely under the control of the Indian Agent. Under the Indian Act, band councils had very narrow jurisdiction and authority.

As a result, First Nations lost control of almost every aspect of their communities while the federal government took over Land holdings, education, resource development, and financial management. The Indian Act has been amended many times, but the basic band council structure and other harmful regulations remain. Suffice it to say that the imposed band council system under the Indian Act was not traditional Indigenous governance. This imposition changed governance forever and in a way not in line with the intention of First Nations to maintain their ways of life.

REDEFINING IDENTITIES

The Indian Act also created and legalized the concept of an "Indian." Today an "Indian," or "Status Indian" according to the Act, is defined as a "person who pursuant to this Act is registered as an Indian or is entitled to be registered as an Indian." When the Act was passed in 1876, there were gendered and assimilative implications for how "Indians" were defined. An "Indian" was "any male person of Indian blood reputed to belong to a particular band" as well as that person's children or spouse. "Indians" could lose their status or become enfranchised if they graduated from university, were women who married non-status men, or between 1876 and 1880 became a Christian minister, doctor, or lawyer. Enfranchisement meant that some Indigenous individuals lost their statutory and treaty rights. Women who married non-status men were compelled to give up their rights. Enfranchisement wasn't removed from the Indian Act until 1985.[13]

The definition of "Indian Status" grew out of cultural assumptions during the British Victorian era (nineteenth century) about race and gender, namely blood quantum theory and the transfer of ownership and property via men. Blood quantum was a colonial measurement system, often through percentages of the mixing of so-called Indigenous and white blood, and it was how a person qualified for Indian Status under the Indian Act. Indian Status flowed through men and their descendants, and subsequent generations could obtain Indian Status only if their parents were deemed Status Indians.

Status Indian women who married a man without status (including a non-Status Indian, Métis, or Inuk or a non-Indigenous man) lost their status rights. An 1880 Indian Act amendment stated that Indigenous women "cease[d] to be an Indian in any respect" if they married "any other than an Indian, or a non-treaty Indian." In other words, they were no longer recognized under the Indian Act. The children of these women lost their rights too. The same rule did not apply to Indigenous men or their children. In other words, Status Indian men could marry anyone they wanted—

despite heritage or race—and retain their status under the Indian Act. Not only did men retain their status, but also their spouses were granted status, even if white women.

Canadian control of Indigenous identities had significant impacts, and Indigenous Peoples have contested the Indian Act repeatedly. In 1967, First Nations women who had lost their status because of the Indian Act came together. Nellie Carlson and Lillian Shirt, from Saddle Lake Cree Nation, and Mary Two-Axe Earley, from Kahnawake, along with others, created the grassroots collective Indian Rights for Indian Women to address gender discrimination in the Indian Act.[14]

The Royal Commission on the Status of Women (also known as the Bird Commission after its chair, Florence Bird) was under way in 1967, and in 1970 it suggested 167 different ways to promote gender equality in Canada, one of which was changing the Indian Act so that First Nations women and their children could retain their status. Changes were made in 1985 with Bill C-31, and as a result status was reinstated for thousands of First Nations women and their children. In 2011, Bill C-3 was passed, and it worked to remove some, but not all, gender inequity in the Indian Act. In 2019, Bill S-3 was enacted to eliminate any residual sex-based inequities in the Indian Act in relation to Indian Status.

To this day, children are no longer eligible for Indian Status after there have been two generations of intermarriage with non-status partners. And the Indian Act still measures Indigenous Peoples by their blood quantum to determine their eligibility. The Native Women's Association of Canada says that there is more work to be done and that the Act "perpetuates sexism, racism, and classism."[16]

CRIMINALIZING CULTURAL PRACTICES

Under the Indian Act, First Nations ceremonies were outlawed, starting in 1884 with the ban on the Potlatch, which Prime Minister Macdonald called "debauchery of the worst kind."[17] Churches and the federal government viewed these ceremonies as threats to "civilization" and "progress." In 1895, "any Indian festival, dance, or other ceremony" was prohibited by an amendment to the Indian Act.

It included the Sundance, the Thirst Dance, and other traditional ceremonies. In 1914, First Nations in western Canada were banned from participating in "costumed" rituals without official permission, and in 1925 dancing was outlawed entirely. Anyone who participated in or assisted with these celebrations could be charged, fined, and even imprisoned under the Indian Act.

These ceremonies were central to the ways of life of First Nations Peoples and enacted their social values regarding collective care, redistribution of resources, and relationships among people and all creation. Consider the Potlatch. As we understand it, for Kwakwaka'wakw, being rich and powerful means giving the most away. Indeed, the English translation of Potlatch is "to give." Since time immemorial, the Kwakwaka'wakw and other coastal BC First Nations have been hosting Potlatches to mark important occasions in their lives, such as naming children, celebrating marriages, transferring rights and privileges, marking important historical moments, and mourning the dead. Elder Agnes Axu Alfred explains that, "when one's heart is glad, he gives away gifts. Our Creator gave it to us, to be our way of doing things, to be our way of rejoicing, we who are [Kwakwaka'wakw].

Everyone on earth is given something. The potlatch was given to us to be our way of expressing joy."[18]

After the Indian Act criminalized Potlatches, some people continued to secretly host them. Barb Cranmer is Kwakwa̱ka̱'wakw and a citizen of the 'Na̱mg̱is Nation. The Cranmer family has kept the Potlatch traditions alive for generations despite Canadian policies intended to destroy the practice. At Christmas in 1921, Barb's grandfather Dan Cranmer held the largest Potlatch recorded on the northwest coast of British Columbia. Federal officials arrested forty-five people, and the participants were given a choice between agreeing to never Potlatch again (and surrendering their Potlatch regalia) or going to jail.

Officials imprisoned twenty-two people and confiscated 750 Potlatch items. Most of the items ended up in three museums: the National Museum in Ottawa (now the Canadian Museum of History), the Royal Ontario Museum in Toronto, and the Museum of the American Indian in New York. This was an incredibly dark time for the community with family members, friends, and sacred items forcibly institutionalized in jails and museums. But the people ensured that their culture and traditions carried on. Indeed, Dan Cranmer saw it as his responsibility to keep the traditions strong regardless of Indian Act policies.

In 1951, the Indian Act was amended to remove the Potlatch ban. By that time, though, so many sacred items had been removed from the coast to museums and private collections across North America. Thus began decades of advocacy work to revitalize the Potlatch and bring the items home again. People all along the West Coast of what is now Canada continue to Potlatch and even did so virtually during the COVID-19 pandemic.

HEALTH CARE

The provision of health care was not part of the Indian Act but it has been grounded for First Nations and Inuit in the kind of racist perceptions that saturated the Act. At treaty making, Indigenous Peoples advocated for their well-being and that of future generations. There is strong evidence for a treaty right to health care. Indeed, scholars have shown that at treaty negotiations Indigenous Peoples initiated discussions on health and well-being. They wanted to maintain their ways of life while also drawing from Western medicine and the emerging medical system.

This was demonstrated in Treaty 11 in 1921 in the Northwest Territories. The report of the commissioner for Treaty 11 noted that "practically all the bands dealt with wanted more provision for medical attendance at each post, schools for their children, and supplies for their old and destitute." Government officials noted that "it was impossible for the Government to furnish regular medical attention" and that "supplies were left at each point for the sick and destitute." None of these wishes made it into the written text of Treaty 11.

Only Treaty 6, signed in 1876, contains any formal wording about health care, in the medicine chest clause: "A medicine chest shall be kept at the house of each Indian Agent for the use and benefit of the Indians at the direction of such agent." There is also a "famine and pestilence" clause in which the state promises to step in and help in case of any emergency.

Even so, the federal government has never formally acknowledged its responsibility for Indigenous health and wellness. In practice, then, health care has been withheld. Historian Liza Piper has written about health care in the North and how Western health care was brought to the northern territories to serve a settler population. The first hospitals were associated with resource development projects and intended for the settler population. Otherwise, churches provided health care on moral grounds and with missionizing tactics.[19]

After the Second World War, the federal government began providing health care to Indigenous Peoples through a separate, segregated network of Indian Hospitals. This separate, racially based hospital system worked in tandem with Indian Act policies to dispossess Indigenous Peoples by removing patients from their Lands, families, and cultural practices to distant hospitals.

In sum, the government of Canada does not acknowledge the treaty right to health care. It is also provided based on Indian Act definitions of who is and who is not considered "Status Indian." This creates a problematic landscape in which Indian Affairs, now Indigenous Services Canada, handles Indigenous health while provinces and territories manage health care writ large.

This patchwork of funding and jurisdiction can be disastrous. For example, Jordan River Anderson, from Norway House Cree Nation in Manitoba, was born in 1999 with multiple disabilities. For more than two years, he lived in a hospital because federal and provincial governments could not agree on who would pay for his at-home care. Jordan passed away before any agreement could be made and therefore was never able to live at home. Today Jordan's Principle tries to prevent this tragedy from happening again.

THE HARMS CONTINUE

We've listed only a few of the colossal harms resulting from settler colonialism. They continued even as assimilative and genocidal agendas shifted toward a program of "integration" of Indigenous Peoples. In 1969, Jean Chrétien, then the minister of Indian Affairs, proposed the White Paper, which called for the end of the Indian Act, the elimination of the category of "Indian," the relationship between the federal government and First Nations to be that of severance (e.g., treaties), the elimination of Aboriginal rights, and no new federal legislation for Indigenous Peoples. In other words, Chrétien's White Paper was widely interpreted by Indigenous leaders as a plan to terminate treaties and inherent rights. This was another way to eliminate "the Indian problem," just as John A. Macdonald had proposed, but in a modern framework of "integration." Indigenous Peoples and many non-Indigenous Canadians fully rejected the proposal, and the government was forced to retreat.

The treaty doublespeak that Venne identified continues today in the way that the Canadian government not only affirms treaty rights (and has been forced to do so by the courts) but also upholds the primacy of Canadian sovereignty. Or in the way that Canada affirms treaty rights but consistently underfunds their full implementation.

When negotiating and signing treaties with the British

Crown and Canada, Indigenous leaders could not have predicted what has happened over the past 160 or so years. Treaty making with the Crown did not bring about many of the positive changes that the First Nations that signed them expected. Treaties were dishonoured by the laws and actions of the Canadian government. These laws and actions have led to deaths and done permanent damage to Indigenous languages, cultures, and communities. But what is the path forward?

Tłįchǫ songwriter David Gon wrote a song related to this

Mediating the Treaties is a piece of public art in downtown Winnipeg, created by Rolande Souliere, that uses a two-headed coin to capture the ambivalence of Treaty 1: the differing and competing understandings of the treaty between the representatives of the Crown and the seven Chiefs of Manitoba, including Chiefs Miskookenew (Red Eagle or Henry Prince, 1819–1899) and Kakekapenais (Forever Bird or William Pennefather or Mann, 1816–1897/1898). *Mediating the Treaties* by Rolande Souliere. City of Winnipeg Public Art Collection. Photo by Carla Hernandez.

"doublespeak" called "The Promise" on his 1987 album *Island Miles Away*. He wrote it and sang it in both English and his language Tłı̨chǫ Yatıì, so that it could be understood by both groups who signed Treaty 11. The song speaks to the dishonouring of treaties and the promises that have not been kept:

When he came to the people in Rae
When he said he was pleased to meet Dene
Said, he wants to make peace, to be as one
So, he made the chief to sign his name
Take my word, nothing going to change your rights
Just as long as the river keep flowing
We have rights every way you can see
Just as long as the sun rise from the east

[*Chorus*] They didn't keep their promise
They didn't even care
They didn't keep their promise
They didn't even dare
They didn't even care.[20]

Akwełǫ̀ǫ̀ eyı dzę̀ę̀ gots'àhtła, hadı,
Dene sìı gılàehtǫ̀ ha.
Hanì de ı̨łè zǫ lats'ı̨ı̨t'e ha.
Eyıts'ǫ dııdzì dek'enèyı̨ı̨tł'è.
Dzǫ dàehsı̨ı̨ sìı wek'è hòʔǫ ha.
Eyı sadaaʔa ts'ǫ̀ wek'è hòʔǫ ha.
Hanì dzǫ eyı sìı godè hǫt'e.
Hanì dzǫ eyı sìı deh nı̨ı̨ʔàa ts'ǫ̀.

Today the Indian Act is still part of Canadian legislation, and you can read it online. It still tries to oppress Indigenous

Peoples, control their identities, and implement rules and regulations to ensure that they assimilate into Canadian society. It has been the main driver of genocide in this country.

But there is another path. Indigenous Elders, scholars, and leaders have proposed ways to honour the treaties, fully and finally. There is much to learn about this.

To start, courts and other institutions need to draw from Indigenous legal principles that are nation-specific. Indigenous legal principles are central teachings or traditional values that structure, organize, and maintain relationships between people and between people and nonhumans. They are still in use today and can shape both relationships and the law going forward.

7.

GENDERING AND QUEERING TREATIES

> I am not a passive woman. I was there, bearing down and shedding blood in the creation process for my children and I will be there should anyone obstruct my nurturing of them. Does this make me violent? No. It makes me a proud and deep lover of creation. I will be there should they decide to invade my tree relatives in the Stein and I will be there for the Oka, should those police run amok again in my community. I don't confuse peace with passive. I don't confuse defense with aggression.[1]
>
> —Lee Maracle, Stó:lō matriarch and writer

Stories of treaty making have usually focused on representatives of the Crown (treaty commissioners and clerks and later Indian Agents and bureaucrats), missionaries (representatives of the Christian churches), and later Indian Act Chiefs, all of whom have been adult men. But in Indigenous societies, women, children, and gender-queer folks have also been involved in decisions on Lands and treaties. While these have been treaty holders with ancestral and ceremonial connections to Lands, their expertise, experiences, and voices have been purposefully excluded from these conversations for a long time. We now know that what happened to Indigenous Peoples on these Lands amounted to genocide, and women, children, and 2SIQTIP (Two Spirit, Indigiqueer, Queer, and Trans Indigenous People) were especially targeted.

When historical treaties were negotiated and signed, Indigenous governance and laws were embedded into everyday life. Children were witnesses to treaties. Sharon Venne reminds us that children were raised to be good listeners so that they could learn the stories that guided Indigenous world views, and Elders led this process.[2] Children and young people who learned the stories kept them alive and well, and retold them over time. Some of these stories were about treaty making, and that is why these oral histories live on today.

Some treaty stories, though, are less prominent or have not been shared in a long time. It depends on the time and location of treaty negotiations and socio-economic conditions, such as food insecurity, diseases and epidemics, and institutionalization at Indian residential schools. The rise and prominence of male-dominated, heteronormative structures, in part because of the Indian Act, has also affected our understanding of these stories.

Girls, women, 2SIQTIP, and other nonmale-gendered identities have been targeted and harmed by the following policies in ways that male-coded Indigenous Peoples have not. Examples include

- children forced into Euro-Canadian gender binaries and segregated by sex at Indian residential schools;
- women as the targets of forced sterilization, which continues to this day;

- children removed from their families during the Sixties Scoop (from approximately the 1930s to 1980s);
- the over-representation of Indigenous women and 2SIQTIP in medical institutions;
- the removal of autonomy for Indigenous women in pregnancy and childbirth by the settler medical system; and
- increased rates of violence against Indigenous women and 2SIQTIP.

Even so, women, girls, and gender-queer folks have been and continue to be fierce and committed activists and Knowledge Keepers, often serving as key decision makers on Land issues. Time and time again, we look to history and see Indigenous women everywhere. They are our matriarchs, Elders, mentors, Knowledge Keepers, and experts. Indigenous women are politically engaged and Land defenders too. And 2SIQTIP are reclaiming their places within their cultures and societies and encouraging Canadians to think about new possibilities. They are leading the way toward mitigating the colonial damage done to Indigenous Peoples.

Here we discuss gender and queer issues in the context of treaty making to add an important lens not typically used.

INDIGENOUS IDEAS ABOUT WOMEN, GIRLS, AND 2SIQTIP

Every Indigenous society has its own ideas and beliefs related to sex and gender. Some of these traditions carry on today. As with treaty histories, it can be hard to fully know or access these histories about sex and gender. Most written histories about Indigenous people before colonization specifically around sex and gender are filed away in church or state archives and were written from the perspective of men, usually non-Indigenous, who held positions of power, such as Indian Agents or missionaries. Colonization changed the way that we understand the role of sex and gender in Indigenous groups today. To counter this, Indigenous Elders and Knowledge Keepers have educated—and continue to educate—their communities and young people about the traditional roles of girls, women, and 2SIQTIP.

It is important to recognize, though, that not all Indigenous societies in the past valued women or 2SIQTIP in the same ways. There is great diversity in understandings of equality and gender freedom based on the time period and culture. The social aspects of gender relations and queer histories in the past are challenging to access and understand. This is true for any society. We should not paint all Indigenous histories with one broad brush or romanticize their worlds. We should try not to generalize or make sweeping statements.

But compared to European patriarchal societies, women were and are respected and celebrated in many Indigenous cultures. They were Knowledge Keepers in all facets of life, including governance and politics. Many nations were matrilineal, meaning that knowledge, family traditions, wealth, and power were passed to future generations through women. Motherhood was revered. Women were not only important caretakers and teachers of children but also cared for their communities more generally. Former Native Women's Association of Canada (NWAC) president and Kanien'keha:ka activist Beverley Jacobs explains that

> women were respected for their spiritual and mental strength and men were respected for their spiritual and physical strength. Women were given the responsibility in bearing children and were given the strength and power to carry that responsibility through. Men had always respected that spiritual and mental strength and women respected the men's physical strength. There was always a balance between men and women as each had their own responsibilities as a man and as a woman.[3]

Before colonization, some Indigenous societies recognized many different genders, some practised polygamy, and allowed sexual fluidity, meaning that sexuality can change over time and in different situations. It was considered normal, in some communities, to have many partners over a lifetime, sometimes simultaneously, and perhaps of the same sex. Prior to colonization, many Indigenous societies supported forms of body sovereignty, allowing people greater control over their own sexual, reproductive, and relational choices.

In Dinjii Zhuh culture, girls and women can be powerful determinants of socio-economic outcomes (e.g., successful hunts) because of a link to medicine power and menstrual cycles. Tłı̨chǫ Elder Rosa Mantla writes about Mǫ̀ht'a gòehk'ǫ (I made campfire) or what a Tłı̨chǫ girl experiences when transitioning to womanhood during her first menstrual cycle. She follows protocols and lives separately, maintaining a small camp. Elders visit her to share their knowledge about womanhood. By the time she returns to camp, the young woman has learned how to care for herself, which protocols she must follow, how to survive, and many other skills.[4]

In other Indigenous cultures, too, menstruating women

are considered too powerful to join in ceremonies, hunts, and other activities. There is so much knowledge to reclaim about women's power in connection with the Land: What does a snow ceremony say about the connection that mothers and babies have with the Land? What is the meaning behind returning a placenta to the earth or nourishing the earth with one's menstrual blood? How did thousands of mothers, midwives, and babies draw from the Land to guide and nourish them during childbirth?

Language can also provide some clues about gender. For example, many of the 200 Indigenous languages that have been spoken in North America have terms to identify individuals outside a man-woman gender binary. There are no gendered pronouns such as *he* and *she* in nêhiyawêwin (the Plains Cree language), and, according to Nêhiyaw physician Dr. James A. Makokis, the word *tastawiyiniwak* means someone "in between" or Two Spirit. In Dinjii Zhuh Ginjìk, there are no gendered pronouns or references to *he* and *she* either. This doesn't mean that gendered binaries didn't exist. The language instead prioritizes kinship ties in the structure of the language. Prefixes are combined to reflect these relationships. For example,

zheh = house
shizheh = my house
dizheh = his/her house
diizheh = our house

The way that Dinjii Zhuh Ginjìk is organized does not allow for gendered pronouns, but this does not mean that there were no gender differences. Language alone cannot always be used to reflect the values that a culture places on gender diversity. But it is interesting that the emphasis in the language is about relationships rather than gender.

Colonial traders and missionaries documented gender terminology of Indigenous languages across North America but not always accurately. For example, nineteenth-century travel accounts and missionary dictionaries introduce the word *berdache*, based on a misinterpretation of a nonbinary person. A settler living in the Great Lakes and Red River regions wrote about an encounter with "one of those who make themselves women." French missionary Albert Lacombe included the word *ayekkwe* in his Cree-language dictionary, recording its meaning as someone who is castrated and thus neither male nor female.[5]

LAND, GOVERNANCE, AND TREATY MAKING

Women and 2SIQTIP have been central to cultural beliefs, governance, and law in Indigenous cultures. 2SIQTIP, in some Indigenous cultures, have had a special connection to the spiritual world with responsibilities essential to ensuring the survival and well-being of their communities. They have been teachers, Knowledge Keepers, healers, herbalists, midwives, child minders, spiritual leaders, interpreters, mediators, and artists. The NWAC reminds us that Indigenous women were (and are) responsible for sacred knowledge transmission across generations and have taken this responsibility seriously.

Writing about the role of Nêhiyawak women, Venne notes that "it is sometimes assumed that Indigenous women held the same inferior status as non-Indigenous women of the same time period. Nothing could be further from the truth."[6] Another example is Haudenosaunee matrilineal clan governance; women often had the authority to determine who served in leadership roles. In the 1790s, for instance, Onöndowa'ga women were consulted about diplomatic decisions and "intervened to urge peaceful negotiation."[7] When representatives from the Council of Six Nations and the United States were negotiating the Treaty of Canandaigua, Haudenosaunee women were consulted and their perspectives informed the process.

Women's activism regarding Lands and treaties continued into the eighteenth century, with Onöndowa'ga women vetoing decisions made by their leaders and asserting that "it is we, the women, who own the land."[8] In *Many Tender Ties*, historian Sylvia Van Kirk shows how First Nations and Métis women were instrumental to the fur trade, contributing their labour, skills, and expertise through marriage. Women played key roles as translators, and their children often served as intermediaries between cultures.[9]

Women and 2SIQTIP have long maintained spiritual connections to the Land. After years of suppression and violence, these practices are now being reclaimed. Central to this is recognizing how the Land teaches fluidity and change, and the affirmation that every organism and spirit has a purpose. Many Indigenous Peoples describe their bond with the Land as maternal, viewing Mother Earth as the source of life and recognizing a shared responsibility for her physical and spiritual well-being.

A quote from the Assembly of First Nations underscores this idea, saying in part that, "from the realms of the human world, the sky dwellers, the water beings, forest creatures and all other forms of life, the beautiful Mother Earth gives birth to, nurtures and sustains all life."[10] Using the term "Mother Earth" reflects a lasting relationship of care, respect, and nurture. Turtle Mountain Ojibwe political scientist Heidi Kiiwetinepinesiik Stark suggests that early treaty making among Indigenous Peoples began with the Land, a perspective that aligns with what we have learned in writing this book.

Scholars have noted that ideas about motherhood, women, childrearing, and Land were included in treaty negotiations. Venne writes that, for Nêhiyawak in the Prairies, the role of women in society made it acceptable that Queen Victoria—the reigning monarch of Canada, also a woman and mother—sought a treaty as a Land-sharing agreement with Nêhiyawak.[11] In other treaties, too, such as Treaty 1 negotiations in 1871, metaphors and narratives of gender were invoked by treaty commissioners that emphasized the maternal aspect of the queen and her desire to care for her children, Indigenous Peoples.

Venne also writes about women's spiritual connection to the Land and to treaty making. The Nêhiyawak Creator linked women to Mother Earth by their ability to bring forth life, and men are helpers to women, not the other way around. Furthermore, Venne says that "because of this spiritual connection with the Creator and Mother Earth, it is the women to own the land."[12] When negotiating treaties, then, male Chiefs had limited authority; they could share the Land but "never . . . sell or surrender it." Nêhiyawak women, who had authority over the Land, did not sign the treaties, and therefore it was implausible that Land possession was transferred to the Crown.[13]

There's more to learn about the role of 2SIQTIP community members with regard to the Land and treaty making given the documented importance of 2SIQTIP to ceremony and culture. We are grateful for queer Indigenous authors such as Billy-Ray Belcourt, T'áncháy Redvers, Jessica Johns, Joshua Whitehead, and others who are exploring relationships with the Land in their writing.

TARGETING WOMEN, CHILDREN, AND 2SIQTIP

Indigenous concepts of gender and sexuality challenged the fabric of colonial society by connecting the body, gender, and sexuality to spirit and the Land. Colonizers who wanted Indigenous Lands used coercion and violence to impose settler genders and a nuclear family model. This was one way to govern and organize relationships with the Land, economy, and political power. Indian Agents caused irreparable damage in intimate spaces because they had the authority to punish Indigenous people who did not adhere to heterosexuality, monogamy, and colonial gender expressions. They could take away children, refuse economic relief, unequally distribute treaty payments, or charge Indigenous people with crimes.

Settler society was based on a hierarchy of sexes in which men were thought to be superior and women inferior and in which homosexuality was criminalized. With the creation of Canada in 1867, and then the imposition of the Indian Act in 1876, there were new and harmful policies directly aimed at Indigenous women and children. The devastation created by the Indian Act cannot be underestimated. It prevented Indigenous women's participation in making key decisions on Lands, treaties, and relationships. The Act also enshrined the exclusion, erasure, and genocide of gender and sexually diverse Indigenous people.

The point of the Act was to eliminate Indigenous cultures in every form: governance, connection to the Land, language, and gender. It was intended to "civilize" Indigenous Peoples to reinforce heterosexuality, the male-female colonial gender binary, and Eurocentric policy and value systems. Today the Indian Act continues to be a driving force in how Indigenous women and 2SIQTIP are classified, and treated, by the state.

Why did the Indian Act target Indigenous women? Newcomers perceived them as dangerous or threatening to white settlement and the formation of the new nation-state of Canada. During the early 1880s, in particular, First Nations and Métis families sometimes set up tipis on the outskirts of newly established white settlements. Men led hunting and trapping activities and were sometimes away for extended periods of time, so white people in the settlements mostly saw First Nations and Métis women. White settlers wanted to prevent any "encroachment" even though their communities were established on Indigenous Lands. Women were rightly perceived to be the backbone of the family and important keepers of knowledge, culture, and language.

First Nations and Métis women were blamed for many of the issues that white bureaucrats labelled dysfunctional within their communities. Meanwhile, the effects of contact with newcomers, the declining bison population, inadequate health care, and—in some areas—the dishonouring of treaties led many Indigenous Peoples to suffer poor health and poverty. Policy makers and bureaucrats viewed Indigenous Peoples as inherently weak, "uncivilized," "savage," and "backward" and held them responsible for these conditions. They especially targeted Indigenous women, portraying them as poor mothers and morally lacking. Sometimes they even used slurs to describe Indigenous women. White settler communities wanted to limit Indigenous women's mobility even though their skills, particularly as midwives and medical practitioners, helped to save the lives of white women and their babies on a regular basis until the establishment of colonial health-care centres and hospitals.

Because of these "threatening" Indigenous women, in 1883 the Department of Indian Affairs (specifically Deputy Superintendent General Lawrence Vankoughnet) proposed a licensing system for tipi dwellers through the NWMP. Indian Commissioner Edgar Dewdney thought that anyone who did not request a tipi licence and therefore did not have a "pass" should be removed under Canada's Vagrant Act. But NWMP Commissioner Acheson Gosford Irvine disagreed and said that such a system could be perceived as a violation of the Numbered Treaties. At this time, then, regulation of the movement of Indigenous Peoples was largely left to local police and Indian Agents.

Women with Indian Status lost their rights if they married someone without status. In addition, the loss of their status meant that First Nations women's involvement with governance was changed. Women were not allowed to run for Chief and band council as dictated by the Indian Act.

Through amendments in 1880 and 1920, the Indian Act mandated compulsory "attendance" (or institutionalization) at Indian residential schools. Girls and women were special targets at residential schools, where sacred knowledge of the Land was disrupted. They were not allowed to harvest medicines from the Land, engage in Land ceremonies, wear traditional clothing or their hair long, or practise traditional menstrual customs.

Survivors share details of having their menstrual cycles tracked, intimate relationships forbidden, and pregnancies banned. Girls were also segregated from boys and young men, severing important relationships and knowledge transmission. It was often at residential schools, too, where Indigenous children—both boys and girls—were abused in violent and criminal ways. There were forced abortions for pregnant girls and young women, the disposal of preterm babies, and the actual extermination of healthy babies. These acts sometimes resulted in the deaths of both girls and young women and their children.

At residential schools, genderful and sexually diverse children had to choose either a male or a female gender and adhere to strict rules. They had to repress parts of themselves and hide their identities to avoid extreme abuse. Two Spirit Elder Laurie McDonald from Enoch Cree Nation explained that 2SIQTIP children experienced intensified abuse at residential schools. Although he felt celebrated and accepted by his family, he felt intense shame and repression at the residential school alongside fear of suffering extreme abuse and being preyed upon.

Relationships with the Land include the capacity to raise future generations of children who can learn about, care for, and steward the Land and animals. Whereas some policies sought to remove Indigenous Peoples physically from their territories, others aimed to control Indigenous women's reproductive autonomy, effectively preventing births altogether. Forced sterilization was seen as a solution that would save the

Laurie McDonald is Two Spirit from the Enoch Cree Nation near amiskwaciwâskahikan. As a child, he was institutionalized at the Ermineskin Indian Residential School, where he faced prejudice, sexual abuse, physical abuse, and neglect. As an adult, Laurie became an educator, social worker, and advocate for Two Spirit people and their allies. Photo courtesy of Laurie McDonald.

state money and solve perceived social problems. Indigenous women were also institutionalized in psychiatric institutions at an alarming rate, and they were sometimes sterilized there too. Most of the sterilizations occurred between the 1920s and 1970s when the Numbered Treaties were supposedly in full effect. Currently, there are lawsuits under way in which Indigenous women sterilized without their consent are now seeking retribution.

Such measures were parts of the broader eugenics movement and fall under the definition of genocide, which includes imposing conditions meant to prevent a group of people from having children.

INDIGENOUS WOMEN'S ORGANIZATIONS AND LEADERSHIP

Indigenous women have been organizing against gender-based repression for centuries. Tk'emlupsemc scholar Sarah Nickel has looked at some of these women's organizations in British Columbia. But overall there are fewer Indigenous women in governance or political leadership positions. There are few if any 2SIQTIP people in such positions. Are these organizations and governments advocating for Indigenous women and 2SIQTIP? Are they trying to get them into leadership positions? Does consultation adequately reflect the needs and perspectives of women and 2SIQTIP?

When the Indian Act was amended to allow Indigenous women to vote in band elections and run for positions on band councils in 1951, women began taking on formal leadership roles within this structure. Elsie Knott was the first woman elected as Chief of the Anishinaabe Curve Lake First Nation in 1954, and she explained that, "when I went in by a real big landslide, it never dawned on me that I was making history."[14]

Inuvialuk woman Nellie Cournoyea was instrumental to the signing of one of the first modern treaties in Canada too. In the 1960s, Inuvialuit of diverse ages and backgrounds—including Elders, harvesters, civil servants, broadcasters, and politicians—united to reclaim their Land rights. In 1970, they formed the Committee for Original Peoples' Entitlement. Cournoyea and Agnes Semmler were instrumental to this work.

The signing of the Inuvialuit Final Agreement in 1984 was the culmination of a fourteen-year struggle fraught with opposition. Cournoyea was later elected to the legislature of the Northwest Territories and became the first Indigenous woman to lead a provincial or territorial government in Canada (in 1991). She played a key role in negotiations leading to the Nunavut Land Claims Agreement, and after leaving politics she led the Inuvialuit Regional Corporation.

2SIQTIP have long been creating spaces to develop community, share knowledge, and reclaim their roles and responsibilities. The first annual gathering of Indigenous LGBTQ2S people was held in Minneapolis in 1988, and today there are numerous collectives that support 2SIQTIP rights, identity, and community building. The terminology has developed over time, from the term "Two Spirit," as shared by Elder Myra Laramee in the 1990s, to the term

The Honourable Nellie Cournoyea in Inuuvik in 1993, wearing a wolverine-trimmed parka. ©NWT Archives/Department of Public Works and Services fonds, G-1995-001: 8174.

A sign made by Nancy MacNeill for a demonstration at the NWT Legislative Assembly in May 2025. Photo by Kate Reid, Member of the Legislative Assembly for Great Slave, Government of the Northwest Territories

"Indigiqueer," coined by Thirza Cuthand in 2004, for those who don't feel comfortable with any gender binary. Indigiqueer writers, artists, and thinkers today are at the cutting edge of cultural resurgence, cultural theory, and artistic production.

Women have been crucial contributors to the persistence and resurgence of Indigenous sovereignty, cultures, and languages in recent years, projects directly connected to the ability and strength of Indigenous Nations to practise sovereignty and exercise their treaty rights. There are dozens of examples to draw from throughout the twentieth century. For instance, Stó:lō women were key organizers in the 1976 occupation of a Canadian Armed Forces building at Coqualeetza in an effort to reclaim Land that settlers had stolen in the nineteenth century.

Women's contributions during the Kanesatake Resistance have not been widely discussed or understood outside the Kanien'keha:ka community until recently. A book by Katsi'tsakwas Ellen Gabriel, titled *When the Pine Needles Fall:*

Indigenous Acts of Resistance, seeks to change that perspective. Women played key roles on the front lines of the resistance, including being subjected to tear gas, assault, and live gunfire. It was a girl, Waneek Horn-Miller, whom the Canadian military targeted and stabbed. And another woman was thrown into a razor wire fence. But women were also victimized when they remained indoors; Doreen Falling Doll Silversmith shared an account of the Quebec police force (the Sûreté du Québec, or SQ) storming a Longhouse and assaulting women as they prepared food. One woman required hospital care as a result of this encounter.

Throughout and after the seventy-eight days, however, women were key decision makers. Kanien'keha:ka clan mothers were advisers who guided the community and reminded its members why the resistance was happening and that it was not a reaction to one isolated event. Waneek Horn-Miller today is an Olympic athlete, known for competing at an elite international level in water polo. She also continues to be a strong activist for Indigenous rights and an advocate for youth involvement in sports.

The Native Women's Association of Canada was established in 1974 and started with women's humanitarian concerns, such as housing, child welfare, and education. NWAC was excluded from important national conversations such as the Charlottetown Accord in 1992, which could have determined important changes to the Canadian Constitution such as Indigenous self-government (and decisions about Lands and treaties) and other law-making processes. This culminated in the 1994 case *Native Women's Association of Canada v. Canada*, in which the Supreme Court of Canada decided that, by not consulting the NWAC in the negotiations for the Charlottetown Accord, the federal government had not violated the Canadian Charter of Rights and Freedoms.[15] Although NWAC did not win this case, it raised the profile of Indigenous women in Canada and the need to consult them regularly.

Importantly, NWAC lobbied for a commission on missing and murdered Indigenous women and girls and organized the Sisters in Spirit vigils on a national scale to promote increased awareness of violence against Indigenous girls, women, and 2SIQTIP. During the years of the National Inquiry into Missing and Murdered Indigenous Women and Girls (2016–21), NWAC kept the federal commission accountable, offering critiques and assessments through published report cards.

In 2021, NWAC also launched the Safe Passage project designed for "missing and murdered Indigenous women, girls, transgender, gender-diverse, and Two-Spirit people" by addressing safety concerns, providing safety resources, educating the public about these missing and murdered people, and commemorating and honouring those taken from us by violence too soon.

In 2012, Canadians learned about the efforts of a remarkable leader, Chief of Attawapiskat First Nation Theresa Spence. On December 11, 2012, Spence used her knowledge and body to advocate for the Land and the rights of her people to it. She went on a hunger strike until Prime Minister Stephen Harper, Governor General David Johnston, and First Nations leaders met to discuss Indigenous rights. She wanted to draw attention to First Nations issues, including a housing and infrastructure crisis in her community.

Spence also acted in support of Idle No More and drew attention to problems with Bill C-45, legislation that would

Chief of Attawapiskat Theresa Spence during her hunger strike in 2013. This photo was taken in the tipi on Victoria Island in Ottawa after speaking with reporters. Photo by Reuters/Chris Watti.

change the rules for environmental assessments of waterways and the leasing of Indigenous Lands. She said that "I am willing to die for my people. No, I am not afraid to die, it's a journey we have to go on and I will go and I am looking forward to it."[16]

Spence did not try to hide that she drank fish broth, medicinal teas, and lemon water. Leanne Betasamosake Simpson has shared that this sort of diet was used historically by Indigenous communities facing poverty and food shortages. Additionally, Indigenous Peoples have various cultural beliefs about and rituals for fasting and its significance. Simpson also reminds us that Spence drank fish broth to signal that colonialism, metaphorically, has kept Indigenous Peoples weak and without nourishment.[17]

This was during a time when Spence camped in a tipi, on Victoria Island in the Ottawa River, directly visible from Parliament Hill. Her demands included a conversation about treaties and the deplorable living conditions in Attawapiskat and northern communities more generally. She told reporters that "I want the Crown, the prime minister and all the leaders to sit down and rebuild that relationship and honour and protect the treaty."[18] Spence gained support from the Assembly of First Nations, which wrote an open letter to Governor General David Johnston calling for a meeting.

It was Indigenous women who kept up Spence's spirit. Women Chiefs from Manitoba visited Spence at her island camp, and they called for other women Chiefs to visit Ottawa to support Spence. They noted the importance of a generative discussion on treaties. Chief Betsy Kennedy of War Lake First Nation said that they shared "Spence's deep concern for the future of our nations and echo Chief Spence's call for restoring our relationship with the Crown to reflect the original spirit and intent of the treaties."[19]

As Spence's hunger strike continued, so did the Idle No More movement. On January 5, 2013, police shut down the Seaway International Bridge in Cornwall, Ontario, after Idle No More demonstrators marched on the border crossing. On the same day, protesters disrupted Via Rail service on the Toronto–Montreal line for seven hours. Prime Minister Harper held a meeting on January 11, and Chief Spence was invited, along with Shawn Atleo, leader of the Assembly of First Nations. But the governor general was not included, so Spence, along with many other Chiefs from across the country, boycotted the meeting. Many First Nations view the treaties as international agreements with the British Crown, so the governor general is essential and not just a figurehead in these situations.

After six weeks, Spence ended her hunger strike. This was after the Assembly of First Nations and the Liberal Party and New Democratic Party caucuses agreed to sign a declaration of specific commitments related to Indigenous issues that Spence had brought forward. Treaties and Lands, for her, were of the utmost concern. She called for the following:

- an immediate meeting among the Crown, federal and provincial governments, and all First Nations to discuss treaty and nontreaty-related relationships;
- a framework and mandate for the implementation and enforcement of treaties on a nation-to-nation basis;
- a plan to reform and modify a Land claims policy;
- a commitment to resource revenue sharing, requiring the participation of provinces and territories;
- a commitment to sustained environmental oversight of First Nations Lands; and
- a plan to ensure that all federal legislation has the consent of First Nations where inherent and treaty rights are affected.[20]

Overall, Spence's actions galvanized Idle No More supporters. Rather than bringing attention to her list, the public took to social media to critique Spence. They argued that it was not a "real hunger strike" and that she was "cheating." When this backlash was shared by the media, the rhetoric changed from Spence being on a "hunger strike" to being on a "liquid diet." Simpson says that this "characterization [of the hunger strike] comes from a place of enormous, unchecked privilege and a position of wealth. It comes from not having to fight for one's physical survival because of the weight of crushing poverty. It comes from always having other options."[21]

Additionally, jokes about diet, fat shaming, and comments about a woman's body were fair game, so it seemed. Racism, misogyny, and body shaming came together in a way that derailed any sort of national conversation about treaties, Indigenous rights, and living conditions. Canada's track record on treatment of Indigenous women is deeply troubling. Recall that there are more than 4,000 missing and murdered Indigenous women and girls on these Lands.

Rather than focusing on Spence's demands around treaties and living conditions, federal officials and media revived a 2011 audit of Attawapiskat finances, alleging poor documentation of $100 million in funding. This is yet another example of how concerns about treaties can quickly be redirected. This is not to say that more than one issue at a time cannot be productively discussed, but treaty rights took a back seat in this conversation.

Women played a prominent role in Idle No More too. Not only were the founders of the movement all women, but also thousands of women took to social media to share messages and news; organized round dances, rallies, and teach-ins; facilitated and engaged in ceremonies; spoke to the media; and undertook so many other tasks essential to the movement.

Dory Nason, an Idle No More activist, said that "the boundless love that Indigenous women have for their families, their lands, their nations, and themselves as Indigenous people . . . motivate[s] Indigenous women everywhere to resist and protest, to teach and inspire, and to hold accountable both Indigenous and non-Indigenous allies to their responsibilities to protect the values and traditions that serve as the foundation for the survival of the land and Indigenous peoples."[22]

Women and matriarchs also took the front lines in British Columbia. In late 2018, Wet'suwet'en citizens set up checkpoints in northern British Columbia, approximately 300 kilometres from Prince George. This tactic had been ongoing for several years and was intended to protest their Land rights in light of Coastal GasLink (CGL) work on a natural gas pipeline. Wet'suwet'en hereditary Chiefs have long expressed their disapproval of pipelines running through their territory. You might be familiar with media reporting about the Wet'suwet'en camp called Unist'ot'en, where CGL and its contractors were unable to pass. In December 2019, the BC Supreme Court granted CGL an interim injunction. An injunction is a legal tool (a judicial order) that "restrains a person from beginning or continuing an action threatening or invading the legal right of another, or that compels a person to carry out a certain act."[23]

In an analysis, the Yellowhead Institute said that this action was designed to "weaponize Canadian law over Indigenous law and rights, as well as the resulting financial and time disadvantage forced upon Indigenous communities defending their territories."[24] As a result of this injunction, there are many implications for the Wet'suwet'en, including the tens of thousands of dollars (if not more) needed for legal fees, the targeting of individuals (people versus corporations), and the notion that Canadian law trumps Indigenous law.

In January 2019, the RCMP arrested fourteen demonstrators at the Gidimt'en camp. Subsequently, the RCMP actions were called "aggressive" and investigated. Later that year a report emerged stating that the RCMP were preparing to use snipers on Wet'suwet'en citizens and that officers were ordered to use "lethal overwatch" and "as much violence toward the gate as you want" in dismantling the roadblock. One of the spokespeople, Molly Wickham (also known as Sleydo'), said that the report shed light on "the reality of the relationship between Indigenous Peoples protecting our lands and RCMP."[25]

In the spring of 2019, Wet'suwet'en hereditary leaders travelled to New York, where the UN permanent forum on Indigenous issues was being held and told the UN special rapporteur on the rights of Indigenous Peoples that their human rights were being violated because of the pipeline development. They were simply asking for recognition of the human right to peacefully express dissent to resource exploitation on their own Lands without being criminalized. Hereditary Chief Na'moks said that her people were "troubled by the ongoing trend in Canada that the interests of corporations for natural resource extraction are superseding the rights of Indigenous people on our lands and territories."[26]

Over time, there were many hostile encounters, including in February 2020. That month marked the arrival of heavily armed RCMP officers, dog squads, and a convoy of more than thirty vehicles and a helicopter at the Unist'ot'en Healing Centre. They were there to arrest women and matriarchs. The women sang as they were arrested and loaded into RCMP vans. These actions occurred alongside raids and arrests at the Wet'suwet'en checkpoint camp, the Gidimt'en camp, and a warming centre. In support of these Wet'suwet'en women, Kanien'keha:ka erected barricades in Kanesatake to support Wet'suwet'en Land defenders. Clearly, very little had changed in thirty years since the days when the SQ and Canadian military invaded Oka.

Delgamuukw v. British Columbia (1997) confirmed that Aboriginal title exists in Canadian law and is constitutionally protected. It defined title as including the right to occupy and use land for a variety of purposes, but left unresolved which specific lands were covered. For the Wet'suwet'en, *Delgamuukw* affirmed in Canadian law what they have always known under their own law: that hereditary Chiefs hold authority over their traditional territories. While Canadian governments continue to privilege agreements with Indian Act band councils, hereditary leaders maintain their responsibility to decide what happens on the land, including whether pipelines are permitted.

Also important to note here is that Wet'suwet'en (and their five First Nations under the Indian Act) have authority over their traditional territories, according to traditional Wet'suwet'en law and governance. Although elected Chiefs and band councils can make legal decisions, current Canadian law does not recognize hereditary Chiefs. In this case, even though CGL says that it consulted Wet'suwet'en band councils, traditional Wet'suwet'en hereditary Chiefs opposed CGL and construction of the pipeline.

RESOURCE EXTRACTION TODAY

Canada is not a safe place for Indigenous women, girls, Two Spirit, questioning, and other genderful folks. They are often at the centre of ongoing colonial oppression in Canada generally and more specifically by the federal government. The National Inquiry into Missing and Murdered Indigenous Women and Girls included 2SIQTIP in its work, but the Royal Commission on Aboriginal Peoples (1996), the UNDRIP (2007), and the TRC (2015) did not.

Big industry is responsible for ongoing resource extraction projects on Indigenous Lands that are either unceded or protected by historical treaties; these Lands have been either stolen outright by Canada or taken where treaties have not been fulfilled. A few examples include hydroelectric power at Muskrat Falls, diamond mines near Attawapiskat, harvesting of ancient trees at Clayoquot Sound, an anti-fracking campaign at Elsipogtog, and lobster harvesting in Mi'kmaq waters.

Treaties that govern these Lands are enduring agreements that symbolize the relationship between the signatories. They speak not only to the sharing of these Lands but also to the survival and prosperity of Indigenous cultures. But, as Ryan Duplassie explains, "Canada's Federal and Provincial governments have historically and continually assumed ultimate authority to make resource-based decisions for all lands and waters without consistent, meaningful consultation and negotiation with First Nations concerned."[27]

The mistreatment and assault of Indigenous women and 2SIQTIP continue to happen at industrial sites. There is often a massive influx of young men with high incomes and ingrained beliefs about masculinity that lead to an increase in the sex trade and related violence, both on site and in nearby Indigenous communities. Conditions can be even worse for Indigenous women who have found gainful employment in this industry, particularly at the more remote "fly in, fly out" sites where there are few support systems and models of social accountability.

Indigenous women who work at these industrial sites have said that they suffer from both gendered violence and structural racism. Although the argument can be made that only a small percentage of the population engages in this toxic and criminal behaviour, far more people are complicit in its inner workings either through silence or moderate encouragement. We must not be bystanders to these actions.

As Stó:lō author Lee Maracle put it, "to call upon us to submit to the organized violence of golfers, corporate logging companies, multinational oil corporations, or any other such truck who seeks to strip mine, clear-cut, or play games on the graves of our ancestors is to distort the meaning of violence. We are being asked to sacrifice our sacred creation, our children, our lineage. We cannot do that."[28]

The growth of industry and resource extraction projects affect Indigenous women and their connection to the Land. For instance, women's knowledge transmission and activities, since they are connected to the Land, have been severely disrupted and, in some cases, severed. Harvesting and using traditional medicines and foods can be impeded because of Land "ownership," new roads and highways, disruption of waterways and supply chains, and changing animal movement patterns because of urban encroachment.

The activities of Indigenous women that can be affected include teaching younger generations about the Land in Indigenous languages; fishing, hunting, animal husbandry, and the gathering of medicines; reproductive ceremonies, such as returning the placenta to the Land or marking a first menstrual cycle; and star and sky gazing.

Toxic substances and chemicals can also be stored at industrial locations and affect the health of Lands and waterways and the animals and plants that people harvest and consume, leading to poor health outcomes. Studies have shown the increased rates of cancer in nearby communities. One example comes from the Peace–Athabasca Delta, where Dënesųłıne, Woodland Cree, and Métis community members have observed contaminated fish and serious health problems in moose linked to nearby oil-sands operations and their tailings ponds.[29] These problems have been connected to serious health risks and rare cancers. The reproductive systems of Indigenous women should also be considered when thinking about harmful toxins, particularly mercury.

Issues related to resource development are also related directly to missing and murdered Indigenous women and girls. For instance, at the Unist'ot'en Healing Centre, Wet'suwet'en hung red dresses to symbolize missing and murdered Indigenous women and girls, reminding observers that industrial development has profound and sometimes deadly consequences for First Nations communities.

Indigenous families have been profoundly affected by violence that has led to missing and murdered loved ones, including children, women, and men. Violence against Indigenous Peoples is higher than that against any other population in Canada. This number includes children, women, men, Elders, Two Spirit folks, and others. We cannot have an exhaustive conversation about genocide here, so we suggest that you consult the findings of the National Inquiry into Missing and Murdered Indigenous Women and Girls readily available online. Canada has not always supported this cause. Indeed, we remember that former Prime Minister Harper said that such a national inquiry "isn't really high on our radar, to be honest."[30]

Indigenous Studies scholar Rob Innes has published work on the scale of violence directed at Indigenous men and makes several contributions to our understanding. He notes that, according to some reports, violence against Indigenous men is higher than that against Indigenous women, that these men experience violence in unique ways, and that the contexts for violence are different and gendered. Innes also notes that violence against men hasn't "been fully acknowledged, articulated, [or] understood in any significant way."[31] This remains true. And despite his calls, we have chosen to focus on women for reasons that we have outlined above.

JOY AS AN ETHICS OF RESISTANCE

We know that Indigenous women, children, and 2SIQTIP had important roles in Indigenous societies since time immemorial. The fact that Indigenous women were warriors and freely breastfed other women's babies is remarkable. We might never know how people in polygamous unions talked about politics and Lands while caressing or holding each other. Or all of the ways in which different genders among Indigenous Nations ensured philosophy, order, and care for the Land. As Indigenous Peoples, we are not so different from our ancestors.

In *A History of My Brief Body*, Billy-Ray Belcourt writes about his experiences on Grindr, during late-stage capitalism, living in a city as an openly gay Cree man.[32] These captivating experiences were not available to our ancestors. But love was. So were intimate and sexual relationships, however fleeting or permanent they might have been. Archives and state records won't tell us these stories. The stories from our families, communities, and nations will, though.

The resurgence of Indigenous gender roles and identities is integral to broader efforts to rebuild Indigenous communities, cultures, and knowledges. We must not be afraid of ingrained Christian and settler ideals present and visible in our communities. We can seek to recognize them. For those who have not yet found a way to reconcile their Christian beliefs with 2SIQTIP lives, we must be patient and gentle in our teachings. We must remind ourselves that Elders and other Knowledge Keepers play a special role in our culture and that we have a responsibility to work toward a fair and equitable society.

We must become comfortable with questioning gender norms and hierarchies that prioritize masculine, cisgender men over other people. The sovereignty of Indigenous Nations depends on the health and well-being of all our people, including women, girls, Two Spirit people, trans people, queer and Indigiqueer people, those who are questioning, intersex people, asexual people, gays, and lesbians.

We must approach leaders in our communities and nations and ask them what they are doing to support 2SIQTIP involvement in conversations about sovereignty, treaty rights, Lands, and bodily autonomy. We must make space for love, care, and joy. As Belcourt writes, "joy is art is an ethics of resistance."[33]

8.

INTERRUPTING MOVEMENT AND MOBILITY

> **The White Man put that [border] there, not us. I don't know why we have to put up with this bullshit.**[1]
>
> —An anonymous Kanien'keha:ka man speaking to another about border issues

Before the creation of Canada, Indigenous Lands and territories extended across what are now provincial, territorial, and international borders. Indigenous Peoples determined their own Land use patterns and movements and created boundaries with their neighbours through treaties and other agreements. There were relationships established across North America prior to colonization and extensive networks of trade and diplomacy. Many of these networks still exist. For instance, Dene from the Northwest Territories travel to and visit with Diné in the American Southwest. Prairie nations on both sides of the Canada-US border gather to engage in celebrations and ceremonies.

How Indigenous Peoples use Lands, travel to our destinations, interact with other people and animals, harvest our food and resources, gather with others, and think about the environment depends on how we understand our connections to those Lands. In *Mohawk Interruptus: Political Life across the Borders of Settler States*, Audra Simpson says that mobility can be a daily condition of life for Indigenous Peoples, and in particular she shows how the cross-border mobility of Kanien'keha:ka equates to their sovereignty. After all, Canada and the United States might have a firm border between their nations, but Kanien'keha:ka can live across it, seeking work as ironworkers on New York City skyscrapers, returning home to families and communities in Canada, and trading goods in local economies.

There are other examples of nations whose territories extend across an international border, such as Dinjii Zhuh and Inuvialuit, whose territories extend from Canada into the United States in Alaska. For example, Niitsitapi, Nêhiyawak, and Métis in the Prairies have territories that extend across the Canada-US border, and seven Indigenous Nations had their territories divided when the US-Mexico border was established: the Yaqui/Yoeme, O'odham, Cocopah/Cucapá, Kumeyaay/Kumiai, Pai, Apache, and Kickapoo/Kikapú.

In the Northwest Territories, the Dene Mapping Project interviewed harvesters and documented their trails, showing a landscape profoundly lived in and visited by many people. The Dene Mapping Project dates to the early 1970s, when Dene leaders directed the Dene Nation to carry out a traditional Land use and occupancy study to document the Dene interest in the Northwest Territories as well as to provide a Land use database to be used in Land claims negotiations and similar applications. Approximately 600 trappers recorded their Land uses, seasons and dates of use, species of animals, modes of transport, and other relevant details on 150 large composite maps. The database was computerized in the 1980s and is now being updated for community use. Dene travel their Lands, and the map below from the Dene Mapping Project shows how extensively they travel.

Over time, Canada has tried to control the mobility of Indigenous Peoples. Settlers did not understand Indigenous Peoples and their cultures well. As we have seen, there were many false assumptions, much misinformation, and great deception in treaty making. Newcomers also underestimated the importance of mobility to Indigenous Peoples. Repeatedly, promises were made that treaty signatories would not be restricted from their ways of life and would be able to hunt, fish, gather, engage in ceremony, visit, and freely move.

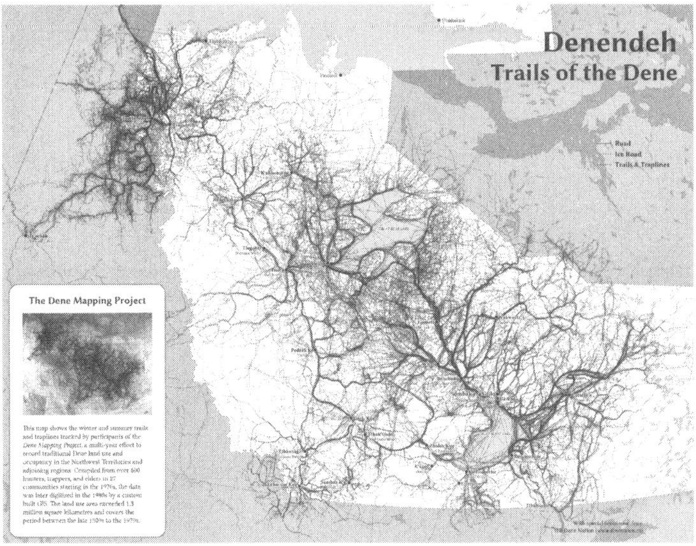

Winter and summer trails and traplines tracked by participants of the Dene Mapping Project. Courtesy of Dene Nation.

But overlooked in subsequent government policy was understanding of and respect for Indigenous Land use patterns, stewardship, and seasonal economies. The government of Canada took it upon itself to define Indigenous Lands as Indian Reserves, Land Claim Settlement Lands, and Indian Lands; create and maintain international, provincial, and territorial borders; and structure and control mobility. But aren't they all "Indian Lands"? How, then, did this come to be?

LANDS HELD IN RESERVE

"Reserves" are Lands literally reserved, or held "in reserve," for First Nations. The Lands are not owned by First Nations or their band councils, governments, or other organizations. Not all First Nations in Canada have reserves, and Métis and Inuit do not have reserves. Some reserves are in urban settings, but most are in rural areas. As of 2022, there were 3,414 reserves in Canada that involved over 600 First Nations.

There are no reserves in Nunavut and only a few in the Northwest Territories and Yukon. The 2016 Canadian census said that about 40 percent of Registered Indians (Indigenous Peoples that the federal government recognizes under the Indian Act) live on reserves. Communities located on reserves tend to be small; 70 percent of them have fewer than 500 residents. Reserves are different from "reservations," the term used in the United States. Overall, reserves are a tiny fraction of the Lands that Indigenous Peoples have inhabited or used since time immemorial.

Generally, Indian Agents and the federal government selected Lands for reserves. They are a direct product of colonization and the resettlement of peoples. Some reserves are very small and have been called "postage stamp" reserves. Some First Nations have more than one reserve, which can border each other, but they can also be located apart from each other.

In *Indigenous Writes*, Chelsea Vowel uses the example of the Alexis Nakota Sioux Nation in Alberta. It has four reserves, two of which are southeast of Hinton, one past Whitecourt (about 175 kilometres northwest of amiskwaciwâskahikan), and one on which most of the citizens of the nation live, at Lac Ste. Anne. Reserve Lands make up less than 1 percent of Canada.[2] Some reserves have also been drastically reduced in size over the years, such as that of the Enoch Cree Nation. Some reserves, though, can contain Lands that the First Nations traditionally used.

The concept of reserve Lands came from treaties in what became known as New France in the 1600s. During this time, Catholic missionaries thought that they would convert more Indigenous Peoples to Christianity if they lived on set parcels of Land. These missionaries then erroneously assumed that all other Lands belonged to them and sought legal title to those Lands. The concepts of Land ownership and title were not parts of Indigenous world views.

As we've seen, there were many early Land agreements that resulted in treaties, such as the Two Row Wampum Treaty in 1613. And then the Royal Proclamation of 1763 acknowledged that Indigenous Peoples had title to Lands and that the Crown was required to negotiate for them.

During this time, pockets of Land were sometimes set aside for Indigenous communities to use until the treaty was finalized. But the specifics of ownership of these pockets was murky, and to prevent squatters, speculators, and others from just taking the Lands the Crown gave itself title to them in order to "protect" them. The Constitution Act says that the Canadian government has power over "Indians, and lands reserved for Indians."[3] These laws were then incorporated into the Indian Act (1876) and enforced during the Numbered Treaties after Confederation.

Amid negotiations for the Numbered Treaties, some Indigenous communities suggested the locations of their future reserves, but Indian Agents had the power to reject their selections, or allot smaller parcels of Land, or assign to them Lands somewhere else. As we discussed in Chapter 4, there have been disputes over reserves, and as a result modern treaties have been negotiated and implemented to compensate for these grievances. The history of reserves in the Northwest Territories and Yukon is different, and we will not discuss it here.

Reserve lands never reflect the extent of traditional territories of First Nations and are very small in comparison. As well, First Nations did not always have a say in the process of assigning reserves. The creation of reserve Lands was meant, in part, to contain Indigenous Peoples. The pass system was then designed to control Indigenous Peoples leaving and returning to reserves.

CREATION OF THE PASS SYSTEM

The North-West Resistance in 1885 was a turning point in terms of how the mobility of Indigenous Peoples was controlled and limited by Indian Affairs and Canada. They viewed First Nations and Métis with suspicion and contempt and sought to control those whom they thought most threatening. Assistant Indian Affairs Commissioner Hayter

Reed thought that the actions of Indigenous Peoples in the 1885 resistance had violated and even negated some of the Numbered Treaties. Interestingly, he did not make the same assessment of Canadian military forces, which had killed dozens of First Nations and Métis in the conflict.

Government officials had pondered the idea of permits or passes during the early 1880s, but no system was implemented until after 1885. It was called the pass system and used mostly in the Prairies. Some people didn't agree with it. For instance, NWMP Commissioner A.G. Irvine thought that it restricted mobility too much and could be a treaty violation. Indeed, the Treaty 6 document says that First Nations had the "right to pursue their avocations of hunting and fishing throughout the tract surrendered."[4] Nonetheless, the pass system was enforced.

In May 1885, Major General Frederick Dobson Middleton wrote to Indian Commissioner Edgar Dewdney to ask that Indigenous Peoples be confined to their reserves so that they would not join the North-West Resistance. Dewdney did not have the authority to implement this restriction, but he issued a notice demanding that people ask permission before leaving the reserve or face arrest. Restricting mobility was not a concern for those Indigenous Peoples perceived as "loyal" by obeying Indian Agents; instead, they were allocated farming equipment and other "rewards."

After the conflict ended, Reed wrote a policy document titled "Memorandum on the Future Management of Indians" that led, in part, to the pass system. It obtained approval from Indian Affairs management and eventually Prime Minister John A. Macdonald, also the superintendent general of Indian Affairs. The pass system took effect in August 1885. Now First Nations had to ask Indian Agents for permission to leave and return to their reserves. Additionally, during this time, the number of Indian Affairs and police staff greatly increased. In Saskatchewan, for example, the number of Indian Agencies increased fivefold, from two to ten. There were more agents of the state to control the movement of people and enforce the pass system.

It was not easy to obtain a pass. The person who sought a pass had to travel to the Indian Agent's home and, if the agent was not there, wait for his return. These sorts of delays could have far-reaching consequences, such as the spoiling of produce meant for the market and financial losses for Indigenous families. Families could not attend large gatherings such as Sundances, powwows, Potlatches, and other important ceremonies. The pass system also limited their ability

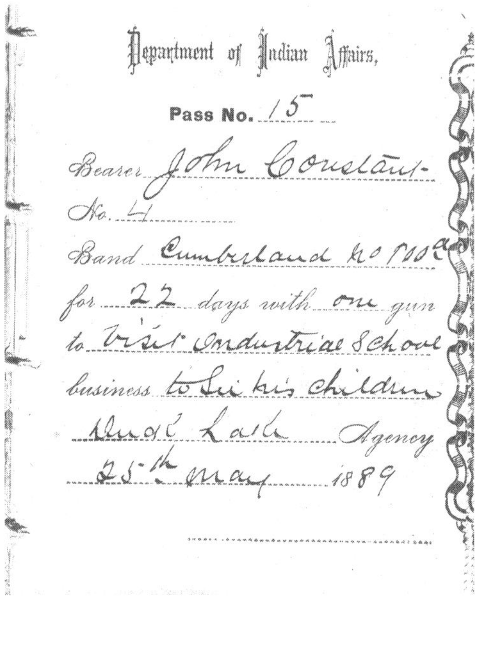

Department of Indian Affairs,

Pass No. 15

Bearer John Constant

No. 4

Band Cumberland

for 22 days with one gun

to visit Industrial School

business to see his children

Duck Lake Agency

25th May 1889

A reserve pass. This travel permit was issued by the Duck Lake Agency in 1889 to John Constant, allowing him to visit his children at an industrial school. Provincial Archives of Saskatchewan, Records of Canada, Department of Indian and Northern Affairs, S-E19, File 35.a.

to gather medicines, harvest seasonal items, check traplines, and hunt and fish. People had to ask permission to pick berries or cut wood if those resources were located off reserve.

The pass system also restricted fur-trading activities and visiting extended family members who lived off reserve. It prevented parents from visiting their children at Indian residential schools or limited their visiting time. It also kept Indigenous and settler communities apart, which contributed to feelings of mistrust and dislike. It limited Indigenous Peoples' ability to gather in large numbers and organize. This restriction was important to Canada since it wanted to limit any threat to white settlements. Additionally, into the 1890s, non-Indigenous sportsmen—specifically the Calgary Gun and Rod Club—complained about Indigenous hunting and petitioned Indian Affairs to confine Indigenous hunters to their reserves. This petition was supported by signatures from the NWMP.

Indigenous Peoples did not always abide by the rules. Despite the consequences, they sometimes left and returned to their reserves without permission or passes. Those caught without a pass were arrested or taken back to their reserves. Alex Williams says in his 2015 documentary, *The Pass System*, that people thus caught could be jailed up to sixty days.[5] Indian Agents also withheld rations as punishment. But it was difficult for Indigenous Peoples to resist this system. Relations with Indian Agents and Indian Affairs more generally were not friendly. Indigenous Peoples were also not allowed to vote federally in Canada until 1960, so there was no likelihood of changing the system through colonial democratic structures.

Policing bodies continued to question the use of the pass system because it was never codified in Canadian law and therefore not enforceable under the law, but Indian Affairs continued to encourage its use. It also suggested that Indian Agents and the NWMP tell Indigenous Peoples that the pass system was part of the law when it was not. The system was in effect, though not evenly enforced, until the 1930s or 1940s.

We still do not have a full understanding of the pass system, especially from Indigenous perspectives. There is evidence that the Canadian government recently attempted to hide the fact that it used the system—illegally—to control the mobility of Indigenous Peoples who lived on reserves. In his documentary, Williams focuses on the oral histories of this form of restriction and segregation.[6] Under the pass system, Williams said, reserves were "open air prisons."[7]

The creation of reserves and the control of their borders were ways in which the mobility of Indigenous peoples was limited. They were encouraged to stay put. However, people sometimes were forced to move to attend a residential school far away from home, family, and community or to go to an Indian Hospital in the South, and occasionally whole communities were forced into new locations.

HIGH ARCTIC FORCED RELOCATIONS

> We were actually on what we called "Prison Island." You were left to your resources, alone, and [no one] worried about running away because you're so far away.[8]
>
> —Larry Audlaluk

Larry Audlaluk and his family were forcibly relocated from Inukjuak, Quebec, to Grise Fiord, Nunavut, in the 1950s when he was two years old. Those relocated suffered greatly and felt like virtual prisoners in the High Arctic, where they were sent to assert Canadian sovereignty. In Inukjuak, the people had the equipment that they needed, and there was plenty of game for food. As Samwillie Eliasialuk recollected, "we lived a secure life at that time, never having experienced hunger." But when they arrived at Grise Fiord, Anna Nungaq said, "there was absolutely nothing, no housing, no medical services. . . . [T]hey just left us there and we saw the ship sailing away and we were just dumped in a place where there was absolutely nothing."[9]

Indeed, this is one of many examples where the state has worked to interrupt the Indigenous right to mobility. At home in Inukjuak, people would have traversed a familiar landscape to harvest, hunt, and visit. Forced relocation interrupted a way of life completely, with ruptures that continue to affect families and communities today.

Unfortunately, Audlaluk's experience is only one of many. There were no treaties or political agreements in place with Inuit when the Canadian government, RCMP, and HBC decided to forcibly move them away from their homelands despite the cost to Inuit life, culture, health, connection to the Land, and economy.

Between 1934 and 1947, Indian Affairs and the HBC thought it appropriate to team up to relocate Inuit living on Qikiqtaaluk (Baffin Island) to Devon Island. This is a revealing example of how, 100 years later, the government and HBC continued to work together in the pursuit of colonial goals. Since time immemorial, Inuit had lived comfortably on Qikiqtaaluk. Fifty-three people, as well as their sled dogs and possessions, were relocated to Devon Island for a two-year period. Conditions there were harsh, and the outcome was not as the government and HBC had anticipated. All fifty-three Inuit elected to leave after two years. But they were not allowed to return home to Qikiqtaaluk. Instead, they were shipped to Arctic Bay, Fort Ross, and Taloyoak (then known as Spence Bay).

This happened against their will, and these families repeatedly asked to return home. This relocation displaced Inuit from their Lands, and it was a complete failure for the state and HBC, but it set the stage for future relocations. The state reframed these relocations as a need to "save" Inuit from the modern temptations of settler lifestyles and white corruption.

In 1949, the federal government "convinced" Inuit living near Ennadai Lake—without the use of a translator—to move more than 100 kilometres away, to Nueltin Lake. When they asked to leave Nueltin Lake and return home, they were then sent to Henik Lake, and then to Tavani, where several Inuit died. In 1953 and 1955, on behalf of the federal government, the RCMP moved just under 100 Inuit from Inukjuak, Nunavik, and Mittimatalik, Nunavut. Taken away from their traditional territories, these families were moved to High Arctic islands, some as far away as 2,000 kilometres, to the Far North. These islands were desolate, whereas the established communities that Inuit were forced to leave had modern services, were rich with wildlife, and had fertile opportunities for socio-economic growth.

As the federal government shuffled Inuit around the North, they eventually ended up in permanent settlements where white people had moved for work and financial gain. If forced relocations weren't bad enough, during this period

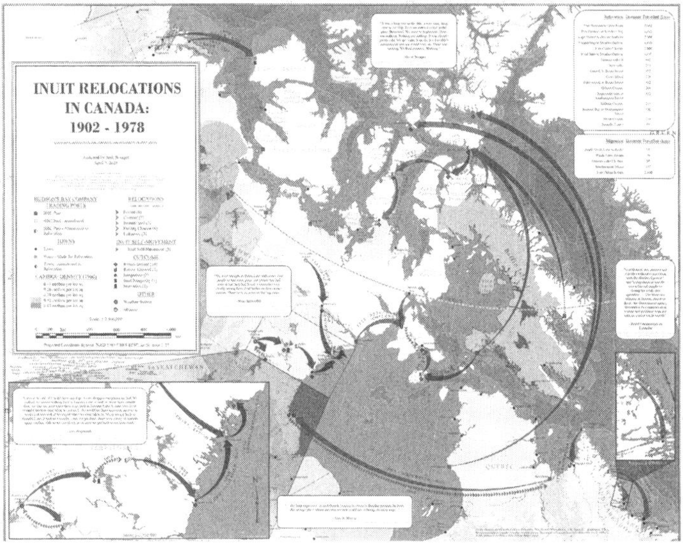

Inuit families were relocated vast distances away from their home communities and ancestral Lands, as this map shows. Map by Josh Bourget, available on the 2024 Esri Canada Map Calendar: https://map-calendar-esricanada.hub.arcgis.com/pages/jan-2024.

the RCMP also killed tens of thousands of qimmitt (sled dogs) belonging to Inuit families. The RCMP claimed that qimmitt were destroyed because of public health and safety concerns, but the Qikiqtani Truth Commission (2007–10) uncovered more to the story. There were some ill qimmitt, and though Inuit wanted to care for them and knew that they'd survive they were targeted anyway. White settlers were afraid of qimmitt and requested that the RCMP kill them, so legal means were adopted to do so.

Inuit perceived the killing of qimmitt as intentional, and done in order to get their families to permanently move off their Lands and into modern communities. The absence of dogs changed Inuit relationships with the Land and reduced their abilities to harvest and gain good incomes for their families. Without qimmitt, Inuit thought that they were unable to engage in their traditional lifestyles.

Remember that, during this period, Inuit children were also removed from their families and sent to residential schools, and Inuit of all ages were sent to tuberculosis hospitals in southern Canada. All of these factors (and others) permanently changed the structure of Inuit families and how they connected to their Lands and cultures.

These relocations and dog killings were not done in the best interests of Inuit. The federal government and RCMP told Inuit that, if they "chose" to relocate, they'd prosper. During the 1930s, the government relocated some Inuit so that they could provide the HBC with furs. By the 1950s, the RCMP continued to promise better hunting grounds, but this promise was false and misleading. The relocations were supposed to contribute to the fur trade, but they also kept Inuit away from modern services. Thus, Inuit could live a more "traditional" lifestyle of gathering and hunting and thereby keep the state's financial obligations to them minimal or nonexistent. Newcomers did not respect Inuit or want their culture to persist, nor did they want the financial commitment to them.

These relocations were also about Canadian Arctic sovereignty. Canada feared that it would lose parts of the Arctic to another country. This fear was behind moving people onto Lands so that another country could not make an ownership claim. During the Second World War, the United States had a military presence in northern Canada and even helped to build critical transportation infrastructure. During the subsequent Cold War, Canada felt threatened not only by Russia but also by the United States, whose forces continued to be stationed in the Arctic and increased their military power. The Canadian government needed to populate the territory.

Echoing the concerns with interpretation and translation of the Numbered Treaties, there are red flags about how the government communicated to Inuit and how they supposedly gave their consent. As noted above, some information about relocations was given with no interpreter present. How would English- or French-speaking officials have communicated the details effectively into Inuktitut without an interpreter? The RCMP also told some Inuit that their family members had already agreed to the relocations. Given the colonial power dynamics at the time, many Inuit thought that they had to agree to the relocations. They were also misled about being able to return home after two years.

Relocated Inuit families were in completely new and different environments, and their knowledge of the Land, hunting patterns, and resources was not entirely relevant to the High Arctic. There were many different factors at play: reduced daylight hours during the winter; a longer and more pronounced winter climate; different animal migration patterns; reduced access to fish, shellfish, and edible vegetation; and limited fuel supplies to keep warm in the winter. Not only were their surroundings different, but also some families were strategically located so that they would not be able to access outside supplies. The government also imposed hunting restrictions that, if defied, could result in being fined or arrested. Even worse, some families were split up during relocations.

Many families requested to return to their homes and traditional territories, promised as an option after two years.

Inuit were then told that they would have to finance the return themselves. To make matters worse, any money that Inuit trappers had earned for their furs was credited to the federal government's Eskimo Loan Fund, making the move unaffordable. Sadly, some were able to leave the High Arctic only through their institutionalization at an Indian Hospital in southern Canada for tuberculosis treatment.

Larry Audlaluk explains that this experience of being exiled to the High Arctic had a role in the creation of Nunavut. He notes that John Amagoalik, an Inuk known as the "Father of Nunavut," was a High Arctic exile, and that experience contributed to how he thought about the North and then later fought for the creation of Nunavut, the biggest Land claim agreement ever signed in Canada. In 1994, the Royal Commission on Aboriginal Peoples investigated the High Arctic relocations and wrote that Inuit families had no way to give free and informed consent to their relocations. Two years later the federal government established a Reconciliation Agreement with a $10 million trust fund for these relocated Inuit, but this fund diminished because of a collapse in the stock market, and payments stopped in 2009.

So, through the creation of reserves and the implementation of the Pass System, Indigenous Peoples were forced to stay put. Yet, through forced relocations, Indigenous Peoples had to move. Either way, they didn't get to decide. Instead, the government decided for them.

INTERNATIONAL BORDERS

I have seen many written documents, and I have seen also my grandparents [had] a sort of written document at the time they

> **crossed to Alaska, to Canada. At that time we didn't know where the border was, as a matter of fact.[10]**
>
> —Peter Thrasher, Akłarvik, Berger Inquiry Community Testimony, 1975

Herman Oyagak is Iñupiaq from Alaska, and Carol Oyagak (née Arey) is Inuvialuk from Akłarvik, Northwest Territories. They met at a drum dance festival in Alaska. In 2018, Herman travelled eighteen hours by snowmobile on traditional trails across the Canada-US border to join Carol in Akłarvik. In 2020, the RCMP arrested him in Akłarvik and transported him to Sǫǫ̀mbak'è; he was then released on bond but faced a deportation order from the Canadian Border Services Agency (CBSA). The order was deferred, but the CBSA could send him back to Alaska at any moment.

The onus was on Herman to prove his case to remain in Canada. His lawyer argued that Indigenous Peoples have a right to undertake traditional cultural practices, including hunting, fishing, participating in ceremonies and celebrations, and engaging in family relationships and marriages. Carol explained that "it's our right. We've always travelled back and forth between Alaska and Canada. And we're always going to continue doing it."[11]

The Oyagaks' experience demonstrates how cross-border restrictions complicate and negatively affect the lives of Indigenous Peoples. Before the creation of the Canada-US border and Land claim agreements in each country, the Oyagaks belonged to one nation: Inuit. For thousands of years, Inuit have travelled these Lands unimpeded, married each other, and harvested and hunted on them. They have made relationships with other Indigenous Peoples as well. International border restrictions prevent families, like the Oyagaks, from exercising their rights to mobility, intimate partnerships, and cultural activities and practices. Inuvialuit Regional Corporation Chair and CEO Duane Ningaqsiq Smith said that deportation is about Canada "blindly following process."[12]

How did this happen? Why wasn't Herman able to reside in Akłarvik and have the right to remain on Inuit Lands?

The creation of a border between the United States and British North America in 1783 was the result of the end of the American War of Independence and the Treaty of Paris. Not everything was resolved, though: the location of the border was still disputed, there were high duties and other restrictions, forts remained occupied in each other's territory, and there were disputes about enslaved people escaping to British territories after the American Revolution of 1776.

There were concerns, too, about the vitality of the fur trade, and officials worried that a decline would affect Indigenous economies. Indeed, there was reason for concern: before the War of Independence, fur trade economies were flourishing, but their success was dependent on the mobility of Indigenous Peoples across their Lands. Drawing a firm border restricted that mobility.

This all led to the need for a new treaty. The Jay Treaty, or Jay's Treaty, of 1794 is also known as the Treaty of Amity, Commerce and Navigation between His Britannick Majesty; and the United States of America, by Their President, with the Advice and Consent of Their Senate. It is primarily a commercial agreement designed to solve the economic and mobility concerns that emerged with the new border.

The Jay Treaty had many terms, but here are the most important, for our purposes, taken from Article III:[13]

- "The Indians dwelling on either side of the said boundary line" shall be free to "pass and repass by land or inland navigation." This means that Indigenous Peoples were freely allowed to cross the border.
- "No duty of entry shall ever be levied by either party on peltries brought by land or inland navigation into the said territories respectively, nor shall the Indians passing or repassing with their own proper goods and effects of whatever nature, pay for the same any import or duty whatever." This means that Indigenous Peoples were excluded from paying duties on goods carried across the border.

Article XXVIII also states that "the first ten articles of this treaty shall be permanent," including Article III noted above. Yet Britain had to continually reassure the Anishinaabeg, Bodewéwadmik, Wendat, and Odawa that the international border would not affect their mobility. These reassurances were necessary, in part, because the United States attempted to regulate and restrict Indigenous traders.

Over the course of twenty years and two subsequent treaties, the right of Indigenous Peoples to pass freely over the border was expressed. Unfortunately, this right doesn't always hold up today.

For two reasons, Canada does not recognize the Jay Treaty in any form. First, Canada claims that the War of 1812 abrogated ("repealed" or "did away with") the Jay Treaty. Second, the Jay Treaty was never sanctioned by legislation (known as ratification) in Canada. So, from Canada's perspective, when entering Canada, anything to do with the Jay Treaty is irrelevant. The only people who have rights to enter and remain in Canada include Canadian citizens, permanent residents, and those registered as Indians under the Indian Act (i.e., they have status cards). The Canadian Immigration and Refugee Protection Act governs all noncitizens.

In 2023, Minister of Immigration Marc Miller said that Canada has no intention of recognizing the Jay Treaty; instead, it is working to increase border movement and flexibility for Indigenous Peoples, an initiative apparently tied to Canada's implementation of the UNDRIP.

When entering the United States, some but not all Indigenous people can use the Jay Treaty to cross the border, legally live and work in the United States, and claim an exemption on duties. In practice, however, US immigration law narrowed the treaty promise: under Section 289 of the Immigration and Nationality Act, only those who can prove they have "at least 50 percent" Indigenous blood are recognized as having this right. As explained earlier, blood quantum is a system of classification used by colonial governments to restrict Indigenous sovereignty and rights or to eliminate or reduce the number of Indigenous people who might qualify for a certain program or agreement. Blood quantum has been harmful and is a part of colonialism. Measuring our ancestral and familial connections against settler-colonial regulations removes our ability to define our nations for ourselves.

Indigenous people who are Canadian citizens must meet US blood quantum requirements to access these benefits. This means that an Indigenous person who is also a Canadian must show documentation from their band/government/nation that they meet the 50 percent blood quantum requirement. The United States considers Inuit to be "Indians" if they meet the 50 percent mark, and Métis can benefit too if they satisfy the blood quantum requisite. Having a Canadian Indian Status card or a band membership card—even if it does state blood quantum—will not be sufficient to gain Jay Treaty benefits.

Also, American Indians born in Canada have the right to enter the United States if they show the proper blood quantum documentation from a "Canadian Indian Band" or a "US Indian Tribe" (according to the US Citizenship and Immigration Services webpage). Indigenous people who cannot prove that they meet the 50 percent blood quantum requirement cannot seek Jay Treaty benefits. The Jay Treaty is therefore a tool, if a limited one, to reinstate freedom of mobility among Indigenous Peoples.

There have been other instances when Indigenous Peoples on both sides of the Canada-US border have challenged border restrictions. In 1924, the United States passed its first Immigration Act, designed to limit immigration from Asia and Southern and Eastern Europe, but it also subjected Indigenous Peoples to the same laws as other non-US citizens. In 1925, the US Department of Immigration arrested Kanien'keha:ka ironworker Paul Diabo and his wife for entering the United States without passports. The couple requested an injunction based on the Jay Treaty but were deported to Canada anyway.

A year later Diabo returned to the United States to challenge his deportation. He was well supported by his ironworker colleagues and community since this international movement had implications for the livelihoods of Kanien'keha:ka families. At the same time, Indigenous Peoples in the United States were organizing, and the Six Nations Defense League emerged to fight on behalf of Indigenous Peoples for cross-border rights. The organization was later renamed the Indian Defense League of America.

In 1927, an American court decided that "international treaties recognized th[e] freedom of Indian people to cross the border between the United States and Canada and that there was nothing in American immigration laws to deny that freedom."[14] Diabo had been unlawfully charged and detained, but the government planned to appeal that decision. This became a discussion about the Jay Treaty and the Treaty of Ghent of 1814.

Ultimately, the court decided that the right to free crossing over the international border was not temporary, that this right had not been abrogated by the War of 1812, and that acts of Congress did not apply to Indigenous Peoples unless clearly stated because of their different legal status. Importantly, the ruling applied specifically to "American Indians born in Canada"—the legal category used in US immigration law—and not automatically to all Indigenous Peoples who cross the border. The case instilled political confidence in Kahnawake and encouraged activism on other issues, such as protesting conditions at Indian day schools and early conversations on the Kahnawake Longhouse movement and sovereignty more generally.

Akwesasne is a Kanien'keha:ka community located in both the United States and Canada, with the border dividing the community. There is a long-standing tension between the right of Kanien'keha:ka to cross the border unimpeded and be exempt from duties and the Canadian and American states enforcing border controls.

In 1956, a Kanien'keha:ka man named Louis Francis from Akwesasne purchased a household appliance on the US side of the Kahnawake reserve. Canadian customs charged Francis duty and tax, which he paid but not without protest. About ten years later, in 1968, leader Mike Mitchell—also from Akwesasne—was arrested when he failed to pay duty on household items that he brought into Canada. In February of the following year, protesters blocked the Seaway International Bridge, part of which was in Akwesasne Kanien'keha:ka territory, forcing Canada to recognize the right to duty-free passage for First Nations.

Twenty years later, in 1988, Mitchell again crossed into Canada from the United States and refused to pay duties on his purchased goods. He challenged the duties in court, and both the Federal Court, Trial Division, and the Federal Court of Appeal affirmed that his right to duty-free passage was protected. However, in 2001 the Supreme Court of Canada, in *Mitchell v. MNR*, overturned those lower-court rulings and held that crossing the border with goods duty-free is not an established Aboriginal right under Section 35 of the Constitution Act, 1982. This final ruling marked a reversal, since earlier courts had sided with Mitchell, but the Supreme Court's decision became binding precedent. It was Chrétien's Liberal government that appealed Mitchell's earlier court victories, leading to the 2001 Supreme Court decision against him.

Mique'l Dangeli of the Tsimshian First Nation in British Columbia was born just outside Canada, on the US Annette Islands Indian Reservation. In 2018, Dangeli sought registration under the Indian Act in Canada so that she could remain in British Columbia, but the approval hinged on obtaining nineteenth-century baptismal records of her great-great-great-grandmother. Dangeli says that "Canada dissects Indigenous territories in ways that sever the lifelines

Kahentinetha Horn, a Kanien'keha:ka activist and model, delivers a message to Buckingham Palace in London in 1969, asserting the continued relevance of the 1794 Jay Treaty. The treaty affirms the right of Indigenous Peoples to cross the US-Canada border freely and in perpetuity. Photo courtesy of Paul Seesequasis.

between First Nation families, communities, languages and ceremonies." Pointing to the fact that Canada doesn't acknowledge the Jay Treaty, she rightly asks "how is it possible that the US, with its extreme policies against immigration, honours the rights of Indigenous peoples regardless of citizenship and Canada does not?"[15]

There are many more examples of how the US-Canada border and the Jay Treaty have complicated and restricted the sovereignty and mobility of Indigenous Peoples in what is now known as Canada. Animals have also been affected by this border. One example is the Porcupine Caribou Herd in Yukon and Alaska, central to the members of the Gwich'in Nation. Indeed, Gwich'in territory and caribou territory overlap each other and cross multiple borders, requiring American-Canadian cooperation on conservation and mobility patterns.

Inuit Tapiriit Kanatami President Natan Obed has also been calling on the Canadian government, including immigration ministers, to rectify border problems. Inuit Nunangat, for example, spans parts of Canada, Greenland, Russia, and the United States. In these regions, Inuit have shared families, hunting areas, and marine management strategies. Obed sees legal reform of the Canadian Immigration Act as "reconstituting our nation in the way that we have always lived in it."[16] For him, changes to Canada's border rules can result in greater Inuit sovereignty.

EXERCISING THE RIGHT TO MOBILITY

> **Too often, our passports are denied by the very countries that took our land.**[17]
>
> —Sid Hill

Indigenous Peoples have a right to mobility. In July 2022, Crystal decided to try crossing the US-Canada border (at the Coutts-Sweetgrass crossing) with her Jay Treaty rights to put them to the test. Information about how to cross the border using Jay Treaty rights was not easy to find. It often feels like the system is designed to withhold knowledge from Indigenous Peoples, and this was the case for exercising Jay Treaty rights under US law.

Crystal's conversation with the US border agent centred on two aspects: blood quantum and documentation. Recall that the United States requires 50 percent "Indian blood" and documentation as proof. First, a letter confirming ancestry and blood quantum cannot come from Indigenous Services Canada because, for the US government, registration under the Indian Act is not sufficient to prove your blood quantum. The letter needs to come from your band or Indigenous government or organization, be written on letterhead, and be signed by a representative.

The letter also needs to include the date of writing, name and date of birth of the traveller, enrolment or membership number related to your nation, Indian Status number, blood quantum in percentage, and detailed information about parents and grandparents (names, birth dates, nationalities, nation/band, Indian Status number, and blood quantum in percentage). It is smart to check with your band, government, or organization about these letters. Some might be quick to respond, but there are accounts of these letters taking more than two years. Bands also have different policies, and some might believe that it is inappropriate to write such a letter.

Second, Jay Treaty border crossing requires an original long-form birth certificate. It can be ordered through the provincial or territorial government of birth. The US border agent told Crystal that not all agents require the long-form birth certificate, but it's still smart to have one. Letters provided by Indigenous bands, governments, and organizations are sometimes incomplete, so secondary documentation (the long-form birth certificate) is necessary. Third, you will need a valid Canadian passport or Indian Status card.

Even if all of your documents are in order, border entry under the Jay Treaty can be complicated depending on the agent and where you cross. There can be delays, verifications, and questions. Border crossings are not always safe because of ongoing stereotyping and racial coding. Indigenous travellers who enter the United States have also noted that, because of the Jay Treaty and the fact that they are perceived not as immigrants but as people with rights, their experiences have been more pleasant than those of their counterparts who enter Canada for a declared purpose.

To be clear, you are not entitled to dual Canadian-American citizenship under the Jay Treaty. You have the right to permanent residency in the United States. According to US Customs, the best option for Indigenous people who cross the border regularly under the Jay Treaty is to obtain a permanent resident card or a green card. How do you get one?

Lawyer Heather Fathali advises that you make an appointment with US Customs and Immigration so that you have dedicated time to discuss your application. According to her, all relevant documents will need to be presented, including a valid Indian Status card (obtained under the Indian Act), a valid Canadian passport, a letter detailing blood quantum in percentage, a long-form birth certificate, and two passport photos. Then you will fill out an I-485 form (used for green card applications). Then you will need another appointment (which might include travel to a major US city) to have digital fingerprints and photographs taken. If your application is approved, then your green card will be mailed to a US address. This process can be tricky, especially if you live in a remote region, such as the North, where you cannot easily travel for appointments or you do not have the financial means to engage in this process.

In 2016, the Standing Senate Committee on Aboriginal Peoples ordered the federal government to address Canada-US border crossing challenges faced by First Nations communities. Indigenous and Northern Affairs Canada appointed Fred

Caron as the minister's special representative on First Nations border-crossing issues. Indigenous Peoples provided Caron with feedback on what can be changed and improved. According to his report, First Nations consider border-crossing mobility issues a significant breach of their treaty rights.

Caron's report summarized a number of concerns:

- a lack of recognition of inherent rights;
- effects on familial and cultural connections, essential to cultural survival;
- current identity documents that do not take into account the desire of Indigenous Peoples to identify themselves as sovereign citizens of Indigenous Nations or as treaty peoples and the length of time that it takes to obtain official identity documents;
- the CBSA treatment of Indigenous people (inappropriate and/or disrespectful treatment, profiling, racism, improper handling of cultural items; and
- the imposition of duties on personal goods and items of historical trade inconsistent with inherent rights.

Solutions put forward in the report include the following:

- the ratification by Canada of the Jay Treaty;
- a legislative or other framework for the recognition of rights;
- a relaxation of Canadian restrictions on entry for Native Americans with criminal offences on their records;
- a review of import restrictions as they relate to traditional medicines;
- modification of the Canadian passport to allow for the identification of an Indigenous person;

- creation of secure identity cards issued by First Nations for travel at Land border crossings;
- improvement of service standards for issuing Status Indian cards;
- mandatory cultural awareness training for CBSA officers and increased hiring of First Nations people as CBSA officers;
- separate lanes for First Nations people at certain ports of entry;
- relaxation of import and export duty rules for goods; and
- the relocation of some ports of entry (e.g., Akwesasne and White River First Nation in Yukon).

Some have suggested that the best solution is to create a separate passport system and framework for Indigenous Peoples.

A passport is a travel document that verifies your identity and nationality. It reflects your membership in a particular nation. That Indigenous people are expected to get a Canadian passport can be viewed as another aspect of colonialism since some Indigenous people think of themselves not as Canadian but as citizens of their own nations. Nevertheless, nearly all Indigenous people have felt compelled to obtain Canadian passports. But some nations have implemented their own passport systems for international travel. Anthropologist Audra Simpson notes that the creation of a separate passport system is just one example of an Indigenous Nation asserting its sovereignty and drawing from Indigenous governance structures.[18]

Haudenosaunee, for example, have made efforts going back more than a century to instill their own passport system. In 1920 and 1923, Haudenosaunee Hereditary Chief Deskaheh (also known as Levi General) travelled to Geneva

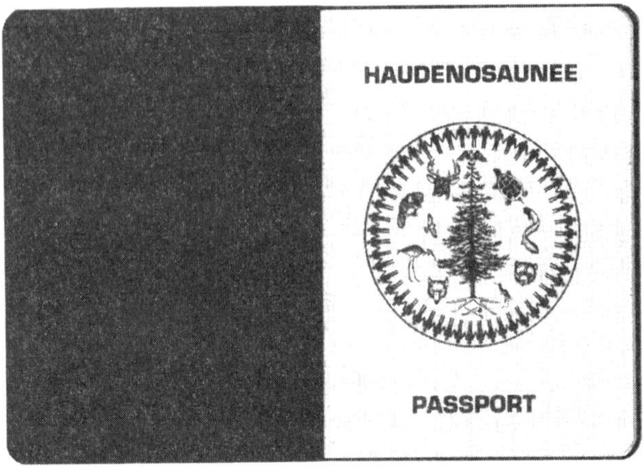

Haudenosaunee have long travelled throughout the world with their own passports, embracing the full rights extended by international law and diplomacy. Unfortunately, not all nation-states recognize their sovereignty or use of the Haudenosaunee passport. Photo courtesy of Susan Hill.

to discuss sovereignty claims with the League of Nations and King George V, under a Haudenosaunee Confederacy–issued passport. The claims to sovereignty rested on Haudenosaunee interpretations of the Treaty of Canandaigua and the Jay Treaty. In Deskaheh's view, these treaties "recognized the collective sovereign status and territorial integrity of the Confederacy and affirmed peace and friendship between it and the United States."[19]

These passports have been used with varying degrees of success. In 1977, the Swiss government accepted Haudenosaunee passports for delegates attending a UN conference on Indigenous rights. In following years, other countries, such as Canada, the United Kingdom, and the United States, also accepted Haudenosaunee passports as official documents for the purpose of travel. In 2005, a delegation travelling on Haudenosaunee passports to Japan was able to enter the country without incident. In 2018, Israel also accepted Haudenosaunee passports but needed reassurances from Canada before doing so. Ireland also accepted them in 2022.

In 2010, three Kanien'keha:ka of Kahnawake were travelling on Haudenosaunee passports, returning from Bolivia. They were delayed for seventeen days in El Salvador. Simpson discusses this delay in *Mohawk Interruptus* and notes that the travellers refused emergency travel documents from Canada (i.e., Canadian passports). Instead, they waited an additional ten days and were finally allowed to enter Canada with their Haudenosaunee Confederacy passports.[20]

In the same year, the Haudenosaunee National Lacrosse Team was denied entry into the United Kingdom because its government refused to recognize the Haudenosaunee passport. The team was supposed to compete in the World Lacrosse League Championship, a sport that the Haudenosaunee themselves had helped to invent a thousand years earlier. The national team did not compete in the United Kingdom that year despite having used Haudenosaunee passports for travel to international competitions for three decades prior.

Some might argue that this refusal was the result of tightened international travel security after the terrorist attacks in 2001. But it could also be an example of how settler states and governments are less willing to understand and support Indigenous expressions of sovereignty in terms of mobility. But the fact that some countries have continued to accept Haudenosaunee passports since 2001 suggests otherwise, even though recognition remains inconsistent. They are sometimes called "fantasy passports," documents that look like passports but are only a souvenir or novelty. Labelling them as such is a tactic to undermine or belittle Indigenous sovereignty more generally but especially in relation to mobility. The problem, of course, with allowing (or tolerating) Indigenous Nations to create their own passport systems and use non-Canadian passports is this: the very act calls Canada's authority and sovereignty into question.

The passport issue will likely remain unresolved for some time. But having these conversations about Indigenous mobility, how it is regulated, and who decides who belongs where is a step in the right direction. Exercising these rights can have profound outcomes for how we practise our cultures and rebuild our nations. We can travel to harvest medicines, visit and reconnect with family members and Elders, engage in celebrations and ceremonies, and even live and work in another country. There can be many other benefits, such as being able to attend a university as a domestic student rather than an international one (saving loads of money on tuition) and purchasing less expensive items in the United States. It's important to note, though, that not all Indigenous Peoples are entitled to these rights.

The conversation also connects to global movements for the right to mobility. For example, the No One Is Illegal movement advocates for the rights of migrants globally. People should be able to stay, move, or return whether they are privileged or not. In many contexts, activists connect migrant rights and Indigenous rights in the sense that no one is illegal on stolen Lands; Indigenous Nations, not settler governments, have inherent authority over migration.

9.

TOWARD SHARED SOLIDARITIES

How about instead of land acknowledgements we do genocide acknowledgements?[1]

—Terese Marie Mailhot, Stó:lō author

TERESE MARIE MAILHOT'S ADVICE TO ACKNOWLEDGE GENOcide is sobering but appropriate as we still reckon with the damage of colonialism on families and communities. In Canada, offering Land acknowledgements has become common. It is a practice growing in the United States too. Governments, organizations, educational institutions, and individuals all regularly make Land acknowledgements. They can be seen in email signatures and books and on websites. Many events begin with Land or territorial acknowledgements: we have heard them at online webinars, book launches, and even hockey games.

The first act in our "150 Acts of Reconciliation" is to "learn the land acknowledgement in your region." We started with this act because we thought that the first thing people should ask is "whose Land do I live on, and what treaties exist here?"[2]

But do Land acknowledgements go far enough? We need concrete actions that support Indigenous sovereignty, encourage the Crown to honour and fully implement the treaties and the UNDRIP, and create a sense of shared solidarity in achieving these goals. Indeed, the spirit and intent of treaty making were to create a shared space within which to decide how different peoples would live together. How can that kind of space be created today?

WHAT IS A LAND ACKNOWLEDGEMENT?

Indigenous Peoples already have protocols to recognize and acknowledge each other via different practices, such as welcoming, announcing, singing, inviting, and offering food. These traditions have carried on since time immemorial. Nêhiyaw scholar Karyn Recollet says that "acknowledging relationships to space and place is an ancient Indigenous practice that flows into the future."[3] These protocols cement Indigenous self-governance and inherent responsibilities to the Land within home territories and guide the role of people visiting from elsewhere. These recognitions sustain relationships with the Land for Indigenous Peoples now and into the distant future.

Métis and Nêhiyaw author Mike Gouldhawke writes that "Land is the terrain upon which all our relations play out, and it can even be seen as a living thing itself, constantly shaping and being shaped by other life forms. Land isn't just a place, it's also a territory, which implies political, legal, and cultural relationships of jurisdiction and care." This is true of settler ways of relating to each other, and the world, based on private and individual rights to property and political representation and through social and economic systems of domination, individualism, competition, and exploitation. According to Gouldhawke, it is also true within Nêhiyawak laws, such as sihtoskâtowin (coming together in mutual support) and miyo-wîcêhtowin (the intentional cultivation of good relations), which stand in stark contrast to settler systems.[4]

But Land acknowledgements, sometimes also called territorial acknowledgements, are something else. They are not Indigenous protocols; they are short statements that usually name the Indigenous territory and treaty area (if there is a treaty) to provide recognition of and respect for local Indigenous Peoples and the shared agreements that govern the territory. Typically, Land acknowledgements are short and to the point. They are usually scripted and stated in a way that does not allow space or time for personal comment or reflection.

A Land acknowledgement should include, at minimum, the names of local Indigenous Nations and/or communities. This alone can be a long list in an area with many nations. Land acknowledgements should also name any political agreements that govern the area. They can include treaties made between Indigenous Peoples, historical treaties with the Crown, and/or comprehensive Land claims (modern treaties).

If there was never a treaty or other agreement with the Crown or Canada, then that should be mentioned too. Often these territories are called "unceded" or "unsurrendered." This is especially important in British Columbia, where about 95 percent of Lands are unceded. In Vancouver, at the Point Grey Campus of the University of British Columbia, for example, the territorial acknowledgement states that "I would like to acknowledge that we are gathered today on the traditional, ancestral, and unceded territory of the Musqueam people."[5] Although the Crown has claimed that treaties involved ceding or surrendering lands, many Indigenous Nations maintain that they never surrendered their Lands.

Land acknowledgements are often complex. Consider the area that includes present-day Toronto, acquired by the British Crown from the Mississaugas in 1787 for "two thousand gun flints, two dozen brass kettles, ten dozen mirrors, two dozen laced hats, a bale of flannel, and ninety-six gallons of rum."[6] The British government purchased the Land for an additional ten shillings in 1805 with the Toronto Purchase. But the area was always contested between Indigenous Nations.

Métis scholar Jesse Thistle says that being correct is important "for the sake of current land claims and also for the sake of basic respect." Working through the complexity, Thistle notes that "Haudenosaunee people, some of them, don't want to recognize that the Anishnabe [*sic*] took control and were here historically. Some Anishnabe people will not recognize that the Haudenosaunee people were here. And both those people sometimes want to erase the Wendat." Moreover, although there were Métis present in Toronto, it was not a homeland for them, and to claim otherwise, for Thistle, "disempowers the Haudenosaunee or the Anishnabe, who do have a rightful claim."[7]

Deciding how to navigate acknowledgement of overlapping territories can be tricky and relies on the person delivering it to understand relationships, power dynamics, contemporary claims, and one's place within them. Land acknowledgements provide opportunities to speak the truth about Canada's relationship with Indigenous Peoples. Often these conversations are not easy or organic. They are good times to share truths about how colonialism and genocide have affected Indigenous Peoples and continue to do so today. A Land acknowledgement is one way to start an important conversation. It can be contentious, and that is okay.

Having such a conversation with respect and relationality is a key part of truth and reconciliation. Land acknowledgements signify that the work is ongoing.

Indeed, to work toward shared solidarity using Land acknowledgements means acknowledging and supporting the continued presence and sovereignty of Indigenous Peoples. The University of California, San Diego, after extensive relationship building with the Kumeyaay Nation, attempted to capture this sense of solidarity:

> The UC San Diego community holds great respect for the land and the original people of the area where our campus is located. The university was built on the unceded territory of the Kumeyaay Nation. Today, the Kumeyaay people continue to maintain their political sovereignty and cultural traditions as vital members of the San Diego community. We acknowledge their tremendous contributions to our region and thank them for their stewardship.[8]

Land acknowledgements have been happening forever. Sometimes they occur at a conference, sometimes you notice them passing a bridge, and sometimes they happen in ways that you could not imagine at first.

THE POTENTIAL TO UNSETTLE

Métis scholar Chelsea Vowel writes that she has been noticing Land acknowledgements at events since at least the early 2000s: "When territorial acknowledgements first began, they were fairly powerful statements of presence, somewhat shocking, perhaps even unwelcome in settler spaces. They provoked discomfort and centered Indigenous priority on these lands."[9]

Certainly, after the TRC's 94 Calls to Action and final report in 2015, more and more individuals and organizations in Canada took up Land acknowledgements within a frame of reconciliation. The 94 Calls to Action did not ask Canadians to offer Land acknowledgements, but they did call for all sectors to work toward a better understanding of treaty relationships and settler responsibilities. Indeed, one of the guiding principles for reconciliation is that "all Canadians, as Treaty peoples, share responsibility for establishing and maintaining mutually respectful relationships."[10] One way to do this is to engage with Land acknowledgements. They can identify and strengthen a treaty relationship. That is a good thing.

A bridge at Garden River First Nation, Ontario. This Land acknowledgement was painted in 1973 by Bob, Darrell, Keith, and Willie Boissoneau, along with Andre and Scott Lesage, to make a statement under the guidance of their ancestors. It has become iconic in the years since and was celebrated publicly in 2023. Photo by James Hopkin/SooToday.

Scholars Teresa Stewart-Ambo and K. Wayne Yang identify Land acknowledgements as a practice that can counter the historical erasure of Indigenous presence on university campuses and other institutional settings. In this way, they are a necessary step in creating inclusive and equitable campus environments. Therefore, they have the *potential* to operate as a mechanism for increasing institutional accountability to Indigenous Peoples. This goes for other places of work and business, too, not just universities or institutions.

Land acknowledgements can also decentre common political narratives. Part of doing so is including animal and plant nations, important inhabitants of these Lands. Nonhuman relatives are our neighbours, key contributors to the environment and human economies, and they play significant roles in cultural practices all over the world.

Looking through the lens of treaty making, and generalizing widely, Indigenous Peoples asked for ongoing access to Lands for fishing, hunting, and gathering, thus maintaining relationships with nonhuman nations and nourishing cultures and economies dependent on those relationships. Yet often we offer Land acknowledgements as though animals are not an integral part of our lives. Sharing stories about urban coyotes, observing the birds in your neighbourhood, or fishing and hunting for food can decentre, disrupt, or unsettle the status quo.

Speaking Indigenous languages can show the failure to maintain total colonial power and the limitation of colonial thought. Indeed, despite centuries of colonialism, Indigenous Peoples are still here. Including (correctly pronounced) place names, customary ways of introducing oneself, or words that express various ways of knowing relevant to good relations across differences in a Land acknowledgement can demonstrate the strength and survival of Indigenous Peoples in light of genocidal policies.

For instance, one key goal of Canadian Indian residential schools was to eliminate Indigenous languages, and we know that—by revitalizing, relearning, and including Indigenous place names—we are working toward truth and reconciliation while supporting Indigenous Peoples in regaining their cultures. Selena Couture writes that a focus on Indigenous languages "is a powerful intervention expressing their survival and resistance."[11]

When Land acknowledgements remind us that other forms of knowledge exist beyond our daily lives, that relationships among peoples on these Lands are ongoing and unresolved, and that they could exist outside colonialism, such acknowledgements have the power to transform.

However, without understanding the relationships and responsibilities that ground transformative Land acknowledgements, they can easily become habitual and empty gestures. For example, political scientist Hayden King helped to craft a Land acknowledgement for Toronto Metropolitan University (formerly Ryerson University) but later said that he had second thoughts. In a radio interview on CBC's *Unreserved*, he explained how, in some cases, Land acknowledgements have become "very superficial" and can fetishize "these actual tangible, concrete treaties. They're not metaphors—they're real institutions, and for us to write and recite a territorial acknowledgement that sort of obscures that fact, I think we do a disservice to that treaty and to those nations."[12]

Have you seen the 2021 Land acknowledgement skit from the *Baroness von Sketch Show*?[13] It is absolutely cringeworthy, perfectly mimicking performative but empty Land acknowledgements. It is a dialogue between two speakers, one who is beginning a performance on a brightly lit stage (S1) and the other who is seated in a full theatre audience (S2):

> S1: Before we begin this evening's performance, we would like to acknowledge that this theatre stands on territory of the Anishinaabe, the Haudenosaunee, the Huron-Wendat, and the Petun First Nations. We are also mindful of the broken covenants and the need to make right with all of our relations. And now please enjoy the show.
> S2: Oh, ah, sorry, hello.
> S1: Oh, oh, I'm sorry.
> S2: Excuse me, um, should we, um, should we go?
> S1: Excuse me?
> S2: Oh, no, no, I just mean, if we're on someone else's Land, shouldn't we, shouldn't we leave?
> S1: Oh, no no no no no, the theatre is here now, and we'd just like to acknowledge whose Land it is.
> S2: I'm sorry, I'm so confused. So, if we're on someone else's Land, shouldn't we do something about that or . . . ?
> S1: Ah, hopefully, we'll enjoy the performance.
> S2: Oh, okay, so some of the money from the ticket sales of the show [is] going to the Indigenous communities?
> S1: Well, no.
> S2: A portion of—of them?
> S1: No, no, the—the ticket sales go to the theatre.
> S2: So is the money from the bottled water sold here going to the First Nations for clean drinking water or . . . ?
> S1: Oh, no, that money goes to Nestlé.
> S2: Nestlé. . . .

S1: They're our sponsor.

S2: I'm so sorry, I'm so confused. Whose land are we on? What are we . . . what are we doing?

S1: It's a dialogue, um. . . .

S2: How are we making [it] right?

S1: Well, there's, uh, uh, there's a plaque you can read in the lobby.

S2: I'm just. . . . I don't understand.

S1: I'm getting a message from the stage manager that we need to begin the show, so please take your seats. Have a good time.

S2: But, um. . . .

S1: Good night. Enjoy the show.

This is an example of how a Land acknowledgement can go so very wrong. It can easily become a romantic statement that does not contain any evidence of action or the existence of hard truths. For example, Land acknowledgements don't usually explain how Canada has failed as a treaty partner. They do not encourage folks to write letters to elected officials, advocate for Indigenous Land rights and sovereignty, or point to the ongoing nature of colonialism in Canada.

One rarely hears about how Indigenous girls and women go missing or are killed on treaty Lands in a Land acknowledgement. The National Inquiry into Missing and Murdered Indigenous Women and Girls, in its Call for Justice 15.2, asked Canadians to "decolonize by learning the true history of Canada and Indigenous history in your local area. Learn about and celebrate Indigenous Peoples' history, cultures, pride, and diversity, acknowledging the land you live on and its importance to local Indigenous communities, both historically and today."[14]

We also don't hear about how the police have removed—and continue to remove—Indigenous Land defenders, sometimes aggressively, from sites of contestation, conflict, or protest at government buildings, pipelines, mines, industrial sites, or railway crossings. People who give Land acknowledgements don't explain how Indigenous children, over generations, were forcibly removed from their Lands and placed in residential schools and sometimes died as a result. Or that uranium was extracted from a mine at Sahtú (Great Bear Lake) in the Northwest Territories and helped to make two atomic bombs during the Second World War. These are real details that inform listeners about the histories of these Lands, and it is possible to make links to how these activities are related to treaties and how they are honoured or dishonoured.

With any truth and reconciliation effort, holding all levels of government accountable is important. After all, many of these governments are making Land acknowledgements in the first place! Settler governments challenge every Indigenous Land claim, hundreds of which are still being processed or are before the courts. Canadians need to take action and insist that their elected officials and other community leaders change the status quo if these acknowledgements are to have meaning for Indigenous Peoples and not just be self-congratulatory moments. King returns to this point: "I want to see the provost of the university or the president of the academic conference or the premier of Ontario saying, 'This is the land that we're on and this is what we're going to do to breathe life into our obligations to those communities and those treaties.'"[15]

So the call is to move to real and uncomfortable truths, as in "genocide acknowledgements" or "burial ground acknowledgements."[16] As Lou Cornum writes, talking about our disposability, and at what cost, is a different way of relating to each other, particularly if you are seeking to better understand the experiences of oppressed peoples. It is through these uncomfortable Land acknowledgements that change can happen. There are other ways to be and other ways to relate to each other:

> When you acknowledge the Land
> Please centre those who have not
> Forgotten its sacredness
> And who have paid a high price
> For honouring their obligations towards it
>
> We ask you to take a moment to remember
> The genocides and ecocides
> That have happened on the Land and to the people of the Land
> . . .
> We ask you to consider that colonialism is anything but
> "settled"
> And to support Indigenous efforts and aspirations
> To have our stolen lands returned
> Our systems of self-governance and treaties recognized
> And our livelihoods restored
>
> Without making this about you

The authors of this poem, entitled "Beyond 'Thank You for the Real Estate,'" wrote it because they found it unsettling to hear settlers repeatedly deliver Land acknowledgements that reference their pleasure and privilege to live, work, and play on these territories. They intervene with this poem to invite settlers to engage in two actions: first, "to recognize the Land as a sacred, living entity from which we all originate"; second, "to acknowledge the intentional complicity of settler systems in genocide and ecocide as the basis for assuming responsibilities towards the Land and Indigenous peoples. These actions encourage settler accountability and responsibility."[17]

So how can Land acknowledgements be meaningful actions that support Indigenous sovereignty? Vowel is hopeful and writes that Land acknowledgements "can be transformative acts that to some extent undo Indigenous erasure."[18] This is true if those speaking and hearing these statements feel uncomfortable. Look for ways to bring the awkwardness and discomfort back.

Diné author Lou Cornum says that feeling uncomfortable represents "the pains of coming into political consciousness."[19] Do not be timid in fully accepting the "truth" part of "truth and reconciliation" when making Land acknowledgements. But discomfort does not mean inflicting harm. Be aware of your audiences and how they can be triggered, and perhaps even give a warning about the conversations that are to come.

Learn responsibilities and obligations based on local protocols, laws, and treaties. Stewart-Ambo and Yang ask "what would it mean for a settler speaker of a land acknowledgment to say, 'I am a visitor, and I hope to become a proper guest?' To be a good guest is to be in good relation to the land—to learn from and to be accountable to the land." They continue to explore this by noting that, "if acknowledegments were an Indigenous protocol, speakers would reflect on their commitments and obligations to the people/place where they are visitors."[20]

King suggests that, rather than using a standard script, each person should write a territorial acknowledgement to reflect on an individual's personal commitments or obligations. We think that this can include everyone in your family, workplace, community organizations, churches, and even children. Children can start to learn about treaties, Indigenous Peoples, and their roles and responsibilities as they grow up—in fact, many are doing so already.

If your child has not learned about treaties and Land agreements, then writing a Land acknowledgement can be a way to start an important conversation. King goes on to write that "it's one thing to say, 'Hey, we're on the territory of the Mississaugas or the Anishinaabek and the Haudenosaunee.' It's another thing to say, 'We're on the territory of the Anishinaabek and the Haudenosaunee and here's what that compels me to do.'"[21] Land acknowledgements should state one's responsibility to Indigenous Peoples, and those who have more power have greater obligations.

We want to hear words that are meaningful, crafted with and in community, with gentle and genuine intentions. We want to hear about the messy and hard and complicated work that had to be done in writing that Land acknowledgement, and then we want to hear about the relationships built through that process. We then want to see bold and brave actions being taken because of Land acknowledgements.

We also think that Land acknowledgements are here to stay. They are not going anywhere. Therefore, we must learn how to think critically about them and move beyond a scripted opening toward action to support reparations for harms done and to ensure Indigenous sovereignty. Regardless of historical treaties, persisting Numbered Treaties, or modern treaties, there is still much to discuss about how Indigenous Nations can regain their sovereignty lost during colonialism. Treaties are not just contracts. They are about relationships. And, if Land acknowledgements get us talking about relationships, then that's a positive thing.

ARE WE ALL TREATY PEOPLE?

Another frame that potentially brings us into relationship with each other is the idea that we are all treaty people. On the one hand, settler and newcomer Canadians need to see themselves as parties to treaties because, as we've shown in previous chapters, these treaties are the agreements that allow people to live, work, play, and profit on these Lands. This teaching is foundational to how Canadians should understand their relationships

On the other, the idea that we are all treaty people is not factual since not all First Nations historically signed treaties with Canada, and Métis and Inuit were excluded. Then there is the fact that settlers and related governments haven't exactly lived up to treaty responsibilities.

The background to this idea comes from the spirit and intent of the original treaties made between Indigenous Peoples and the British Crown and later the Canadian government. By the 1960s, it was clear that colonialism had warped this relationship. Led by Harry Hawthorn of the University of British Columbia, a federal study concluded that failed government policies had had profoundly negative effects on Indigenous Peoples across the country. In 1969, the Canadian government published the White Paper and used Hawthorn's findings to argue for the elimination of Indian Status and the Indian Act but failed.

During the 1970s, the first modern treaties were signed, and in 1996 the Royal Commission on Aboriginal Peoples completed a final report, which echoed the findings of decades earlier in the Hawthorn report. But this time RCAP showed how moving forward meant looking back to the original relationship envisioned (and never realized) between Indigenous Peoples and newcomers.

Settlers typically think about treaties as an "Indigenous thing" or relevant only to Indigenous Peoples. Many Indigenous families know the treaty histories, which of their ancestors signed or were present at them, and attend local celebrations of of those treaties. But the fact is that Canadians have treaty rights; they just don't think about or act on them. In other words, settler Canadians are often very disconnected from treaty histories, celebrations, obligations, and responsibilities.

In our experience, many people are quite surprised to discover that Canada would not exist if it was not for treaties with Indigenous Peoples, that their ancestors had roles in these treaty histories, and that they should keep their own government accountable for the agreements that they made.

We have both lived in Treaty 6 territory: Sara grew up in this territory, and Crystal lives there now. What does it mean to say that we exercise a treaty right by living here or by having lived here? Practically speaking, the Royal Proclamation required the Crown to purchase Land from First Nations before settlement, a principle later applied to the Prairies through treaty making. Within settler law, then, treaties needed to be signed with Indigenous Peoples to settle the Lands. Furthermore, Indigenous Peoples asked for treaties to set out their relationships with settlers.

It was not until the treaty was signed here, on Treaty 6 Lands, that the Canadian government initiated a massive immigration campaign that invited settlers from Eastern Europe, such as Sara's ancestors, to live here and farm the Land. Without the Royal Proclamation and Treaty 6, would there be a city like amiskwaciwâskahikan, with a provincial government and a university where we both studied and Crystal now works? Treaties were not mere formalities; they were essential to the long-term goals of the Crown.[22] Living on, working on, and owning these Lands are treaty rights.

Acknowledging that we are all treaty people means that, in addition to rights, we all have responsibilities and relationships outlined in the treaties. Respect and noninterference were pictured in the Two Row Wampum Treaty, in which each row is a boat:

> One boat is the canoe with the Haudenosaunee way of life, laws, and people. The other is the Dutch ship with their laws, religion, and people in it. The boats will travel side by side down the river of life. Each nation will respect the ways of each other and will not interfere with the other. "Together we will travel in Friendship and in Peace Forever; as long as the grass is green, as long as the water runs downhill, as long as the sun rises in the East and sets in the West, and as long as our Mother Earth will last."[23]

This is part of Indigenous understandings of subsequent treaties, too, in phrasing such as "we will not be prevented from our way of life." This responsibility to treat others with respect and noninterference can extend to how we relate to newcomers, too, such as not requiring new immigrants to Canada to assimilate into the Canadian mainstream.

Indigenous understandings and practices of sovereignty also emphasize relationality rooted in kinship and the central role of consent. As Rauna Kuokkanen, Sheryl Lightfoot, Gina Starblanket, and Matthew Wildcat point out, ideas of sharing related to Indigenous territories, jurisdictions, and intersecting or coexisting sovereignties are also widespread. The concept of sharing is inherent in the Dish with One Spoon covenant, which established a framework for peacefully sharing and stewarding the territories and resources around the Great Lakes.

Another example is the contemporary community of Maskwacis, a group of four First Nations that has found ways to work in the spirit of both individual autonomy and collective responsibility. Similarly, the values of sharing and coexistence ground Indigenous conceptualizations of treaty making; these values create the potential for multiple systems to flourish in relation to each other.

Traditional Indigenous governance structures often employ leadership and decision-making models that are consensual, community oriented, and integrative, grounded in a profound interconnection with the Land and each other. This emphasis on relationships and interdependencies extends not only between humans but also to Lands, waters, and animals.[24]

According to Indigenous perspectives, generally, treaty making is not about ceding and surrendering the Land or handing over ownership. Rather, it is about living well together, with the Land, to ensure the best future for the generations to come. We thus think that following the original laws would be a good start. This means the laws central to the Indigenous Peoples of the territory.

In Treaty 6 territory, for example, a central concept in Nêhiyawak law is wahkohtowin, a set of laws, obligations, and practices to honour and respect the fact that all of creation is related and interconnected. In Treaty 8 and 11 territories, Dene practise their own set of laws (sometimes called Dene Laws) that guide relationships between people and all creation. Inuit also have maligait (laws) that support living a good life. These laws include working for the common good, respecting all living things, maintaining harmony and balance, and continually planning and preparing for the future.

Nêhiyaw writer Emily Riddle says that treaties thus have the possibility to prescribe how people can live together in a "good way," which defines a respectful and reciprocal relationality. She says that "our ancestors imagined lives for us that are contained in the treaty and provide guidance about how to live with these new relatives in our territory." This is a nonhierarchical interdependence that includes nonhuman relationships. It encompasses mutual aid, Land sharing, and dissemination of Indigenous knowledge. For Riddle, all of us could be working together to live up to and benefit from the treaty agreements.[25]

This aligns with how Gina Starblanket describes the possibilities of treaty making to envision our collective future and shape our everyday interactions.[26] Starting with treaty making informs how we think about current events. How might we use a treaty lens to help us handle a pandemic, navigate a wildfire evacuation, plan for the education of our children, and respond to global wars?

Some people have come together to try to figure it out.

The Treaty Land Sharing Network exists in the Prairies and consists of farmers and ranchers who share their Lands with Indigenous Peoples so that they can gather medicines, harvest plants, hunt game, or engage in ceremony. The network started in 2018 since Indigenous Peoples found that trying to access Lands in the Prairies was becoming increasingly dangerous.

Several recent incidents demonstrated this danger. The 2016 death of Colten Boushie as a result of Gerald Stanley's actions (and then his subsequent acquittal in 2018) and the deaths of two Métis hunters, Maurice Cardinal and Jacob Sansom, who tried to access hunting Lands in Alberta in 2020, made people rethink how to be safe. Landholders in Saskatchewan met at Wanuskewin to better understand their responsibilities as treaty people and to take steps toward restoring safe Land access and sharing Lands with Indigenous Peoples, as treaty relationships indicated. As of spring 2025, the network includes sixty locations and 40,000 acres across Treaty 4 and Treaty 6 territories.[27]

Using this lens, it becomes possible to see that treaties are relevant to everyone and everything on these Lands. Treaties—by design—can create a framework for lasting relationships among settlers, newcomers, and Indigenous Peoples on these Lands. Indeed, Chelsea Vowel reminds us that "people who are living on these lands need to understand, renew, and insist on having better relationships with one another."[28]

One act in our "150 Acts of Reconciliation" in 2017 reads thus: "If you live in an area where there is a Treaty relationship, read the treaty document." This is probably a good first step, but looking back on it today we notice that we didn't have any act about engaging with oral histories of treaty or contemporary Indigenous scholarship about treaties or treaty making.

Another treaty responsibility is to always keep future generations in mind. This, again, is one reason that Indigenous Peoples signed treaties, in order to ensure that future generations would be healthy, protected, and in good relationships with others (including the Land, animals, and plants). What does it mean to think about our day-to-day lives, our work, and our politics in terms of their impacts on the future? Instead of fixating on benefits, profits, or Western ideals of success, how can we look out for *all* future generations? Riddle thinks that treaties "can be a way to make sure that we have enough for future generations. They should be so forward-thinking that the decisions we make will impact generations we never meet."[29]

And, in keeping with long-standing practice, Indigenous Peoples continue to make treaties with each other and with animal and plant nations. These treaties are outside colonial law but draw from the long histories of treaty making that Indigenous Peoples have in making relationships with each other and with other living beings. One contemporary example is the Buffalo Treaty. Prairie Indigenous Nations, whose way of life centred on their relationship with bison since time immemorial, came together to draft and sign a treaty in 2014. The stated objective of the treaty is

> to honor, recognize, and revitalize the time immemorial relationship we have with BUFFALO, it is the collective intention of WE, the undersigned NATIONS, to welcome BUFFALO to once again live among us as CREATOR intended by doing everything within our

> means so WE and BUFFALO will once again live together to nurture each other culturally and spiritually. It is our collective intention to recognize BUFFALO as a wild free-ranging animal and as an important part of the ecological system; to provide a safe space and environment across our historic homelands, on both sides of the United States and the Canadian border, so together WE can have our brother, the BUFFALO, lead us in nurturing our land, plants and other animals to once again realize THE BUFFALO WAYS for our future generations."[30]

The treaty is about returning bison as a keystone species to the Prairies and centring bison in relationships between different groups in the Prairies. Returning bison to the centre of life reawakens concepts, values, and customs and allows for building and sustaining prairie Indigenous political relationships and solidarities outside colonial governance structures. This is an example of how Indigenous Peoples are revitalizing Indigenous concepts of treaty making.

Treaties ask us to be in relationship with each other, but in general settler society pushes us to perceive ourselves as independent, not in relationship with each other at all. In fact, that is one of white feminist researcher Peggy McIntosh's points about white privilege: "I can remain oblivious of the language and customs of persons of color who constitute the world's majority without feeling in my culture any penalty for such oblivion."[31] This is especially important considering how treaties have been dishonoured by successive settler governments over the years. Settler Canadians cannot say that they are treaty people without seeing themselves in a reciprocal and respectful relationship with Indigenous Peoples.

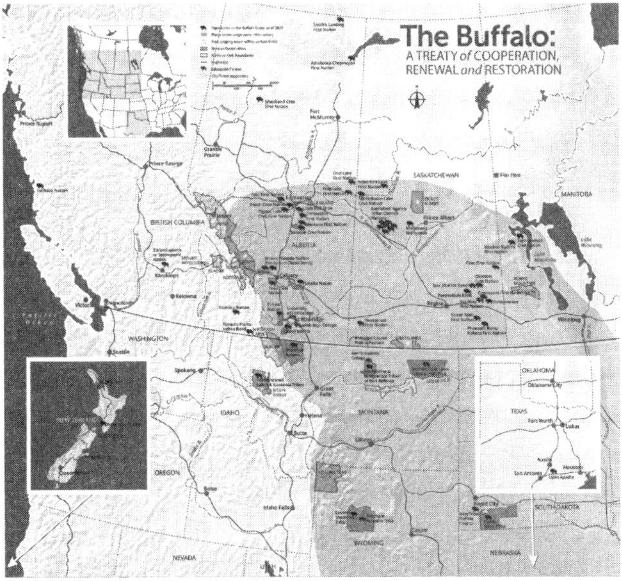

The Buffalo Treaty, a treaty of cooperation, renewal, and restoration, extends across the US-Canada border within the historical range of the bison and has over forty signatories. Map courtesy of the Buffalo Treaty, Buffalotreaty.com.

Additionally, the playing field is not equal. Some have benefited more than others from treaties. We know that Indigenous Peoples have benefited the least from treaties, but settler Canadians have benefited differently as well. This can be seen in both the past and the present. For instance, lucrative Land acquisition deals or invasive resource extraction projects have ensured that some settlers have profited immensely, both financially and socially.

These "projects" often happen on Lands where treaties have not been implemented or, in some cases, have been completely dishonoured. Eve Tuck and K. Wayne Yang remind us of the phrase "settler move to innocence," and that rings true here when thinking about the saying "we are all treaty people." For Tuck and Yang, stating that "we are all treaty people" doesn't allow for any consideration of the power dynamics that we live within, and instead disconnects the past from the present, making settlers innocent recipients of treaty benefits. But in truth settlers continue to enjoy privilege, occupation of stolen Lands, and failed promises, as they have for some time now.[32]

Changing settler-colonial structures to allow for life as responsible and ethical treaty people isn't easy, especially within government structures. In response to the RCAP report in 1996, the government of Canada wrote that a "vision of the future should build on recognition of the rights of Aboriginal peoples and on the treaty relationship."[33] In Saskatchewan, this was taken up by the Federation of Saskatchewan Indian Nations, the government of Saskatchewan, and the government of Canada, which began negotiations in 1996 to imagine Indigenous self-determination outside state categories and to jointly articulate a vision of treaty-based governance.

After years of discussions, the vision was proposed in an agreement in principle (AIP) in 2003. It was founded on the inherent right of Indigenous Peoples to self-determination, and the AIP recognized First Nations jurisdiction and law-making power in many areas and proposed to build governance "from the bottom up." Each First Nation could decide whether and how to participate through a process called "delegating forward."

As we understand it, consenting self-determining First Nations would participate provincewide in making decisions in areas in which they wanted jurisdiction. However, agreements were never finalized. Although negotiators articulated a vision of treaty-based governance in Saskatchewan, they were unable to deviate from the path set out by the Indian Act and other colonial policies. In other words, the process, unfortunately, was unable to break away from Canada's colonial path and fully embrace the reality that "we are all treaty people."

Understanding a treaty as a negotiated relationship of independence, friendship, and sharing between Indigenous Peoples and settlers creates space to think about a contemporary treaty relationship as "a space of negotiated understanding." Thinking of yourself as a treaty person can help in working to create and understand the kind of mutually beneficial and respectful relationships at the heart of the treaties. No doubt, a first step would be to use any influence that each of us has to ensure that the Crown fulfills historical treaty obligations as they were mutually understood and as a basis from which to strengthen contemporary relationships.[34]

In June 2023, after more than a decade of litigation, the government of Canada made a commitment to twenty-one Anishinaabe communities, along the north shore of Lake Huron, to pay them $10 billion to honour original promises made in the Robinson-Huron Treaty. Signed in 1850, the treaty promised annual payments to Anishinaabeg in exchange for the right to use their Lands. A clause tied the value of annual payments to resource revenues, but annual payments were capped at four dollars per person in 1874 and never increased. Meanwhile, mining, lumber, and fishing industries in the region generated billions of dollars in profits.

Here's what Chief Shingwaukonse said in August 1948 about the promise of compensation if Anishinaabe Lands were ever wanted:

> The English promised our Fathers that they would never take any land from them without purchasing it. We believed their words, and have not as yet been deceived. Whenever the English have required any of our lands, they have held councils and purchased such lands as they required from us. For those reasons we consider the land to be ours and were not a little astonished to find that the money (minerals) on our lands has been taken possession of by the White Children of our Great Mother, without consulting us. We rested on the belief that it was only a preparatory step taken by the Governor to fix a value on it and then purchase [it] from us.[35]

Canada has many debts to settle and relationships to repair before we can collectively say that "we are all treaty people."

This aligns with Glen Coulthard's argument in his influential book *Red Skin, White Masks: Rejecting the Colonial Politics of Recognition*.[36] Coulthard shows that the colonial relationship between Indigenous Peoples and the Canadian state cannot be adequately transformed through "recognition," meaning a nation-to-nation relationship based on Indigenous rights.

Instead of generating the kind of coexistence envisioned by treaties—as grounded in reciprocity, respect, and noninterference—recognition reproduces the existing power relationship that we currently experience and suffer from. To change the dynamic, society would basically have to start from scratch. That's not an easy proposition for many people! Indigenous Peoples, conversely, could refuse to participate in settler politics and instead focus on Indigenous cultural, legal, and political resurgence.

10.

LAND DEFENDERS FROM WAY BACK TO LAND BACK

Canada no longer had its shit together with respect to managing the so-called "Indian Problem."[1]

—Glen Coulthard, Dene political scientist

Glen Coulthard was writing about a period in the 1990s when Indigenous-led direct actions and blockades were happening with increased frequency. Indigenous Peoples took up space, stopped development, and in so doing enacted sovereignty. Indeed, they have always defended their Lands and ways of life. From the earliest days of contact and treaty making, Indigenous leaders sought to ensure that they could access their Lands and continue their ways of life even as colonialism and capitalism wrought changes in their families, communities, and the continent.

Mistahimaskwa, or Big Bear, for example, refused to sign a treaty and worked to unite the Nêhiyawak in the Prairies. He was afraid that signing a treaty and the future it would bring would be a "rope around our necks"—signifying the loss of freedoms—and only signed an adhesion to Treaty 6 in 1882 under duress, when there was no other option available to prevent his people from starving.[2]

Many Inuvialuit declined to sign Treaty 11 in 1921, viewing it as offering little benefit for their people. In the Northwest Territories, over the years, Dene have refused treaty payments in protest when their rights were infringed. According to the Dene Nation, this happened multiple times between 1920 and 1980 to protest game regulations, question the fairness of treaties, protest the cede and surrender clause, and assert their rights.

In 1969, the federal government's White Paper, as discussed, proposed new tactics of assimilation, including eliminating Indian status, dismantling the Indian Act, and effectively ignoring treaties. If these tactics were successful, then all First Nations, Métis, and Inuit would have been fully assimilated into Canadian society.

Mistahimaskwa (*standing, fourth from left*) at Fort Pitt in 1884. The others in the group include Four Sky Thunder, Mistahimaskwa's son Okemow Peeaysis or King Bird, Matoose, and Napasis. Provincial Archives of Saskatchewan R-A7516.

Indigenous leaders in Canada were furious, and there was a sharp increase in activism to protect the rights of Indigenous Peoples. This led to the publication of *Citizens Plus*, also known as the Red Paper. Presented to members of the federal cabinet in 1970 by Harold Cardinal and a delegation of 150 Chiefs, the Red Paper shared a counter-vision of the future of Canada in which federal authorities admitted to past mistakes; committed to preserving the Lands, rights, statuses, and traditions of Indigenous Peoples; recognized historical treaties; and worked toward self-sufficient models for education and economic development in Indigenous communities.

Opposition to the White Paper also galvanized organizations, such as the National Indian Brotherhood (currently called the Assembly of First Nations), operating at a national level to advocate for Indigenous rights. It also laid the groundwork for future self-government negotiations and modern treaties.

By the 1990s, Indigenous Peoples and communities did not want to wait any longer. They had waited long enough. Coulthard writes that Indigenous youth were "no longer willing to play by Canada's rules" and would use various means to advance their communities' rights and interests. He says that this time period was "the inevitable culmination of a near decade-long escalation of Native frustration with a colonial state that steadfastly refused to uphold the rights that had been recently 'recognized and affirmed' in section 35 (1) of the Constitution Act, 1982" and that "this frustration was clearly boiling over, resulting in a marked rise in First Nations' militancy and land-based direct action."[3]

National Chief of the Assembly of First Nations Georges Erasmus warned Canada in 1988 that, "if you do not deal with this generation of leaders, then we cannot promise that you are going to like the kind of violent political action that we can just about guarantee the next generation is going to bring to you." Consider this "a warning," Erasmus continued. "We want to let you know that you're playing with fire. We may be the last generation of leaders that are prepared to sit down and peacefully negotiate our concerns with you."[4]

TAKING DIRECT ACTION

There were events unfolding all over Canada in this spirit, and one of them drew national and international attention. In 1990 in southwestern Quebec, Kanien'keha:ka protesters took action to stop the development of new housing and the expansion of a golf course on their Lands and in an area that included sacred burial grounds. The Kanesatake Resistance (also known as the Oka Crisis) took place over seventy-eight days in the community of Kanesatake (near the town of Oka).

This was the flashpoint of a centuries-long struggle that Kanien'keha:ka had been engaged in to regain sovereignty over their Lands. They were part of the Haudenosaunee Confederacy and a party to the Two Row Wampum Treaty. However, their Lands are on territories claimed by two colonial nations: England and France.

The king of France had granted in 1717 a Roman Catholic order, called the Sulpicians, authority over their Lands, working under the Doctrine of Discovery. When Britain conquered New France in 1760 and implemented the Royal Proclamation in 1763, the Kanien'keha:ka saw an opportunity to regain control over their Lands and began engaging with British officials on this question. But those officials ignored their demands, and the Sulpicians retained authority.

For the next 150 years, the Kanien'keha:ka continued to diplomatically assert their Land rights. Britain and then Canada repeatedly ignored them and even reaffirmed Sulpician authority. By the end of the Second World War in 1945, the Kanien'keha:ka lived on six square kilometres, a mere fraction of the 687 square kilometres to which they wanted the rights. This small parcel of Land was known as the Pines.

A golf course was built on the Pines in 1961, but the Kanien'keha:ka continued to reassert their claims to their Lands, petitioning the government in 1975, 1977, and 1986, with no success. In 1989, Mayor of Oka Jean Ouellette announced an expansion of the golf course and the construction of a luxury townhouse complex on the Pines, on Land where the ancestral cemetery was located. Since Canada had rejected all the claims of the Kanien'keha:ka to these Lands, they were not consulted in this decision.

In an attempt to halt construction, local Kanien'keha:ka, along with a social justice group called the Mohawk Warrior Society, barricaded the road leading into and out of the Pines. When the protesters ignored requests to remove the roadblocks, Oka called in the Quebec provincial police force, the Sûreté du Québec (SQ). On July 11, 1990, the SQ engaged Kanien'keha:ka demonstrators with tear gas and weapons, Corporal Marcel Lemay was killed in the crossfire, and the SQ retreated.

In the following weeks, supporters from across Canada joined Kanien'keha:ka in their fight for justice.

Kanien'keha:ka blocked traffic on the Mercier Bridge in Montreal and sharpened their demands, which now included their right to full sovereignty. By mid-July, the Canadian army had been called in, and 4,000 Canadian soldiers arrived with a full display of military force, including armoured vehicles, artillery, and air and water support.

Police blocked the protesters' supply routes, harassed supply drivers, and raided community food banks. In September, the military and the SQ engaged hundreds of Kanien'keha:ka with tear gas and warning shots and assaulted them with their rifles. In defence, Kanien'keha:ka responded with rocks. By the time the gas cleared, nearly 100 people had been injured.

When Parliament began the fall session that year, Prime Minister Brian Mulroney promised to meet some Kanien'keha:ka demands. The resistance ended two days later, and Kanien'keha:ka women and children left the building where negotiations had taken place. Waneek Horn-Miller, fourteen at the time, was carrying her four-year-old sister. As they left the building, a Canadian soldier stabbed Horn-Miller with a bayonet in the chest. Thankfully, she survived. Several Kanien'keha:ka were arrested and charged by the SQ. Five were convicted of crimes, and one served time in prison.

The Kanesatake Resistance sparked national attention and interest. Some Quebecers were angry about the protest and the idea that Kanien'keha:ka could stop development. Some held anti-protest demonstrations and marches, stoned vehicles that contained Kanien'keha:ka women and children, and at one point burned an effigy of a Kanien'keha:ka person. There were others, though, who supported and stood with Kanien'keha:ka and engaged in solidarity protests and blockades across Canada.

This all happened because Canada had ignored Kanien'keha:ka attempts to discuss Land issues for more than a century. In 2022, Kanesatake spokesperson Katsi'tsakwas Ellen Gabriel said that, "at the end of the day, they do not have the papers that say that we have surrendered this land to them. I don't care about their versions of history—this is plain theft and we shouldn't have to go to the courts to defend our lands."[5]

As a result of the Kanesatake Resistance, Prime Minister Mulroney said that resolving Land claims was a priority for his government. To do so, it committed to overhauling its approach to modern treaties. It also lifted a six-claim cap, meaning that, before this, the federal government would only accept six ongoing Land claims at any given time.

Other examples from around the time of the Kanesatake Resistance in which Indigenous Peoples took direct action to defend their Lands and rights include

- the Innu occupation and blockade of the Canadian Air Force/NATO base at Goose Bay, Labrador, in 1989;
- the Lubicon Cree's boycott of the Calgary Olympics in 1988 as a response to oil and gas development in Alberta;
- blockades across British Columbia throughout the 1990s in support of the Kanesatake Resistance, in opposition to logging, and in support of local Land claims;
- attempts by the Algonquins of Barriere Lake in Quebec to stop clear-cut logging on their Lands in 1989, 1991, 2008, and 2010;

- a series of protests and blockades to stop clear-cutting in Clayoquot Sound in 1993;
- the Temagami First Nation blockades on Red Squirrel Road to stop development in 1989;
- Kettle and Stony Point First Nation's demands that Land taken for a military camp be returned in Ipperwash, Ontario, in 1995;
- the Gustafsen Lake Standoff in the summer of 1995 between a group of Secwépemc Sundancers and the RCMP over access to Land for ceremonial purposes on private property; and
- Elijah Harper's rejection of the Meech Lake Accord in 1990 because of the lack of consultation with Indigenous Peoples.

From the perspective of Indigenous Peoples, relations with settler-colonial Canada had already undergone significant strain before this time. Canada should have come to the

Innu protesting against NATO military flight training in Goose Bay in 1989. This was one of many examples of direct action taken by Indigenous Land defenders in the late 1980s and early 1990s. Photo by Bob Bartel.

same conclusion. CBC reporter Rosemary Barton described this as a time "when many thought the wheels were coming off Confederation."[6]

As in Kanien'keha:ka territory, these issues had been brewing for quite some time, and each act of resistance and refusal had a backstory. The story behind Ipperwash demonstrates this. In 1942, the federal government—using the War Measures Act—appropriated the Stony Point Reserve to use as a military camp. This came after the reserve had already surrendered 377 acres (including shoreline) to commercial developers in 1928 under considerable pressure from the Department of Indian Affairs. Citizens of the Kettle and Stony Point First Nation demanded again and again that this Land be returned. After being consistently ignored, they occupied the military camp twice, in 1993 and 1995. On September 4, 1995, their occupation extended to nearby Ipperwash Provincial Park, Land included in the 1928 surrender.

The Ontario Provincial Police confronted these Land defenders and killed Dudley George, an Anishinaabe demonstrator. This happened after Premier of Ontario Mike Harris reportedly said that he wanted "the f—king Indians out of the park."[7] There was no official investigation of these events under Harris, but one was called in 2003. It revealed several problems with government approaches to the situation, at both provincial and federal levels. The Ontario government was prompted to establish a Ministry of Aboriginal Affairs, to transfer Ipperwash Provincial Park back to the Kettle and Stony Point First Nation, to return the reserve Land eventually, and to offer a $95 million settlement.

The Gustafsen Lake Standoff in British Columbia also had a backstory. Before it was the largest paramilitary operation in the history of the province, it began as a dispute between a small group of Secwépemc Sundancers and the RCMP over Land access for ceremonial purposes on private property near 100 Mile House. Lyle James, an American rancher, had previously allowed the Sundancers to hold their ceremonies on his property, and he had even hired some of them to work on his ranch at times.

When the relationship deteriorated, James served them with an eviction notice, and there were allegations that his staff fired warning shots at the Sundancers. Calling themselves the Ts'Peten Defenders, the group of Sundancers argued that they maintained their sovereign rights to Lands claimed by James since they had not ceded or surrendered them to the Crown. Even so, the Ts'Peten Defenders were accused of "undisputed lawlessness."

Police were planning tactical operations when, on September 11, 1995, a vehicle driven by two Ts'Peten Defenders near the camp ran over an explosive device planted by the RCMP. When the Sundancers fled on foot, gunfire was exchanged for forty-five minutes, and thousands of rounds of ammunition were shot. No one was seriously injured or killed. On September 18, the remaining Ts'Peten Defenders surrendered to the police.

Over the following year of investigation and criminal trials, RCMP officers were accused of launching a campaign of disinformation, refusing to allow the media on site to talk with activists, and engaging in a smear campaign against First Nations leaders.

In this context, the federal government announced in 1991 that it would establish a royal commission to investigate the relationship among Indigenous Peoples, the Canadian government, and Canadian society as a whole. The RCAP team had prominent Indigenous people as commissioners, including Paul Chartrand, J. Peter Meekison, Viola Robinson, Mary Sillett, and Bertha Wilson, and it was chaired by René Dussault and Georges Erasmus. To come up with a strategy, the commissioners visited ninety-six First Nations communities, held 178 days of public hearings, and heard from more than 2,000 people. The RCAP also commissioned more than 350 research studies. The commissioners called this a "new beginning with Indigenous peoples."[8]

When it ended two years behind schedule in 1996, the commission had spent $58 million, published a 4,000-page report, made 440 recommendations, and established a twenty-year agenda. The RCAP studied many different issues, including historical relations, self-government, the Royal Proclamation of 1763, the Indian Act, the Numbered Treaties, and Aboriginal case law. In a nutshell, the commissioners called for "mutual recognition, mutual respect, sharing and mutual responsibility."[9]

Key themes in the final report include

- legislation, including a new royal proclamation, stating Canada's commitment to a new relationship and treaty process that recognize Indigenous Nations and governance;
- recognition of an Indigenous order of government that would give Indigenous Nations authority over their own people, within the parameters of the Canadian Charter of Rights and Freedoms;
- replacement of the Department of Indian Affairs with two departments, one to facilitate new relationships with

Indigenous Nations, the other to provide services for non-self-governing communities;
- establishment of an Indigenous parliament;
- recognition of Métis self-government, a Land base, and right to hunt and fish on Crown Land;
- initiatives to address social, educational, health, and housing needs, including training 10,000 health-care professionals over a decade, establishing an Indigenous Peoples' university, and recognizing Indigenous Nations' authority over their own child welfare;
- acknowledgement that Canadian legislation had unilaterally defined "Indians" in harmful and homogenizing ways;
- recognition of the need to significantly increase the Land holdings of First Nations in southern Canada;
- special recommendations for the North, including political and economic development; and
- creation of a new federal Department of Aboriginal Relations to assist Indigenous Nations to transition to self-government and support for communities not yet ready for change.

How did the federal government respond to the RCAP findings? Well, it agreed to study the report but immediately ignored the recommendation to hold a first ministers' conference within six months of the release of the report. Instead, the Chrétien Liberal government released a list of state achievements since 1993, seemingly doubling down on established rhetoric that everything was fine.

When the government did formally respond to the report in 1998, it suggested nonconstitutional and nonspecific approaches: renewing partnerships; strengthening Indigenous governance; developing a new fiscal relationship; and supporting strong communities, peoples, and economies. It also published *Gathering Strength: Canada's Aboriginal Action Plan*, which included a statement of reconciliation and a commitment of $350 million to facilitate community healing, especially for former students of Indian residential schools. Provincial and territorial governments didn't respond to the report at all since they viewed the RCAP as an initiative of the federal government.

The RCAP called on Canada to create a new framework for Indigenous rights through the negotiation of modern treaties, treaty renewals, and new agreements. The 440 recommendations were more far reaching than those of any other federal commission. However, without meaningful and impactful action to follow up on the recommendations, one royal commission could not fix the magnitude of fractured relationships between the Crown (first Britain and then Canada) and Indigenous Nations that had been souring, sometimes, for hundreds of years.

Today the majority of the RCAP recommendations have not been implemented, and there remains very little political appetite for constitutional discussions. Yet, in its final report, the TRC said that the RCAP and its findings "opened people's eyes and changed the conversation about the reality for Aboriginal people in this country."[10]

IDLE NO MORE

It was a bitterly cold day in amiskwaciwâskahikan in 2012, but that did not dissuade hundreds of people who bundled up and gathered in the river valley with signs and banners to march in the streets. In Sǫǫ̀mbak'è, supporters danced across a downtown intersection on Franklin Avenue. Shopping malls around the country echoed with drumming and singing as people gathered for flash mobs.

These events were all part of the Idle No More movement, an Indigenous-led, national conversation on Lands and rights in Canada. The movement began in November 2012 to protest Bill C-45, an omnibus bill proposed by the Harper Conservative government that sought to dismantle many environmental protections. It called for new "nation-to-nation relations based on mutual respect."[11] Since then, Idle No More has grown to support, more broadly, Indigenous rights, sovereignty, treaty promises, and protection of Lands, waters, and skies.

Four women—Nina Wilson, Sylvia McAdam, Jessica Gordon, and Sheelah McLean—created, led, and mobilized the movement. It was grassroots but gained international support and action, all in the name of Indigenous rights. Idle No More organizers said that their vision "revolves around Indigenous Ways of Knowing rooted in Indigenous Sovereignty to protect water, air, land and all creation for future generations."[12] The focus was on treaties, the environment, consultation, and nation-to-nation relationships.

By 2012, the Harper Conservative government had already been in power for six years and had introduced several omnibus bills with sweeping changes. One was Bill C-45, formally known as the Jobs and Growth Act. It would affect over sixty acts, including the Indian Act, the Environmental Assessment Act, and the Navigable Waters Protection Act of 1882. The changes would make it easier for the government and corporations to approve large-scale projects without a

Idle No More demonstrators dance across a downtown intersection in Sǫǫ̀mbak'è in December 2012. Supporters danced, drummed, and walked in communities all across Canada that winter. Photo by Tessa Macintosh Photography.

thorough environmental assessment process. This was particularly concerning in regard to waters, for many waterways pass through traditional First Nations Lands. At the time, the government had been trying for a few years to get the Enbridge Northern Gateway Pipeline approved and the infrastructure in place to connect the oil sands to the Pacific Ocean. There was also the disturbing language of "absolute surrender" in Section 208. The rights and authority of Indigenous Peoples were at risk if the proposed changes were passed. Nêhiyaw iskwew and legal rights scholar Janice Makokis called this the "Harper Indian Act."[13]

During this time, Indigenous Peoples reflected on their relationship with the federal government, including the many bills that had been proposed to improve living conditions for them. Many of those bills, including the Kelowna Accord (2005) and the Family Homes on Reserves and Matrimonial Interests or Rights Act (2008), had died. Additionally, the compounding failure of Canada over the centuries to implement treaty rights led to the souring of relationships between Indigenous Nations and Canada.

Idle No More also unfolded at a time when an increasing number of people were mobilizing on cellular networks, the internet, and other digital media platforms as forms of rapid and reliable communication. By January 24, 2013, approximately 113,000 people had tweeted nearly a million times, and the majority of them were women. Tens of thousands of people were using Facebook to share their thoughts, pictures, and stories about Idle No More events.

By January 5, close to 50,000 people were following the movement's Facebook page. Idle No More was prominent on social media, and there were teach-ins, flash mobs, round dances, rallies, demonstrations, and blockades, both on the streets and in shopping malls. Action and support were on an international scale, including in the United States, Egypt, New Zealand, Greenland, France, the United Kingdom, and other countries.

Co-founder Sylvia McAdam spoke publicly about the importance of peaceful protests "within the legal boundaries."[14] There were many examples of this. In January 2013, six youths and a guide started walking to Ottawa, over 1,600 kilometres from Whapmagoostui, Quebec. By the time they arrived in March, the group consisted of 400 people and was later called the Journey of Nishiyuu. This was all because of the Idle No More movement.

The actions of Chief Theresa Spence figured prominently in media coverage of the movement, but she was not a spokesperson for it. Media coverage was extensive. All of this put pressure on the Harper government and led to a meeting between Harper and the Assembly of First Nations, led at the time by National Chief Shawn Atleo.

The largest Idle No More public event was on January 11, 2013, on Parliament Hill; 3,000 people showed up to voice their concerns and support the movement. This event was related to the meeting that Spence had asked for with Harper, a representative of the Crown (Governor General David Johnston), and First Nations leaders. After Spence ended her hunger strike, media attention to Idle No More declined significantly, and in many ways Canada went back to being its settler-colonial self.

In the spring of 2013, Idle No More aligned with a group of activists, called Defenders of the Land, and issued a joint declaration calling on all levels of government to undertake the following:

- to repeal provisions of Bill C-45 that infringed treaty rights and environmental protections;
- to strengthen democratic practices by implementing proportional representation and ensuring a process of consultation related to legislation on collective rights and environmental protections;
- to fully implement the UNDRIP, including the right of Indigenous Peoples to refuse developments on their Lands;
- to cease the government policy of "extinguishing" Aboriginal title and affirm Aboriginal title and rights according to Section 35 of the Constitution (and as recommended by the RCAP);
- to honour and implement historical treaties; and
- to establish a National Inquiry into Missing and Murdered Indigenous Women and Girls.

At the time, the energy and activity that Idle No More generated were remarkable. One reason was that there was unity among some Indigenous Peoples and settler Canadians. Environmentalists were also deeply concerned about the impacts of the omnibus bill and wanted the government held accountable.

And Idle No More was framed in a way that spoke to relationships and coexistence not just for Indigenous Peoples but also for settlers. This cause was assisted by well-known public figures, such as Wab Kinew, able to reach wide audiences. Kinew spoke about the "recognition of treaty rights, [the] revitalization of Indigenous cultures, and an end to legislation imposed without meaningful consultation," noting that this was the responsibility of "Canadians of all backgrounds."[15]

Since 2013, Idle No More has been a key organizer of rallies and a supporter of related causes. For example, it called for changes to the justice system after the murder of Colten Boushie in rural Saskatchewan and subsequent acquittal of the man accused of his murder, Gerald Stanley. The movement also supported Justice for Jon Styres after he was shot by Peter Khill for breaking into his truck in Ontario in 2016.

The facts remain that Indigenous Peoples are still seen as dispensable within larger society and that Indigenous communities are not served by Canada's justice system. In these cases, ideas about private property and one's right to defend it are seen as more important than Indigenous lives. Today, although not as active as it was a decade ago, Idle No More continues to support important causes such as the Wet'suwet'en Land Defenders.

1492 LAND BACK LANE

> When I hear Indigenous youth and land protectors chant "Land Back!" at a rally, I know it can mean the literal restoration of land ownership. When grandmothers and knowledge keepers say it, I tend to think it means more the stewardship and protection of mother earth. When Indigenous political leaders say it, it often means comprehensive land claims and self-governing agreements. No matter what meaning is attached, we as Indigenous nations have an urge to reconnect with our land in meaningful ways.[16]
>
> —Ronald Gamblin, Anishinaabe, Inninew, and Métis community organizer

Conversations about Lands and treaties are ongoing, and Land defenders continue to take direct action. In July 2020, Haudenosaunee Land defenders occupied a housing development site in Caledonia, Ontario. They said that this location was unceded Six Nations Land, and the location became known as 1492 Land Back Lane. This site in particular represents a long-standing issue between Haudenosaunee and newcomers dating back to the Haldimand Proclamation of 1784, when the governor of Quebec compensated the Haudenosaunee for their support for British forces during the American Revolution. Since then, the Haudenosaunee and Crown have disputed this tract of Land, and 1492 Land Back Lane is part of the ongoing Land Back movement.

Arnell Tailfeathers, a Niitsitapi from Kainai, helped popularize the phrase in 2018, and by 2019 the NDN Collective in the United States had launched Land Back as an international

Indigenous movement. Land Back activities have been undertaken in Canada, the United States, Mexico, New Zealand, and Fiji. Broadly speaking, Land Back is meant to inspire a process of regaining Indigenous sovereignty and political authority over Indigenous Lands, with various sub-interests, including the environment, language and culture, food security, and housing. Importantly, though, the Land Back movement has never called for non-Indigenous peoples to leave unceded Indigenous Lands. It does call, however, for a shift in power and control over Lands. It means getting Lands back under the jurisdiction of Indigenous Peoples.

There are many examples of the Land Back movement beyond 1492 Land Back Lane. For instance, the NDN Collective (pronounced "Indian Collective") in the United States gained critical momentum for the Land Back campaign during Donald Trump's 2020 presidential campaign event at Mount Rushmore. They wanted Mount Rushmore closed and their Land—the Black Hills—returned. Molly Swain and Chelsea Vowel, self-described as "landless Métis," created Back to the Land: 2Land2Furious Landraiser so that they could fundraise to purchase ancestral Land in Lac Ste. Anne County, Alberta, about ninety kilometres west of amiskwaciwâskahikan.

Land Back is also embedded in popular culture. In 2020, the legendary music group A Tribe Called Red (now called The Halluci Nation) produced a song called "Land Back" to support the movement. The following year Łingít and Unangax̂ artist Nicholas Galanin created an "Indian Land" sign later inscribed with the words *Land Back*.

Even before Land Back was a movement, people found ways to give Land back. For instance, a Cape Breton doctor who worked with Indigenous Peoples for his entire career donated 350 acres of Land to the Eskasoni First Nation in 2016. In 2018, the City of Vancouver returned an ancient burial site to the xʷməθkʷəy̓əm (Musqueam). In 2020, the Tsartlip First Nation in British Columbia received Land back, and Swain and Vowel's dream of Métis homelands came true after a wealthy donor in the United States gave them the money to purchase the Lands. And nearly thirty years after the Kanesatake Resistance, the Quebec Land developer signed an agreement with the Kanien'keha:ka Council of Kanesatake in 2019. This agreement returned approximately sixty hectares of Land, including that fought for in the resistance. It was labelled an "ecological gift through a federal government program." The developer, Gregoire Gollin, said that this action was "my contribution to reconciliation."[17] Although this was a positive outcome, Gollin would have received significant tax benefits for such a "gift."

It's curious, though, that churches and the federal government aren't lining up to return Lands.

When we think about the events at Oka and other places, and how the Canadian state has engaged with Indigenous rights to Lands and sovereignty (armed intervention and violence), it becomes clear that Canada's strategy has not changed much over the years.

And, whether it's a domestic process such as the RCAP, initiated by the federal government in 1991 in response to land disputes and crises, or an international framework such as the UNDRIP, it seems that Canada can't get its act together to uphold treaty agreements and grant human rights to everyone on these Lands. Canada often supports foreign for-profit corporations that seek to exploit Indigenous Lands for financial gain over Indigenous Nations despite having repeatedly said that it is prioritizing "nation-to-nation" relationships. The stakes for Canada, after all, are incredibly high. According to the Yellowhead Institute, Canada

- leads the world in mining extraction, mining over sixty minerals and metals, with total domestic exports valued at $81.4 billion per year;
- has a forest sector that "generated $24.6 billion to Canada's GDP in a single year, $24.2 billion to Canada's trade balance, and 186,838 jobs in 2017, not counting all of the secondary industries to which it contributes";
- has high fossil fuel production, including crude oil, natural gas, and coal; and
- has a large pulp and paper industry that leads international production and injects $9.8 billion into the Canadian economy.[18]

Land Back rock in Sǫǫ̀mbak'è. Photo courtesy of Roxane Poulin.

Importantly, though, Indigenous Peoples in the settler state of Canada continue to have their basic human rights denied in myriad ways. In six weeks in the summer of 2024 and as we were writing this book, six Indigenous people died in Canada via encounters with police. Thousands more died before them. Canada is more concerned about protecting its statehood, sovereignty, and economy than about implementing human rights for all. Every day we live out historical Land agreements—and injustices—whether we choose to think about them or not. This is why, today and every day, Land Back is vital.

CONCLUSION
LAND, KNOWLEDGE, AND RESPONSIBILITY

> Well, since the white man came in this country, since then the white people never tell the Indian . . . what they [are] going to do. . . . They just sneak around. They don't want to let the Indian know, they just do it.[1]
>
> —Gwichyà Gwich'in Chief Hyacinthe Andre, Tsiigehtshik (Arctic Red River), Berger Inquiry testimony, 1976

Ah gwįįnzii, shilakut! Good to see you, friend and relative! Thank you for taking this journey with us. We have presented you with a lot of information, and we hope that it was not overwhelming. You might want to revisit chapters as you think through treaties on these Lands and your responsibility as a treaty partner. Some content might not be relevant to you at this moment, and, if you're anything like us, you might learn something completely new the next time you revisit this book.

Perhaps you are a settler Canadian who is just learning that word and how to claim it. Or maybe you are an Indigenous Person who has the blessing of keeping oral histories related to treaty making. Perhaps you have been a long-time advocate for truth and reconciliation and are unsure what your next steps are. Or maybe you are a recent newcomer to Canada, and you're trying to figure this all out. You are not alone in your journey. We hope that we have offered you all something useful in this book.

In it, we invited you to talk treaty with us. In the Introduction, we wrote that treaties are the bedrock of this country called Canada, and they are the basis for how we understand the country, the provinces and territories, and the cities and towns where we live. Understanding treaties is crucial to our future too. These discussions are not easy, but it is critical to know about the history of treaties, the ongoing process of treaty making in Canada, and our responsibilities as citizens of various nations, whether Canada or an Indigenous Nation. At the core of this book, we explored how we can do this in partnership: What do we have in common, and how are we related? How can we better learn about and understand each other? How can we talk treaty together?

Now that you have this information, what are you going to do with it? It's our hope that, after reading *Talk Treaty to Me*, non-Indigenous readers will better understand their relationships with and responsibilities to Lands and treaties and have the desire to learn more about Indigenous histories and issues in contemporary Canada. We also hope that through this work Indigenous readers (especially youth) will be inspired to assert our treaty rights and hold Canada accountable for its missteps as a so-called treaty partner.

IN PURSUIT OF TRUTH AND RECONCILIATION

The TRC's foundational 94 Calls to Action published in 2015 remain relevant ten years later, and we argue that the work needed to accomplish them is more important now than ever. It has been a decade since this landmark commission and its calls to action. According to the TRC, guiding principles for reconciliation include recognizing and respecting Indigenous rights, including treaty, constitutional, and human rights.

Survivors took Canada to court for the harms done by residential schools, resulting in our country's largest ever class action lawsuit. It resulted in the Indian Residential Schools Settlement Agreement. The agreement, among other stipulations, included the establishment of a Truth and Reconciliation Commission to help educate Canadians and to facilitate reconciliation among former students of Indian residential schools, their families, their communities, and all of Canadian society.

There is no reconciliation without a treaty between us. Here's Call to Action 45, which calls for the government of Canada, with the Crown, to build on existing frameworks to create a "Royal Proclamation of Reconciliation":

> We call upon the Government of Canada, on behalf of all Canadians, to jointly develop with Aboriginal peoples a Royal Proclamation of Reconciliation to be issued by the Crown. The proclamation would build on the Royal Proclamation of 1763 and the Treaty of Niagara of 1764, and reaffirm the nation-to-nation relationship between Aboriginal peoples and the Crown. The proclamation would include, but not be limited to, the following commitments:
>
> 1. Repudiate concepts used to justify European sovereignty over Indigenous Lands and Peoples such as the Doctrine of Discovery and terra nullius.

2. Adopt and implement the United Nations Declaration on the Rights of Indigenous Peoples as the framework for reconciliation.
3. Renew or establish Treaty relationships based on principles of mutual recognition, mutual respect, and shared responsibility for maintaining those relationships into the future.
4. Reconcile Aboriginal and Crown constitutional and legal orders to ensure that Aboriginal peoples are full partners in Confederation, including the recognition and integration of Indigenous laws and legal traditions in negotiation and implementation processes involving Treaties, land claims, and other constructive agreements.

In 2015, the TRC commissioners—more than 250 years later, when discussing the legacy of Indian residential schools—identified the Royal Proclamation, treaties, and Land issues in Canada as central pillars of the work that needs to be done today. This book builds upon the ideas that we published in 2017 in "150 Acts of Reconciliation for the Last 150 Days of Canada's 150." Today those acts remain relevant as well.

How has your perspective of treaty making changed after reading this book? You can revisit the definitions of a treaty that we provided in the Introduction. Does one ring truer for you? Are there other aspects of a treaty that you'd add?

As treaty partners, we owe it to ourselves and to each other to implement and practise the principles of truth and reconciliation.

WHAT'S NEXT: "A STORY FOR THE FUTURE"

> Atachuukaii has been travelling beyond the boundaries of the known world for longer than anyone now living can remember, but it is said that the world will not come to an end before he returns from those distant parts. Not all of the stories that began during ts'ii deii days have reached their conclusion yet. Then he paddled out into the ocean. . . . You're going to see him come back, before the end of this world. Until then, he said, he'd stay out there, somewhere in the ocean. Into the sea with the small birch bark canoe. . . . I asked mom, "Did you see Atachuukaii go out of sight?"—"No," she said, "that's what my dad's dad told us—generations, generations, telling one another about this story." That's a real true story.[2]
>
> —Tony Andre, Gwichyà Gwich'in Elder

As humans, we are all visionaries. We wonder what tomorrow will bring, we imagine our futures and our children happy, and we dream of scenarios in which promises are honoured and a society that is fair and equitable. So it is sometimes hard not to wonder what Canada would look like if Indigenous communities had complete sovereignty over their Lands. What if treaties with Canada were first negotiated on a fair playing field and then each party honoured them responsibly? If Indigenous communities had the same resources as big industry, then what would they choose to do with them and according to which social conventions? How would this change the social conditions for Indigenous women and 2SIQTIP? What would our nations look like today if Canada had not subjected Indigenous Peoples to harmful and genocidal policies?

Gina Starblanket's work reminds us that, when treaties were made that invoked the sun, water, grass, and even in some contexts rocks and mountains, Indigenous Peoples looked to a relationship that would be everlasting and contribute to the mutual flourishing of peoples, Lands, and animals.

Indeed, treaties are not static, one-time transactions from the past; they were intended to provide frameworks that future generations could work within to govern their relationships too. This is true. Our relationships now are the results of relationships formed 600 years ago or a few decades ago. We are making new relationships today, too, and we want to do that in a good way.

We cannot change the past, but we can change the future. And we can do it together. We can do it by talking treaty together.

APPENDICES

TIMELINE OF TREATIES AND RELATED EVENTS

Time immemorial/Ingilraani/ts'ii dęįį—origin of the world and agreements between people and animals

1000 Dish with One Spoon

1000–1450 Great Law of Peace

1400s Papal bulls/Doctrine of Discovery

1492 Christopher Columbus's first voyage to the Americas

1494 Treaty of Tordesillas

1534 Jacques Cartier claims territory for France

1600s–1700s Dutch West India Company expands settlement and trade in North America

1600s–1700s Peace and friendship treaties

1613–1842 More than 400 negotiations carried out by the Haudenosaunee Confederacy with Dutch, French, English, and later American entities

1600s–1700s Covenant Chain alliances between the Haudenosaunee and Dutch and then British

1613 Gaswéñdah (Two Row Wampum Treaty)

1620 First residential school for Indigenous students opened by the Roman Catholic religious order Récollets at Notre-Dame-des-Anges in Quebec

1670 Hudson's Bay Company founded

1674 Dutch relinquish New Netherland to the British

1692 Nêhiyaw-Pwât (Iron Alliance)

1700 Great Peace of Montreal with presentation of Dish with One Spoon Wampum Belt

1713 Treaty of Utrecht—France cedes mainland of the Maritimes to the British

1725 Treaty of Mascarene/Mascarene's Treaty between Mi'kmaq, Maliseet, Passamaquoddy, and Penobscot Nations and the Nova Scotia government

1730s–1850s Commercial whaling in the Arctic Ocean

1763 Treaty of Paris—France renounces all claims to territory in mainland North America to Britain

1763 Royal Proclamation
1764 Treaty of Niagara
1764–1860s Upper Canada Treaties
1776 US independence from Britain
1794 Jay Treaty
1800s peace between Edzo and Akaitcho at Gots'okàtì
1800s peace between Nêhiyawak and Dene at Peace River
1805 Toronto Purchase
1812–1815 War of 1812
1817 Selkirk Treaty
1828 Opening of Mohawk Institute in Brantford, Ontario (the first long-term, state-supported residential school in Canada)
1850s Robinson Treaties
1850–54 Douglas Treaties
1860s Decreased influence of the Nêhiyaw-Pwât due to collapse in bison herds and decline of the fur trade
1867 British North America Act/Canadian Confederation
1870 Dominion of Canada purchase of Rupert's Land from the Hudson's Bay Company
1870 Manitoba Act
1871 Last treaty between Nêhiyawak and Niitsitapi at Bear Hills
1871 Treaty 1
1871 Treaty 2
1873 Creation of the North West Mounted Police
1873 Treaty 3
1874 Treaty 4
1875 Treaty 5
1876 Treaty 6
1876 Indian Act
1877 Treaty 7
1884 and 1920 Indian Act mandates compulsory attendance at Indian residential schools
1884 Potlatch ban in the Indian Act
1885 North-West Resistance
1885 Establishment of the pass system
1895 Prohibition of "any Indian festival, dance, or other ceremony" in the Indian Act
1899 Treaty 8
1905–06 Treaty 9
1906 Treaty 10

1920 and 1923 Haudenosaunee Hereditary Chief Deskaheh travels to Geneva under a Haudenosaunee Confederacy passport
1921–22 Treaty 11
1921 Inuvialuit refusal of Treaty 11
1923 Williams Treaties
1924 US Immigration Act
1930s First Indian Hospitals—Fort Qu'Appelle Indian Hospital and Dynevor Indian Hospital
1934–55 Inuit relocations to the High Arctic
1930s–80s Sixties Scoop
1942–60 Eldorado Mine on Great Bear Lake producing uranium for the Manhattan Project and the atomic bomb
1949 Newfoundland and Labrador join Confederation
1951 Potlatch ban removed from the Indian Act
1960s Indian Hospitals transferred or closed
1960s Creation of Committee for Original Peoples' Entitlement
1967 Indian Rights for Indian Women
1969 White Paper released by Jean Chrétien, then minister of Indian Affairs
1970 *Citizens Plus* (the Red Paper) presented to the federal government by Harold Cardinal and the Indian Association of Alberta
1971 Alaska Native Claims Settlement Act
1973 *Paulette et al. v. The Queen* (Paulette Caveat)
1973 *Calder v. British Columbia* (*Calder* case)
1973 *Together Today for Our Children Tomorrow* presented to the federal government by Elijah Smith and a delegation of Yukon Chiefs
1973 Comprehensive Land Claims policy
1974 Native Women's Association of Canada established
1974–77 Berger Inquiry/Mackenzie Valley Pipeline Inquiry
1975 James Bay and Northern Quebec Agreement
1976 *Dene Declaration and Manifesto*
1976 Stó:lō women organize occupation of Canadian Armed Forces building at Coqualeetza
1978 Northeastern Quebec Agreement
1980–94 Clayoquot Sound protests
1982 Repatriation of the Canadian Constitution
1982 Assembly of First Nations established
1984 Inuvialuit Final Agreement
1985 Bill C-31 allowed women and children to regain Indian Status
1986 shíshálh Nation Self-Government Act
1988 Lubicon Cree boycott of the Olympics

1988 First annual gathering of Indigenous LGBTQ2S people held in Minneapolis
1989 Innu occupation and blockade of the Canadian Air Force/NATO base at Goose Bay, Labrador
1989 Temagami First Nation blockades
1989 Barriere Lake Algonquin blockades
1990 Kanesatake Resistance/Oka Crisis
1990 Elijah Harper's rejection of the Meech Lake Accord
1991–96 Royal Commission on Aboriginal Peoples
1992 Gwich'in Comprehensive Land Claim Agreement
1993 Sahtú Dene and Métis Comprehensive Land Claim Agreement
1993 Nunavut Land Claims Agreement
1993 Council for Yukon Indians Umbrella Final Agreement
1995 Champagne and Aishihik First Nations Final Agreement
1995 First Nation of Nacho Nyak Dun Final Agreement
1995 Teslin Tlingit Council Final Agreement
1995 Ipperwash Crisis
1995 Gustafsen Lake Standoff
1996 Last residential schools in Canada close
1997 Little Salmon/Carmacks First Nation Final Agreement
1997 Selkirk First Nation Final Agreement
1997 *Delgamuukw v. British Columbia*
1998 Tr'ondëk Hwëch'in Final Agreement
1999 Creation of Nunavut
2000 Nisg̱a'a Final Agreement
2000 Land acknowledgements start to be delivered at events
2002 Ta'an Kwach'an Council Final Agreement
2003 Tłı̨chǫ Land Claims and Self-Government Agreement
2004 Kluane First Nation Final Agreement
2005 Labrador Inuit Land Claims Agreement
2005 Kwanlin Dun First Nation Final Agreement and Self-Government Agreement
2005 Westbank First Nation Self-Government Agreement
2005 Death of Jordan River Anderson leads to Jordan's Principle developed by the First Nations Child and Family Caring Society
2006 Carcross/Tagish First Nation Final Agreement
2007 United Nations Declaration on the Rights of Indigenous Peoples
2007–10 Qikiqtani Truth Commission
2008 Start of the Truth and Reconciliation Commission of Canada
2008 Nunavik Inuit Land Claims Agreement

2009 Tsawwassen First Nation Final Agreement
2010 Eeyou Marine Region Land Claims Agreement
2011 Maa-nulth First Nations Final Agreement
2011 Bill C-3 removed gender inequity in the Indian Act
2012 Idle No More and Chief Theresa Spence's hunger strike
2014 Sioux Valley Dakota Nation Self-Government Agreement
2014 Buffalo Treaty
2015 Final report of the TRC
2016 Tla'amin Nation Final Agreement
2016 Délı̨nę Final Self-Government Agreement
2016 Death of Colten Boushie
2016 Standing Senate Committee on Aboriginal Peoples ordered the federal government to address Canada-US border-crossing challenges faced by First Nations people
2016–21 National Inquiry into Missing and Murdered Indigenous Women and Girls
2017 Canada 150
2018 Cree Nation Governance Agreement
2018 Wet'suwet'en checkpoints set up in protest of a natural gas pipeline
2018 Treaty Land Sharing Network established
2018 Land Back movement initiated
2019 Bill S-9 removes any residual sex-based inequities in the Indian Act
2020 UNDRIP Act passed by the government of Canada
2020 Deaths of Maurice Cardinal and Jacob Sansom, Métis hunters attempting to access Land
2020–21 Fairy Creek Blockades
2020 Establishment of 1492 Land Back Lane
2021 Discovery of 215 unmarked graves outside the former Kamloops Indian Residential School by the Tk'emlups te Secwépemc Nation
2023 UNDRIP Act Action Plan 2023–2028
2023 Settlement to honour original promises made in the Robinson-Huron Treaty
2023 Vatican repudiates the Doctrine of Discovery
2023 A Self-Government Treaty Recognizing the Whitecap Dakota Nation/Wapaha Ska Dakota Oyate
2024 Red River Métis Self-Government Recognition and Implementation Treaty
2025 Chiix̱uujin/Chaaw K̲aawgaa "Big Tide (Low Water)" Haida Title Lands Agreement
Tłegǫhłı̨ Got'ı̨nę Self Government Agreement (At the time this book

went to press, the agreement had been ratified but not yet passed into law.)

CHAPTER ACTIVITIES

Want to take your learning further? Here are some calls to action that you can take on!

CHAPTER 1: Find and engage with a creation story from your region. Read or listen to it, and be attentive to its lessons. Share your experience and knowledge with someone you know.

CHAPTER 2: See if you can find out about the first Europeans in your region. What can you learn about the relationship between European newcomers and First Nations at that time?

CHAPTER 3: Read the written text of a historical treaty from your region and find at least one oral history account of the treaty to read or listen to. Which promises were made?

CHAPTER 4: Access the website of an Indigenous government. Read its story, learn about its work, and follow it on social media.

CHAPTER 5: Engage with the story of an Indigenous matriarch or 2SIQTIP from your region. Learn about their life, whether it be from a museum display, in a book, or through an artistic lens of painting, writing, drawing, performance, or song.

CHAPTER 6: Read or listen to the experiences of a residential school Survivor. There are podcasts and books now widely available, and all of the reports of the Truth and Reconciliation Commission of Canada are available online.

CHAPTER 7: Draw out the borders in your area. Include political borders; treaty borders; city, county, community, or reserve borders; cultural borders; and landscape features such as rivers or mountains. How do these different boundaries affect your everyday life? How do you think this is different for you compared with others in your community?

CHAPTER 8: Try writing and delivering a Land acknowledgement. You can start by looking at examples from your area. Consider involving your family members, friends, and co-workers in this exercise.

CHAPTER 9: How do you understand your treaty responsibilities? If you don't know the answer, then talk with someone about them, and try to find out what your responsibilities are.

CHAPTER 10: Learn about Land defenders in your region. Learn about the current actions they are taking and the history behind them.

ACKNOWLEDGEMENTS

Hàįį' to Treaty 6, 8, and 11 territories and the relationships that these Lands hold (and have held) for us.

Rick Broadhead reached out to us after reading "150 Acts of Reconciliation," and we are so happy that he did. Rick, hàįį' for your enthusiasm for our work and your steady guidance seeing this through!

We lucked out with Brad Wilson at HarperCollins Canada. Hàįį' Brad and the whole team for seeing this project through and helping us to bring our vision to life.

Hàįį' Stef Kennedy for sharing an idea and letting us run with it! This was definitely not the usual route from idea to book, but we are so grateful that you are part of it.

We were fortunate to have Matthew Wildcat and Stephen Mussell read an initial manuscript draft and share insightful feedback with us. They strengthened our thinking, made sure that we were as accurate as possible, and shared their expertise. Their contributions and attention to detail made this book better. We thank Matthew for encouraging us to write a much stronger analysis of the Doctrine of Discovery, and we thank Stephen for ensuring that we maintained a sharp focus on Indigenous rights and sovereignty. Hàįį to you both, Matthew and Stephen.

Hàįį to all those who contributed work that appears in this book. Thank you to Eric Leinberger who created maps. Thank you to Jenn Harris for creating the index. Thank you to Bob Bartel, Susan Hill, James Hopkin, Carla Hernandez, Laurie McDonald, Roxane Poulin, Kate Reid, Paul Seesequasis, Rolande Souliere, Tessa MacIntosh Photography, Gwich'in Tribal Council, Inuvialuit Regional Corporation, Dene Nation, Toronto Metropolitan University, Glenbow Museum, Library and Archives Canada, Library of Congress, Manitoba Museum, Provincial Archives of Saskatchewan, NWT Archives, and the Buffalo Treaty for generously sharing photos, art, and maps. Masì cho to David Gon for allowing part of his song "The Promise" to appear, and to Mary Siemens for translating the lyrics into Tłı̨chǫ Yatıì.

We are grateful for financial support provided by Prairie Indigenous Relationality Network and the Critical Approaches to Indigenous Relationality project at the University of Alberta.

CRYSTAL'S GRATITUDE

The Land brings me joy every day. Thank you to the Land, waters, and all living things, especially the caribou, moose, deer, muskrats, wolverines, weasels, rabbits, chickens and other birds, fish, dragonflies, butterflies, and plants that routinely spark my curiosity. Thank you Quinn and Jett for reminding me about these relationships and responsibilities when life gets busy.

Hàį' to my northern Elders and teachers who, at different times, have nourished my connection to our Lands, animals, stars, and spirits: Robert Alexie Jr., Robert Alexie Sr., Alestine Andre, James Andre, Julie-Ann Andre, Mickey Andre, Paul Andrew, Billy Archie, Kristi Benson, Jane Bullock, Juliet Bullock, Marka Bullock, Peter Clark, Elizabeth Colin,

Evelyn DeBastien, Leonard DeBastien, Richard DeBastien, Lillian Elias, Sharon Anne Firth, Danny Gaudet, Gloria Gaudet, Annie B. Gordon, Sharla Greenland, Sarah Jerome, Norma Kassi, Itai Katz, Douglas Kendo, Ingrid Kritsch, Beverly Lennie, Johnny Lennie, Les Lokos, Lorraine Lokos, Denise McDonald, Agnes Mitchell, Morris Neyelle, Annie Norbert, Jordan Peterson, Mary-Effie Snowshoe, Sharon Snowshoe, Julienne The'dahcha, Jennie Vandermeer, Karen Wright-Fraser, Norman Yak'eula, and John B. Zoe.

Hiy hiy to my academic friends, mentors, and colleagues who encouraged me to think more deeply about our Lands, our connections to them, and how our relationships guide those connections: Chris Andersen, Lianne Charlie, Harley Crowshoe, Jess Dunkin, Shalene Jobin, Hayden King, Mandee McDonald, Aidan Burghardt, Gina Starblanket, Leanne Betasamosake Simpson, Kisha Supernant, Matthew Wildcat, Zoe Todd, and Kristine Wray. A big thank you to my writing partner and collaborator, Sara Komarnisky. We did it!

Thank you to my partner, Charlie, who helps to make my dreams come true.

SARA'S GRATITUDE

I am grateful to all of the colleagues, friends, mentors, and teachers who I've learned from and with over the years about Land, treaties, languages, cultures, and reconciliation. There are so many to list! Here, I wish to say masì cho to these people in particular: Paul Andrew, Lindsay Bell, Mary Rose Blackduck, Lianne Charlie, Julia Christensen, Debbie DeLancey, Jess Dunkin, Lois Edge, Georgina Franki, Sarah Hazell, Beverly Lemire, Mandee McDonald, Agnes

Pascal, Zoe Todd, Joni Tsatchia, Jennie Vandermeer, Cam Welch, Kelsey Wrightson, Mahalia Yakaleya Newmark, and John B. Zoe. Thanks to the Gordon Foundation and Tłı̨chǫ Government, I was able to attend a treaty simulation workshop in Behchokǫ̀ in 2023 and learned a lot from observing the youth negotiations. Thank you to the Northwest Territories Treaty Talks team for running virtual treaty education sessions during the pandemic in 2021 and continuing to inspire me. To my parents, my siblings, my nieces and nephews, and my friends (especially Teija, Ryan, and Marlee, who I haven't listed yet): thank you for the love and support. Thank you to the families of Pilot's Lane: I feel very lucky to live where I do. Hàı̨ı̨' to my co-author (but also my friend) Crystal Fraser: I'm grateful to continue to think, write, and laugh together with you. It is my life's journey to live as a good guest on Indigenous Lands and to teach my children the same. I feel very lucky to have my partner, Chris, and our children, Ingrid and Nils, along on this journey with me.

NOTES

EPIGRAPH

Harold Johnson, *Two Families: Treaties and Government* (Purich Publishing, 2007), 85.

INTRODUCTION: TALK TREATY TO ME

1. Harold Cardinal and Walter Hildebrandt, *Treaty Elders of Saskatchewan: Our Dream Is That Our Peoples Will One Day Be Clearly Recognized as Nations* (University of Calgary Press, 2000), 53.
2. Leanne Simpson, "Looking after Gdoo-naaganinaa: Precolonial Nishnaabeg Diplomatic and Treaty Relationships," *Wicazo Sa Review* 23, no. 2 (2008): 38.
3. *Oxford English Dictionary*; this usage is now obsolete but was common from approximately 1427 to 1753.
4. *Oxford English Dictionary*; this is the prevailing sense today but has been in use since approximately 1430.
5. Gina Starblanket, "Constitutionalizing (In)Justice: Treaty Interpretation and the Containment of Indigenous Governance," *Constitutional Forum constitutionnel* 28, no. 2 (2019): 21.
6. Eva Jewell and Ian Mosby, *Calls to Action Accountability: A 2023 Status Update on Reconciliation* (Toronto: Yellowhead Institute, 2023), 5, https://yellowheadinstitute.org/wp-content/uploads/2023/12/YI-TRC-C2A-2023-Special-Report-compressed.pdf.
7. Douglas Irvin-Erickson, "The History of Raphaël Lemkin and the UN Genocide Convention," in *Handbook of Genocide Studies*, ed. David Simon and Leora Khan (Edward Elgar Publishing, 2023), 13–14.

CHAPTER 1: TREATY MAKING SINCE TIME IMMEMORIAL

1. Elizabeth Yakeleya et al., *We Remember the Coming of the White Man*, ed. Sarah Stewart (Uproute Print, 2020), xii.
2. *Taimani: At That Time, Inuvialuit Timeline Visual Guide*, ed. Charles Arnold et al. (Inuvialuit Regional Corporation, 2011), 15.
3. Gwich'in Social and Cultural Institute, *Gwich'in Place Names Atlas*, https:/atlas.gwichin.ca.

4. Michael Heine et al., *Gwichya Gwich'in Googwandak: The History and Stories of the Gwichya Gwich'in as Told by the Elders of Tsiigehtshik*, rev. ed. (Gwich'in Social and Cultural Institute, 2007), 18.
5. Sharon Snowshoe and Johnny Semple, "The Boy in the Moon," *Xàgots'eèhk'ò Journal* 2, no. 2 (2023–24): 7–10.
6. Shalene Jobin, "Cree Peoplehood, International Trade, and Diplomacy," *Revue générale de droit* 43, no. 2 (2013): 614.
7. Danny Musqua, in *Treaty Elders of Saskatchewan: Our Dream Is That Our Peoples Will One Day Be Clearly Recognized as Nations*, ed. Harold Cardinal and Walter Hildebrandt (University of Calgary Press, 2000), 39.
8. Yellowknives Dene First Nation Elders Advisory Council, *Weledeh Yellowknives Dene: A History* (Yellowknives Dene First Nation, 1997).
9. Rene M.J. Lamothe, "It Was Only a Treaty: Treaty 11 According to the Dene of the Mackenzie Valley," unpublished paper for the Dene Nation and the Royal Commission on Aboriginal Peoples, 1996, 11–12.
10. Willie Okemow, quoted in Lamothe, "It Was Only a Treaty," 10–11.
11. Jobin, "Cree Peoplehood, International Trade, and Diplomacy," 629.
12. Doug Cuthand, "How the Cree, Blackfoot Confederacies Achieved, Maintained Peace," *StarPhoenix* [Saskatoon], June 17, 2022.
13. Haudenosaunee Confederacy, "Who We Are: About the Haudenosaunee Confederacy," https://www.haudenosauneeconfederacy.com/who-we-are.
14. Arthur C. Parker, *The Constitution of the Five Nations or The Iroquois Book of the Great Law* (University of the State of New York, 1916), 9.
15. Neta C. Crawford, "A Security Regime among Democracies: Cooperation among Iroquois Nations," *International Organization* 48, no. 3 (1994): 345–385.
16. Onondaga Nation, People of the Hills, "Wampum," https://www.onondaganation.org/culture/wampum.
17. Barbara A. Mann and Jerry L. Fields, "A Sign in the Sky: Dating the League of the Haudenosaunee," *American Indian Culture and Research Journal* 21, no. 2 (1997): 107.
18. Lorrie Gallant, Jasmine Wong, and Erez Zobary, "Facing Canada, a Facing History Community Blog: The Dish with One Spoon Wampum (Webinar 2)," *Facing History and Ourselves*, October 29, 2020, https://facingcanada.facinghistory.org/the-dish-with-one-spoon-wampum.
19. Leanne Simpson, "Looking after Gdoo-naaganinaa: Precolonial Nishnaabeg Diplomatic and Treaty Relationships," *Wicazo Sa Review* 23, no. 2 (2008): 36.
20. Yakeleya et al., *We Remember the Coming of the White Man*, xii.

CHAPTER 2: WHEN THINGS BEGAN TO CHANGE

1. Michael Heine et al., *Gwichya Gwich'in Googwandak: The History and Stories of the Gwichya Gwich'in as Told by the Elders of Tsiigehtshik*, rev. ed. (Gwich'in Social and Cultural Institute, 2007), 4.
2. Heine et al., *Gwichya Gwich'in Googwandak*, 4–5.
3. A summary of elements in the Doctrine of Discovery is found in Robert J. Miller, "The Doctrine of Discovery," *Indigenous Peoples' Journal of Law, Culture, and Resistance* 5 (2019): 35–46. See also Robert J. Miller, *Native America, Discovered and Conquered: Thomas Jefferson, Lewis and Clark, and Manifest Destiny* (Praeger Publishers, 2006). We thank Matthew Wildcat for working with us to highlight some of the most important elements here.
4. Ray Fadden, quoted in Tom Keefer, "A Short Introduction to the Two Row Wampum," *Briarpatch*, March 10, 2014.
5. Robert Venables, Onondaga Nation, People of the Hills, "Polishing the Silver Covenant Chain: A Brief History of Some of the Symbols and Metaphors in Haudenosaunee Treaty Negotiations," October 4, 2010, https://www.onondaganation.org/history/2010/polishing-the-silver-covenant-chain-a-brief-history-of-some-of-the-symbols-and-metaphors-in-haudenosaunee-treaty-negotiations.
6. Andrea Bear Nicholas, "Mascarene's Treaty of 1725," *University of New Brunswick Law Journal* 43 (1994): 3.
7. Bear Nicholas, "Mascarene's Treaty"; Peskotomuhkati First Nation, "At the Root of the Relationship: The 1725 Treaty," https://qonaskamkuk.com/peskotomuhkati-nation/the-1725-treaty; Atlantic Policy Congress of First Nations Chiefs Secretariat, "Mascarene's Treaty of 1725," https://www.apcfnc.ca/wp-content/uploads/2020/06/mascarenestreaty.pdf.
8. Brian Slattery, "The Royal Proclamation of 1763 and the Aboriginal Constitution," in *Keeping Promises: The Royal Proclamation of 1763, Aboriginal Rights, and Treaties in Canada*, ed. Terry Fenge and Jim Aldridge (McGill-Queen's University Press, 2015), 20.
9. Talking Treaties Collective, "Treaty of Niagara: Pontiac's War and the Royal Proclamation," in *A Treaty Guide for Torontonians* (Talking Treaties Collective, n.d.), https://talkingtreaties.ca/.
10. John Borrows, "Wampum at Niagara: The Royal Proclamation, Canadian Legal History, and Self-Government," in *Aboriginal and Treaty Rights in Canada: Essays on Law, Equality, and Respect for Difference*, ed. Michael Asch (UBC Press, 1997), 163.
11. Quoted in Alan Ojiig Corbiere, "Ojibwe Chief Shingwaukonse: One Who Was Not Idle," *Muskrat Magazine*, June 6, 2013.

12. Sharon Venne, "Understanding Treaty 6: An Indigenous Perspective," in *Aboriginal and Treaty Rights in Canada: Essays on Law, Equality, and Respect for Difference*, ed. Michael Asch (UBC Press, 1997), 184.
13. René Fumoleau, *As Long as This Land Shall Last: A History of Treaty 8 and Treaty 11, 1870–1939* (University of Calgary Press, 2004), 60.
14. Tłı̨chǫ Government, "*Ìłè dǫ gha gǫta,*" *in Tłı̨chǫ Unity: Our Strategic Framework and Intentions 2021–2025* (Tłı̨chǫ Government, 2021), 23.

CHAPTER 3: WRITTEN TREATIES, FALSEHOODS, AND ORAL HISTORIES

1. Stephen Kakfwi, *Stoneface: A Defiant Dene* (Caitlin Press, 2023), 84.
2. Kakfwi, 84.
3. Sheldon Krasowski, *No Surrender: The Land Remains Indigenous* (University of Regina Press, 2019).
4. Sheldon Krasowski, "To Understand Why the Land Remains Indigenous, Look to History," *Globe and Mail*, April 19, 2019.
5. Harold Johnson, *Two Families*, 41–42.
6. James A.J. McKenna to Clifford Sifton, in René Fumoleau, *As Long as This Land Shall Last: A History of Treaty 8 and Treaty 11, 1870–1939* (University of Calgary Press, 2004), 58.
7. James Daschuk, *Clearing the Plains: Disease, Politics of Starvation, and the Loss of Aboriginal Life* (University of Regina Press, 2013), 114.
8. Krasowski, *No Surrender*, 70.
9. Paul Andrew and Patrick Scott, *We Are a River: 100 Years of Treaty 11* (Native Communications Society of the Northwest Territories, 2024).
10. Fumoleau, *As Long as This Land Shall Last*, 228.
11. Krasowski, *No Surrender*, 160.
12. Krasowski, *No Surrender*, 159.
13. Bob Beal, "Treaty 6," in *Indigenous Saskatchewan Encyclopedia* (University of Saskatchewan, n.d.). Also see Peter Erasmus, *Buffalo Days and Nights* (Fifth House Books, 2015).
14. Fumoleau, *As Long as This Land Shall Last*, 274.
15. Fumoleau, *As Long As This Land Shall Last*, 218.
16. Rene M.J. Lamothe, "It Was Only a Treaty: Treaty 11 According to the Dene of the Mackenzie Valley," unpublished paper for the Dene Nation and the Royal Commission on Aboriginal Peoples, 1996, ii–iii.
17. Fumoleau, *As Long as This Land Shall Last*, 79–80.
18. Sharon Venne, "Understanding Treaty 6: An Indigenous Perspective," in *Aboriginal and Treaty Rights in Canada: Essays on Law, Equality, and Respect for Difference*, ed. Michael Asch (UBC Press, 1997), 191.
19. Gordon Oakes, in *Treaty Elders of Saskatchewan: Our Dream Is That Our Peoples Will One Day Be Clearly Recognized as Nations*, ed. Harold Cardinal and Walter Hildebrandt (University of Calgary Press, 2000), 63.

20. Elizabeth Yakeleya et al., *We Remember the Coming of the White Man*, ed. Sarah Stewart (Uproute Print, 2020), 181.
21. Lamothe, "It Was Only A Treaty," ii–iii.
22. Lamothe, "It Was Only a Treaty," 113–15.
23. Johnson, *Two Families*, 29.
24. Yakeleya et al., *We Remember the Coming of the White Man*, 181.

CHAPTER 4: REFUSAL, UNCEDED TERRITORY, MÉTIS SCRIP, AND MODERN TREATIES

1. Katherena Vermette, *river woman* (House of Anansi Press, 2018).
2. René Fumoleau, *As Long as This Land Shall Last: A History of Treaty 8 and Treaty 11, 1870–1939* (University of Calgary Press, 2004), 265.
3. Fumoleau, *As Long As This Land Shall Last*, 265.
4. Nuligak, *I Nuligak* (Peter Martin Associates, 1966), 163.
5. Wendy Wickwire, *At the Bridge: James Teit and an Anthropology of Belonging* (UBC Press, 2019), 176.
6. Métis National Council, "Citizenship," https://www.metisnation.ca/about/citizenship.
7. Chris Andersen, *Métis: Race, Recognition, and the Struggle for Indigenous Peoplehood* (UBC Press, 2014), 24.
8. Chelsea Vowel, *Indigenous Writes: A Guide to First Nations, Métis and Inuit Issues in Canada* (Highwater Press, 2016), 49–50.
9. Andrea Sandmaier, "Opinion: Canada Must Address Injustice of Métis Scrip System," *Edmonton Journal,* December 27, 2024.
10. Quoted in Fumoleau, *As Long as This Land Shall Last*, 270.
11. Larry Chartrand, *Métis Treaties in Canada: Past Realities and Present Promise* (Indigenous Law Centre, University of Saskatchewan, 2020), 3.
12. Vowel, *Indigenous Writes*, 254.

CHAPTER 5: THE ONGOING FIGHT FOR INDIGENOUS RIGHTS

1. CBC Learning, "Natives Speak Out," *Canada: A People's History* (2001), https://www.cbc.ca/history/.
2. Georges Erasmus, "We the Dene," in *Dene Nation: The Colony Within*, ed. Mel Watkins (University of Toronto Press, 1977), 178.
3. Manitoba Métis Federation, "Manitoba Métis Federation and Canada Sign First-of-Its Kind Self-Government Treaty," press release, November 30, 2024, https://www.mmf.mb.ca/news/manitoba-metis-federation-and-canada-sign-first-of-its-kind-self-government-treaty.
4. Georges Erasmus, "Address to First Ministers' Conference on Aboriginal Constitutional Matters, 26–27 March 1987," in *Governments in Conflict? Provinces and Indian Nations in Canada*, ed. J.A. Long and M. Boldt (University of Toronto Press, 1988), 256–57.

5. John A. Borrows, "Genealogy of Law: Inherent Sovereignty," *Osgoode Hall Law Journal* 30, no. 2 (1992): 295.
6. Hayden King, "Editor's Introduction: The Declaration of Slow," in *Special Report: The UN Declaration on the Rights of Indigenous Peoples in Canada: Lessons from B.C.* (Yellowhead Institute, 2020), 6–8.
7. Truth and Reconciliation Commission of Canada, *What We Have Learned: Principles of Truth and Reconciliation* (Truth and Reconciliation Commission of Canada, 2015), 3.
8. United Nations General Assembly, *United Nations Declaration on the Rights of Indigenous Peoples*, Article 46(1), A/RES/61/295 (September 13, 2007).
9. Quoted in Cassandra Blondin Burt, "Dene Nation Opposes UNDRIP Clause That Threatens Indigenous Sovereignty," *Northern News Services Ltd.*, September 14, 2022.
10. Terry Mitchell, "Realising Indigenous Rights in the Context of Extractive Imperialism: Canada's Shifting and Fledgling Progress towards the Implementation of UNDRIP," *International Journal of Critical Indigenous Studies* 12, no. 1 (2019): 46–59.

CHAPTER 6: THE (DIS)HONOURING OF TREATIES AND CANADIAN SETTLER COLONIALISM

1. Tanya Tagaq, *Split Tooth* (Viking Press, 2018), 119.
2. Patrick Wolfe, *Settler Colonialism and the Transformation of Anthropology: The Politics and Poetics of an Ethnographic Event* (Cassell, 1999), 2.
3. Quoted in Ashleigh-Rae Thomas, "Who Is a Settler, According to Indigenous and Black Scholars," *Vice*, February 15, 2019.
4. Eve Tuck and K. Wayne Yang, "Decolonization Is Not a Metaphor," *Decolonization: Indigeneity, Education and Society* 1, no. 1 (2012): 6–7.
5. Thomas, "Who Is a Settler."
6. Kwet'į̀ translates to "stone or rock people." Some scholars have speculated that the term is a reference to English HBC traders who built stone forts. See Tom Andrews and John B. Zoe, "The Įdaà Trail: Archaeology and the Dogrib Cultural Landscape, Northwest Territories, Canada," in *At a Crossroads: Archaeology and First Peoples in Canada*, ed. George P. Nicholas and Thomas D. Andrews (Archaeology Press, 1997), 160.
7. Quoted in Jovana Jankovic, "Filmmaker Q&A: *Qallunaat! Why White People Are Funny*," NFB Blog, January 13, 2014, https://www.blog.nfb.ca.
8. Robin DiAngelo, *White Fragility: Why It's So Hard for White People to Talk about Racism* (Beacon Press, 2018).
9. Rene M.J. Lamothe, "It Was Only a Treaty: Treaty 11 According to the

Dene of the Mackenzie Valley," unpublished paper for the Dene Nation and the Royal Commission on Aboriginal Peoples, 1996, 149.

10. Sharon Venne, "Treaty Doubletalk in Canada," *Indigenous Law Bulletin* 5, no. 1 (2000).
11. Vine Deloria, "Conquest Masquerading as Law," in *Unlearning the Language of Conquest: Scholars Expose Anti-Indianism in America*, ed. Four Arrows (Don Trent Jacobs) (University of Texas Press, 2006), 94–107.
12. *House of Commons Debates*, 46 Vict. (May 9, 1883), 14, 1107–08.
13. Canada, *The Indian Act*, 1876, 39 Vict., c. 18, Statutes of Canada (1876).
14. After being evicted from their apartment in 1969, Lillian Shirt lived in a tipi in Churchill Square in amiskwaciwâskahikan, drawing attention to many important issues faced by Indigenous Peoples. She is even said to have inspired John Lennon. Lillian Shirt et al., "Lillian Piché Shirt, John Lennon and a Cree Grandmother's Inspiration for the Song 'Imagine,'" *Active History*, December 5, 2016.
15. Wayne Brown, "Mary Two-Axe Earley: Crusader Fought for Equal Rights for Aboriginal Women," *Windspeaker*, February 18, 2017.
16. Native Women's Association of Canada, "Indian Act," n.d.
17. Indigenous Corporate Training Inc. "10 Quotes John A. Macdonald Made about First Nations." Indigenous Corporate Training Inc., June 28, 2016, https://www.ictinc.ca/blog/10-quotes-john-a.-macdonald-made-about-first-nations.
18. The Kwa̱kwa̱ka̱'wakw Potlatch on the Northwest Coast, "Potlatch," n.d., https://www.umistapotlatch.ca.
19. Liza Piper, *When Disease Came to This Country: Epidemics and Colonialism in Northern North America* (Cambridge University Press, 2023).
20. David Gon, "The Promise," Island Miles Away (CBC Northern Service Broadcast Recording, 1988), Tłı̨chǫ Yatıı̀ translation by Mary Siemens.

CHAPTER 7: GENDERING AND QUEERING TREATIES

1. Lee Maracle, "Peace," *The Womanist* 2, no. 2 (1990): 9.
2. Sharon Venne, "Understanding Treaty 6: An Indigenous Perspective," in *Aboriginal and Treaty Rights in Canada: Essays on Law, Equality, and Respect for Difference*, ed. Michael Asch (UBC Press, 1997), 174.
3. First Nations and Indigenous Studies Program, University of British Columbia, "Marginalization of Aboriginal Women," Indigenous Foundations, n.d.
4. Rosa Mantla, "Mǫ̀ht'a Gòehk'ǫ, I Made Camp Fire, Tłı̨chǫ Worldview: The Role of Language in Tłı̨chǫ Puberty Camp" (MEd thesis, University of Victoria, 2017).

5. 2SLGBTQQIA+ Sub Working Group, "MMIWG2SLGBTQQIA+ National Action Plan: Final Report," https://www.mmiwg2slgbtqqia.ca/.
6. Venne, "Understanding Treaty 6," 191.
7. Joan M. Jensen, "Native American Women and Agriculture: A Seneca Case Study," *Sex Roles* 3, no. 5 (1977), 427.
8. Jensen, "Native American Women and Agriculture," 428.
9. Sylvia Van Kirk, *Many Tender Ties: Women in Fur Trade Society, 1670–1870* (Watson and Dwyer, 1980).
10. Margot A. Hurlburt and Ranjan Datta, "When the Environment Is Destroyed, You're Destroyed: Achieving Indigenous Led Pipeline Justice," *Energy Research and Social Science* 91 (2022), 5.
11. Venne, "Understanding Treaty 6," 192.
12. Venne, "Understanding Treaty 6," 191.
13. Venne, "Understanding Treaty 6," 191–92.
14. Government of Canada, "Elsie Knott, 1922–1995," https://www.canada.ca/en/women-gender-equality/commemorations-celebrations/women-impact/trailblazers/elsie-knott.html.
15. *Native Women's Association of Canada v. Canada*, [1994] 3 S.C.R. 627 (Supreme Court of Canada).
16. Quoted in Mark Blackburn, "Attawapiskat Chief Spence Says Not 'Afraid to Die' as She Launches Hunger Strike," *APTN National News*, December 10, 2012.
17. Leanne Simpson, "Think Chief Spence Is on a 'Liquid Diet'? I Think You're Ignorant," *Huffpost Blog*, January 20, 2013, https://www.huffpost.com/archive/ca/entry/think-chief-spence-is-on-a-liquid-diet-i-think-youre-ignoran_b_2517450.
18. Quoted in Blackburn, "Attawapiskat Chief Spence Says."
19. Quoted in "Chief Theresa Spence to End Hunger Strike Today," *CBC News*, January 23, 2013.
20. Spence made additional calls, but the ones related to Lands and treaties appear here. See "Chief Theresa Spence to End Hunger Strike Today."
21. Simpson, "Think Chief Spence Is on a 'Liquid Diet'? I Think You're Ignorant."
22. Quoted in Jérôme Melançon, "Idle No More: A Movement of Dissent," *Aboriginal Policy Studies* 7, no. 1 (2018): 137.
23. *Coastal GasLink Pipeline Ltd. v. Huson*, 2019 BCSC 2264 (Supreme Court of British Columbia).
24. "An Analysis of Coastal GasLink's Notice of Application for Injunction," (Yellowhead Institute, November 2019), https://redpaper.yellowheadinstitute.org/community-tools-resources/.
25. Jon Hernandez, "Reports of RCMP Snipers Dispatched to Wet'suwet'en Blockade 'Concerning,' Says Indigenous Services Minister," *CBC News*, December 19, 2019.

26. Quoted in Chantelle Bellrichard, "Wet'suwet'en Hereditary Leaders Level Human Rights Complaint during Speeches at United Nations Forum," *CBC News*, April 26, 2019.
27. Ryan Duplassie, "'Idle No More': Indigenous People's Coordinated Reaction to the Twin Forces of Colonialism and Neo-Colonialism in Canada," in *Globalization and "Minority" Cultures: The Role of "Minor" Cultural Groups in Shaping Our Global Future*, ed. Sophie Croisy (Brill, 2014), 188.
28. Maracle, "Peace."
29. Alex Birrell, "As the Toll of the Tar Sands on Indigenous Communities Grows, Canada Continues to Fail in Its Obligations to UNDRIP," *The Council of Canadians*, November 9, 2022.
30. "Full Text of Peter Mansbridge's Interview with Stephen Harper," *CBC News*, December 17, 2014.
31. Rob Innes, "Moose on the Loose: Indigenous Men, Violence, and the Colonial Excuse," *Aboriginal Policy Studies* 4, no. 1 (2015): 47.
32. Billy-Ray Belcourt, *A History of My Brief Body* (Penguin Canada, 2020), 56–62.
33. Belcourt, *A History of My Brief Body*, 8.

CHAPTER 8: INTERRUPTING INDIGENOUS MOBILITY

1. Quoted in Audra Simpson, *Mohawk Interruptus: Political Life across the Borders of Settler States* (Duke University Press, 2014), 115.
2. Chelsea Vowel, *Indigenous Writes: A Guide to First Nations, Métis and Inuit Issues in Canada* (Highwater Press, 2016), 260–61.
3. Canada, *Constitution Act, 1867* (UK), 30 & 31 Vict., c. 3, reprinted in *Revised Statutes of Canada* 1985, app. II, no. 5, s. 91(24).
4. Government of Canada, "Treaty Texts: Treaty No. 6" (Queen's Printer and Controller of Stationery, 1964).
5. Alex Williams, dir., *The Pass System* (V Tape, 2015).
6. Williams, *The Pass System.*
7. Quoted in Kerry Benjoe, "First Nation Reserves Prior to 1960s Were 'Open-Air Prisons,' Says Saskatoon Filmmaker behind *The Pass System*," *Regina Leader Post*, November 26, 2015.
8. Quoted in Jane Sponagle, "We Called It 'Prison Island': Inuk Man Remembers Forced Relocation to Grise Fiord," *CBC News*, June 30, 2017.
9. Quoted in Royal Commission on Aboriginal Peoples, *The High Arctic Relocation: A Report on the 1953–55 Relocation* (Canada Communication Group Publishing, 1994), 25.
10. Peter Thrasher, testimony to the Mackenzie Valley Pipeline Inquiry, community hearing, Aklavik, N.W.T., April 2 1975, in *Mackenzie Pipeline Community Hearings 1975–1976*, vol. 1 (Allwest Reporting Ltd., 2003, electronic ed.), 12.

11. "Family in Aklavik, N.W.T., Hopeful after Minister Says Indigenous People Have Right to Move Freely: Federal Immigration Minister Said It Should Be Easier for Indigenous People to Cross International Borders," *CBC News*.
12. Quoted in Emma Tranter, "'We're Going to Fight This': Deportation of Inupiaq Man Living in Canada Deferred," *The Canadian Press*, December 10, 2021.
13. Great Britain and United States. *Treaty of Amity, Commerce, and Navigation* ("Jay Treaty"), signed November 19, 1794, art. III.
14. Gerald F. Reid, "Illegal Alien? The Immigration Case of Mohawk Ironworker Paul K. Diabo," *Proceedings of the American Philosophical Society* 151, no. 1 (March 2007): 71.
15. Quoted in Amy Smart, "Indigenous Woman Fights to Stay in Canada, Says Traditional Tsimshian Territory Is BC," *National Post*, June 20, 2018.
16. Olivia Stefanovich, "Immigration Minister Says He Wants to Make It Easier for Indigenous People to Cross Borders," *CBC News*, September 29, 2023.
17. Sid Hill, "My Six Nation Haudenosaunee Passport Is Not a 'Fantasy Document,'" *The Guardian*, October 30, 2015.
18. Simpson, *Mohawk Interruptus*, 19.
19. Reid, "Illegal Alien?," 78.
20. Simpson, *Mohawk Interruptus*, 18.

CHAPTER 9: TOWARD SHARED SOLIDARITIES

1. Terese Marie Mailhot, *Heart Berries: A Memoir* (Counterpoint, 2018); Lou Cornum, "Burial Ground Acknowledgements: Land Acknowledgments as Acts of Institutional Inclusion Obscure the Antagonism that Follows from Genocide," *New Inquiry*, October 14, 2019.
2. Crystal Fraser and Sara Komarnisky, "150 Acts of Reconciliation for the Last 150 Days of Canada's 150," *Active History*, August 4, 2017, activehistory.ca/150Acts.
3. Quoted in Teresa Stewart-Ambo and K. Wayne Yang, "Beyond Land Acknowledgment in Settler Institutions," *Social Text* 39, no. 1 (2021): 27.
4. Mike Gouldhawke, "Land as a Social Relationship," *Briarpatch*, September 10, 2020.
5. UBC Ceremonies and Events Department and the Musqueam Protocol Office, *Guidelines for Incorporating and Honouring Musqueam Protocol at UBC*, https://ceremonies.sites.olt.ubc.ca/files/2024/08/UBC-Guidelines_Musqueam-Protocol-for-Events.pdf.
6. Stephen Marche, "Canada's Impossible Acknowledgment," *The New Yorker*, September 7, 2017.

7. Quoted in Marche, "Canada's Impossible Acknowledgement."
8. Stewart-Ambo and Yang, "Beyond Land Acknowledgment," 40.
9. Chelsea Vowel, "Beyond Territorial Acknowledgments," September 23, 2016, https://apihtawikosisan.com/2016/09/beyond-territorial-acknowledgments/.
10. Truth and Reconciliation Commission of Canada, *What We Have Learned: Principles of Truth and Reconciliation* (Truth and Reconciliation Commission of Canada, 2015), 126.
11. Selena Couture, "Land Acknowledgements: Speaking Colonial Failure," *Rethinking the Practice and Performance of Indigenous Land Acknowledgement*, special issue of *Canadian Theatre Review* 177 (2019): 28.
12. Hayden King, "'I Regret It': Hayden King on Writing Ryerson University's Territorial Land Acknowledgement," CBC Radio, *Unreserved*, January 18, 2019.
13. "Land Acknowledgement," *Baroness von Sketch Show* (Frantic Films/CBC Comedy, 2021).
14. "Call for Justice for All Canadians, 15.2," in *Reclaiming Power and Place: The Final Report of the National Inquiry into Missing and Murdered Indigenous Women and Girls* (Privy Council, 2019), 199.
15. Stewart-Ambo and Yang, "Beyond Land Acknowledgment," 32–33.
16. Mailhot, *Heart Berries*; Cornum, "Burial Ground Acknowledgements."
17. Cash Ahenakew et al., "Land Acknowledgement Poem," n.d., *Indigenous Peoples' Wellbeing Blog*, https://blogs.ubc.ca/ahenakewcrc/land-acknowledgement-poem/.
18. Vowel, "Beyond Territorial Acknowledgments."
19. Cornum, "Burial Ground Acknowledgements."
20. Stewart-Ambo and Yang, "Beyond Land Acknowledgment," 34.
21. King, "'I Regret It'."
22. Janique Dubois, "'We Are All Treaty People': Assessing the Gap between the Dream and the Reality of Treaty-Based Governance in Saskatchewan," *Nouvelles pratiques sociales* 27, no. 1 (2014): 35.
23. Onondaga Nation, "Two Row Wampum—Gaswéñdah," https://www.onondaganation.org/culture/wampum/two-row-wampum-belt-guswenta/.
24. Rauna Kuokkanen et al., "Are Indigenous Conceptions of Sovereignty as Non-Interference Patriarchal?," *Review of International Studies* 51, no. 1 (2025): 8.
25. Amei-Lee Laboucan, "How to Be a Better Treaty Person: No Two Treaty Agreements Are Alike, But All of Them Offer a Lot to the People Who Reside on Treaty Territory," *New Trail*, July 23, 2021.
26. Gina Starblanket, *Beyond Rights and Wrongs: Towards a Treaty-Based Practice of Relationality* (PhD diss., University of Victoria, 2017), 2–4.

27. Treaty Land Sharing Network, "About Us," https://treatylandsharing network.ca/about.
28. Quoted in Laboucan, "How to Be a Better Treaty Person."
29. Quoted in Laboucan, "How to Be a Better Treaty Person."
30. "The Buffalo: A Treaty of Cooperation, Renewal and Restoration," https://www.buffalotreaty.com.
31. Peggy McIntosh, "White Privilege: Unpacking the Invisible Knapsack," *Peace and Freedom*, July–August 1989, 11.
32. Eve Tuck and K. Wayne Yang, "Decolonization Is Not a Metaphor," *Decolonization: Indigeneity, Education and Society* 1, no. 1 (2012): 23–28.
33. Dubois, " 'We Are All Treaty People.' "
34. Kelsey Wrightson, "We Are Treaty Peoples: The Common Understanding of Treaty 6 and Contemporary Treaty in British Columbia" (MA thesis, University of Victoria, 2010), 122.
35. Quoted in "Robinson-Huron Treaty Rights: 1850 and Today," n.d., Anishinabek Nation.
36. Glen Sean Coulthard, *Red Skin, White Masks: Rejecting the Colonial Politics of Recognition* (University of Minnesota Press, 2014).

CHAPTER 10: LAND DEFENDERS FROM WAY BACK TO LAND BACK

1. Glen Coulthard, "#IdleNoMore in Historical Context," *Decolonization: Indigeneity, Education and Society* (blog), December 24, 2012, https://decolonization.wordpress.com/2012/12/24/idlenomore-in-historical-context/.
2. Hugh A. Dempsey, *Big Bear: The End of Freedom* (Douglas & McIntyre, 1984), 74–75.
3. Coulthard, "#IdleNoMore in Historical Context."
4. Quoted in Coulthard, "#IdleNoMore in Historical Context."
5. Quoted in Laurence Brisson Dubreuil, "Oka Backtracks on Land Protection," *Toronto Star*, January 24, 2022.
6. Rosemary Barton, "Over 20 Years Ago, We Had a Plan to Repair the Crown-Indigenous Relationship. What Happened?," *CBC News*, February 28, 2020.
7. Tabitha de Bruin, "Ipperwash Crisis," *The Canadian Encyclopedia*, August 14, 2013, https://www.thecanadianencyclopedia.ca/en/article/ipperwash-crisis.
8. Quoted in Barton, "Over 20 Years Ago."
9. Canada, Royal Commission on Aboriginal Peoples, *People to People, Nation to Nation: Highlights from the Report of the Royal Commission on Aboriginal Peoples* (Minister of Supply and Services Canada, 1996), 3.
10. Truth and Reconciliation Commission of Canada, *Canada's Residential Schools: Reconciliation*, Final Report of the Truth and Reconcilia-

tion Commission of Canada, vol. 6 (McGill-Queen's University Press, 2016), 3.

11. "An Indigenous-Led Social Movement," n.d., Idle No More, https://idlenomore.ca/about-the-movement.
12. Idle No More Founders and Organizers, "Idle No More—World Day of Action," press release, January 10, 2013, Indigenous Food Systems Network, https://www.indigenousfoodsystems.org/content/idle-no-more-world-day-action.
13. Quoted in Jérôme Melançon, "Idle No More: A Movement of Dissent," *Aboriginal Policy Studies* 7, no. 1 (2018): 131.
14. Sylvia McAdam, interview on *CTV Question Period*, quoted in "Idle No More Co-Founder Supports Spence, Not Blockades," *CTV News*, January 13, 2013.
15. Quoted in Melançon, "Idle No More," 133.
16. Ronald Gamblin, "LAND BACK! What Do We Mean?," 4Rs Youth Movement (blog), n.d., https://4rsyouth.ca/land-back-what-do-we-mean/.
17. Sidhartha Banerjee, "Developer to Return Disputed Land to Kanesatake Mohawks as Ecological Gift," *The Canadian Press*, July 13, 2019. Yellowhead Institute Red Paper," 2019, http://redpaper.yellowheadinstitute.org/.

CONCLUSION: LAND, KNOWLEDGE, AND RESPONSIBILITY

1. Hyacinthe Andre, testimony to the Mackenzie Valley Pipeline Inquiry, community hearing, Arctic Red River, N.W.T., March 13 1976, in *Mackenzie Pipeline Community Hearings 1975–1976*, vol. 47 (Allwest Reporting Ltd., 2003, electronic ed.), 4530–34.
2. Michael Heine et al., *Gwichya Gwich'in Googwandak: The History and Stories of the Gwichya Gwich'in as Told by the Elders of Tsiigehtshik*, rev. ed. (Gwich'in Social and Cultural Institute, 2007), 5–6.

INDEX

*Image locators are indicated in bold